James Alexander McLellan

Applied Psychology

an introduction to the principles and practice of education

James Alexander McLellan

Applied Psychology
an introduction to the principles and practice of education

ISBN/EAN: 9783337313234

Printed in Europe, USA, Canada, Australia, Japan

Cover: Foto ©Andreas Hilbeck / pixelio.de

More available books at **www.hansebooks.com**

APPLIED PSYCHOLOGY.

AN INTRODUCTION

TO THE

PRINCIPLES AND PRACTICE
OF EDUCATION.

BY

J. A. McLELLAN, M.A., LL.D.

Director of Normal Schools, for Ontario.

Author of " Mental Arithmetic," " Elements of Algebra," etc.
Joint Author of " Algebraic Analysis."

Learn to Do by Knowing and to Know by Doing.

Toronto:
THE COPP, CLARK COMPANY, LIMITED,
1889.

PREFACE.

This volume has been prepared at the request of many teachers and Inspectors that I should publish some of my lectures on the Psychology, Principles and Practice of Education, which have been given from time to time before Teachers' Associations. It was urged that though there are many excellent books on general Psychology, there is still room for one which more directly meets the needs of the teacher. Some of these works are too abstract and deal with philosophical questions that very remotely concern the science of education ; others are too superficial, *i.e.*, in their attempts to make psychology easy, they have made it worthless for the educator as well as for the student of philosophy. Most writers on psychology declare that a knowledge of that subject is indispensable in the training of the teacher ; but it must be confessed that the ordinary teacher, even after reading psychologies that claim to be specially prepared for teachers, fails to see the direct bearing of the subject on the work of instruction.

What is wanted, say the teachers who have the worth of psychology so often dinned in their ears, is a more practical work, that is, one that will show explicitly the relation of psychology to education, and give the teacher a clearer and more thorough knowledge of the principles which underlie true methods of instruction. It would be too much to expect that this volume will fully meet these requirements ; but it is hoped that teachers will find in it some justification of the opinion now generally held by educationists, and tersely expressed by Herbert Spencer, that " with complete knowledge of the subject which a teacher has to teach, a co-essential thing is a knowledge of psychology ; and especially of that part of psychology which deals with the evolution of the faculties."

Attention may be called to certain features of the book :

1. The general mode of treatment in the part on mental science is that of Professor Dewey, whose work on Psychology has been so well received by students of philosophy. In preparing an analysis of lectures on Educational Psychology, I consulted the lamented Professor Young, who, while favouring me with his own ideas on the subject, specially recommended Dewey's " Psychology." On the basis of that work, accordingly, lectures were prepared and delivered before Teachers' Associations ; perhaps it is not too much to say that the deep interest these lectures have awakened among teachers is a fair test of the practical worth of the method.

2. The book is not a series of baby-talks on mind. The psychology which requires no thinking is worthless for both teacher and student. If " education is the hardest and most difficult problem ever proposed to man," its science cannot be mastered without thought. But while the book has not ignored scientific method—and so may not be useless as an introduction to more advanced work—the subject, it is hoped, has been so plainly illustrated that it will prove interesting and intelligible to the general reader and certainly to any student of common industry and ability.

3. As intimated, an attempt has been made to make the book of practical value to teachers. Besides the deduction of educational principles from each important topic as discussed, there is a summary chapter which gives a clear and concise view of the Basis, Aims and Methods of Instruction, as grounded on psychology.

4. It is believed that the chapters on the Method of Interrogation will show still more clearly the relation of psychology to educational method, and prove helpful to the teacher who wishes to acquire skill in the art of questioning, the *ars artium* of his calling.

5. The chapter on Kindergarten Work and Self-Instruction in Public Schools, abounds, it is thought, in hints and suggestions which will be found of real value in the practical work of the school-room. The plans and work recommended have stood the test of experience ; if faithfully carried out they will lighten the labour of both teachers and pupils, and greatly increase the efficiency of the public schools.

6. The outline methods on some important branches— based on explicit psychological principles—will, perhaps, prove more serviceable to the teacher than a whole volume of empirical " ways and devices."

7. The full analytical table of contents will help the student to such a mastery of educational principles as established in this volume that he will be fairly able to test independently any of the innumerable methods which are urged upon his attention by distinguished inventors.

To Professor Dewey, whose book on Psychology,—already mentioned—should be read by every student of the subject,

I must express my obligations for most valuable assistance in the preparation of this work.

For the practical part of the chapter on Kindergarten work and on geography, my thanks are due to Mr. J. Suddaby, who is regarded as one of our most progressive teachers, and whose work—which I have often inspected—has placed the Berlin Model School in the front rank of training schools.

For nearly forty years the Professional training of teachers has been—perhaps from the force of circumstances—largely empirical and imitative ; the essence of this method of training may be expressed by the single formula, " Observe and Imitate." This has made teaching a mere " trade," and, as Mr. Fitch says, " teaching is the sorriest of all trades though the noblest of all professions."   But it has been, and is, plainly the policy of the Hon. G. W. Ross to " change all that," to insist on a knowledge of the laws, principles and results of mental evolution as a necessary part of a teacher's preparation, to make professional training something worthy of the name by placing it on a rational, *i.e.*, a psychological basis, and, in a word, to substitute for a " sorry trade " the noblest of *professions*.   I sincerely hope that this book will help, in some degree, to give effect to that wise and far-seeing policy.

Toronto, March, 1889.

CONTENTS.

CHAPTER I.

Psychology and its Relations to the Teacher

CHAPTER II.

The Bases of Psychical Life (A).

II.—Interest.

III.—Impulse.

CHAPTER III.

The Psychical Processes (B).

INTRODUCTION.

III. Voluntary Attention.

III.—Educational Principles.

IV.—Apperception and Retention.

CHAPTER IV.

Forms of Intellectual Development.

(First Division of C or Mental Products.)

§ 1.—Principles of Intellectual Development.

§ 2.—Stages of Intellectual Development—Training of Perception.

§ 5.—Stages of Intellectual Development—continued—Training of Thought.

I.—Indirect Training Brought About by Training other Lower Stages

Illustrated by :

II.—Direct Training.

CHAPTER V.

The Forms of Emotional Development.

(Second Division of C or Mental Products.)

I.—Conditions of Interest.

II.—Principles of Emotional Growth.

CHAPTER VI.

Forms of Volitional Development.

(Third Division of C or Psychical Products.)

I.—Factors of Volitional Development.

CHAPTER VII.

Mind and Body.

CHAPTER VIII.

Summary of Principles.

IV.—Relation of Knowledge, Feeling and Will............. 177

V.—Criticism of Maxims.

CHAPTER IX.

The Method of Interrogation, Art of Questioning.

CHAPTER X.

The Method of Interrogation—Continued.

A. Objects of Questioning—*Continued.*
II.—Training of Apperception.

CHAPTER XI.

Kindergarten Work and Self-Instruction in Public Schools.

VII. Self-Instruction in Common Work.

CHAPTER XII.

Outline Methods in Special Subjects.

PRINCIPLES AND PRACTICE

OF

EDUCATION.

CHAPTER I.

PSYCHOLOGY AND ITS RELATION TO THE TEACHER.

On hearing the oft-repeated assertion of the high value of a knowledge of psychology as a preparation for teaching, the teacher may reasonably ask :—What is psychology, and what relation does it bear to the work of the teacher?   Is it essential or at least important, that he should have a knowledge of the subject?   If it is important what makes it so, and how shall the teacher avail himself of it in order to become a better educator?   To a brief consideration of these questions, this chapter will be devoted.

Psychology Defined.—What is psychology?   For the teacher's purpose, the simplest answer that can be given to this question is that it is the science of the minds of those whom he has to teach—the term mind being used to include the entire psychical (Greek, *psyche*, soul) nature, the WILL, and the EMOTIONS, as well as the INTELLECT.   Since the teacher has to do, on the whole, with the body, the physical nature of the pupil, only on account of its close connection with moral and intellectual habits, it is plain that this definition is almost equivalent to saying that for the teacher psychology is the science of the pupil himself; *it is a systematic and orderly account of the mind that the educator must reach, of the nature of this mind and of the laws, principles and results of its activity.*

Formal Definition and Terms.—A more technical definition of psychology is that it is the science of the facts or phenomena of self. By self is meant that the mind exists *for itself*: that it is conscious of its own processes and states. Other terms used are *Ego* implying that the self recognizes itself as I in distinction from things and from other persons. *Soul* as generally used, suggests the close relation between the mind and its organ, the body. *Subject* is used to imply that the mind is a unity binding together all feelings, ideas, and purposes, and distinguishes it from the object which lies over against self. The term *spirit* suggests the higher moral and religious activities of mind.

Methods of Psychology.—There are various methods used for investigating and explaining psychical facts. A person may set himself to study his own mind ; may watch the origin and progress of his own thoughts ; may analyze them as they come and go and note the ties that seem to connect them. In other words, he may observe himself as he would observe any phenomena. This is the method of *introspection*—of looking within. Many of our ideas come to us primarily through the connection of soul with body in the form of sensations, and many of our states, as our desires, express themselves through the body. We may, therefore, experiment with our sense organs as a means of changing our ideas. This is the *experimental* method. We may also study the minds of others. We may observe (1) children with a view to ascertaining the original forms and gradual development of what we know introspectively only as finished products. Or we may study (2) animals, with a view to learning about instincts, and the lower stages of psychical life ; or (3) the minds of those defective or disordered, like the blind, the deaf, or the insane, and thus discover the effect of withdrawal or alteration of any factor. In these three cases, we are following the comparative method. Or, finally, instead of studying mind directly, we may study its products and then reason back to those activities of mind necessary to produce such results. Language, the growth of science and of art, political and religious institutions, we may consider and study as manifestations, embodiments of intelligence, and hence infer some laws of intelligence itself. This is the *objective* method.

The Basis of Educational Method.—More particularly, psychology is an account of the various ways in which the mind works. Some of these ways are what constitute the process of learning, and it is of prime importance that the teacher should know them. In all his educational work it is to these processes that he must appeal, and upon them that he must build.

A method of teaching which does not rest upon these processes will be arbitrary, and either barren of good results or positively harmful. Such a method, having no connection with any activity native to the learner's mind, either hangs "in the air" utterly without practical significance, or tends to thwart some activity instead of aiding its development. A child's psychical processes will doubtless go on whether he is taught well or ill, or indeed whether he is taught at all or not ; but left to themselves—to the education of "nature"—or directed by wrong methods, they are almost sure to stop short of their highest capacity, to operate feebly or only intermittently, and to be exercised in a wasteful and inefficient way : thus the true end of education— *the harmonious and equable evolution of the human powers*—is never reached. Methods find their place in stimulating the instinctive activities into ever-renewed movement, in keeping them directed in the right line, and progressing upon that line in the simplest, most economical and most vital way. They must rest, therefore, upon knowledge of the activities of the mind and of the laws governing them. This knowledge psychology aims to give.

Value of Method.—The position thus given to method does not detract from its high value—a value so high, that the whole question of education on its practical side, is a question of method. It only shows what is the reason for this high value. It shows that methods have such an important place *because they are tributary* to the natural processes of the mind. Methods are brought into disrepute not by giving them this subsidiary function, but by making them mere mechanical devices which the teacher is required to master in order to give instruction in certain subjects. A method regarded as a mere contrivance for imparting knowledge is *at best* formal and lifeless, and *at worst*, degenerates into a mere stereotyped trick, the repetition of which is deadening to the pupil, and degrading to the teacher. But exactly the same outward procedure when not the result of blind obedience to an assumed educational rule, but followed as clearly auxiliary to some activity on the part of the pupil, places the work of the teacher on a *rational* basis, gives it vitality and effectiveness, and makes the teacher an *artist* rather than a *tradesman.* It should ever be remembered that the servile imitation of what in the hands of another may be a right method, or the mechanical adherence to empirical rules, is not educational method in any true sense of the term. True educational methods are ways of approach to the learner's mind, and ways of directing its activities according to well understood laws. They are *not* the blind observance of formulæ, pedagogical, or otherwise ; but are skillful adaptations to the mental processes of the concrete subject who is learning, the actual individual self. Upon this fact and this alone is based the claim of the great educational importance of psychology.

Limitations of Psychology.—But it is important to know what psychology cannot do as well as what it can do. The following limitations are accordingly to be noticed. In the *first place* teaching deals with individuals, while psychology, like every science, is generic. That is to say, as a science, it deals with classes ; it gives the laws of mind in general, but overlooks the specifically different circumstances under which these laws operate in different individuals. Botany, for example, while giving the laws of plant life in general, does not deal with the individual roses, geraniums, etc., about which the chief interest of the florist centres. Similarly psychology says and can say nothing about this and that boy and girl ; yet it is just with this and that boy and girl that the teacher has continually to do.

In the *second place*, psychology as a science is theoretical, while teaching is practical. That is to say psychology can give the teacher knowledge of the laws of the workings of the mind; but it cannot give him the tact and skill and insight necessary to apply these laws with the best possible results in his actual experiences. Just as one may know the laws of the physiology and pathology of the human body and yet be a poor physician through lack of the practical qualities, the sympathy, the insight, the energy necessary to apply this knowledge, so one who lacks sympathy may be able to state all that is known of psychology and yet be a poor teacher; for science is a weak substitute for sympathy. On the other hand, great sympathy with pupils will often give the teacher a power of insight into their mental processes, and thus enable him to adjust his teaching methods with good effect, although he has but slight theoretical knowledge; in this case, sympathy is, in part, a substitute for philosophy.

But these limitations, after all, only amount to saying that personal skill based partly on inborn qualities, and partly on acquired experience, counts for much in teaching as in everything else. The best teacher will be he who unites high personal qualities with knowledge of the theory of his subject which has been perfected by experience; for "studies perfect nature and are perfected by experience."

Mode of Treatment.—We may begin our study of the theory which underlies teaching by comparison of a finished manufactured article to completely developed mental states. Just as a piece of broadcloth was not always cloth, but was made from the raw material by certain mechanical processes, so an act of thought or will was at first psychical *raw material* which had to undergo certain psychical *processes* in order to become a finished *product*. The teacher will naturally desire to know something about each of these, something about the capacities which are the beginnings, the raw material—something about the processes which act upon the raw material, and something about the finished products. Accordingly we shall take up I.

The Bases of Psychical Life. II. The Processes of Psychical Life, and III. *The three forms of psychical development*,
viz., the Intellectual, the Emotional, and the Volitional,
with something about the various classes of facts coming under
each head

Note.—Regarding Psychology and its Methods consult Dewey's Psychology, Chapter I.

CHAPTER II.

THE BASES OF PSYCHICAL LIFE.

As just said, the development of mind takes its origin from
certain capacities which are at once the stimulus to further
progress and the raw material out of which the more complex
forms are made. These bases are, upon the intellectual side,
Sensations; upon the emotional, Interests; upon the volitional, Impulses. We begin with a study of the facts concerning

§1. SENSATION.

Sensation may be defined as *any* Mental State *which
arises from a* bodily stimulus, *and upon the basis of which we
get knowledge of the* world around us. A few examples will
make this clear. We smell of an orange, and get the
sensation of odor; we put a part of it in our mouth, and get the
sensation of taste; we look at it, and get the sensation of color;
we explore its surface with our hands, and get the sensation of
contact, of pressure, and of temperature; we drop it, and get
the sensation of sound. If we apply these examples to our definition we see (1) That smell, taste, sight, touch and hearing
are all *mental states*, for the mind's content is changed as soon

as each occurs; (2) That the means which occasion these mental changes are *bodily organs*, the eye, ear, hand, etc., together with the nerves connecting these organs with the brain ; and (3) That through each of these states we learn something about *our surroundings*. If, now, we regard the orange as an illustration of the whole world about us, we see how the first step in knowledge of this world is taken.

Sensations are Immediate and Presentative.—By *immediate* is meant that the last antecedent of the mental state is a physical change and not an intervening psychical process. Sensations of yellow, of the peculiar taste and smell of the orange follow as soon as the eye or the proper organ is directed by the mind upon this fruit. The mind does not have to remember, or imagine or think in order to have these feelings. But, if the eye falls upon the figures, 7, 9, 8, 6, 5, 4, the intellect must go through a series of processes and come to a conclusion before discovering that the sum is 39. Such knowledge is accordingly called *mediate*, that is, depending upon intermediate processes, and is opposed to sensation. We may illustrate again by the difference between simply hearing a sound and comprehending the meaning of the words uttered. The sound is heard as soon as the stimulus reaches the brain ; the meaning of the words is not apprehended until certain processes of interpretation, to be studied hereafter, are brought to bear.

The term *presentative* has somewhat the same significance as immediate. A sensation is called presentative because it is formed wholly of original elements, without any reproduced factors entering in. Thus the pain that I feel as I cut my finger is immediately *presented* to me, and is a sensation, while the memory of this pain, or the pain that comes from the hearing of the death of a friend, is *representative*, being based upon the recalling of past experiences. The sensation, in a word, is presentative because occasioned by some object actually affecting the organ of sense ; while memories, abstract ideas, conceptions like those of justice, of education, of arithmetic, not being produced by some direct affection of the sense-organ, are representative in character.

Sensation, to sum up, is primary and original, not secondary and derived, and has no antecedent excepting the *physical* stimulus of the sense-organ. Sensation is, therefore, the *simple* and *elementary material* out of which knowledge of the world about us is built up, and hence our account of how the mind gains its knowledge must begin with a study of sensations.

Characteristics of Sensations.—From these general considerations we must turn to a study of the particular characteristics of sensation. We may continue to illustrate by the sensations occasioned by the orange—say the visual sensation of color. This sensation, like every other, possesses *quality*, *extensity*, *intensity*, and *tone*. By quality is meant the peculiar nature or *content* of the sensation—in this case, that it is a color and not a sound or taste, and furthermore that it is yellow in color, and not green nor red. *Extensity* refers to the extent of impression produced, to its *voluminousness*. A small portion of orange skin does not make so extensive an impression as the whole orange, nor this as a whole basket of oranges. *Intensity* is not to be confounded with extensity. The latter, as just said, means the largeness of the impression. But any sensation of yellow, whatever its extent, has a certain *degree* of intensity according to the amount of light which produces it. This intensity would be nothing in pitch darkness, and at its brightest, of course, in noonday light, while at twilight it would be feeble, etc. Similarly the intensity of a sound may vary from the slightest whisper to the loudest roar of artillery. Finally, as to *tone*, the yellow may be more or less painful, because the color is crude and glaring, or it may be pleasant because refined and pure in quality. The tone thus refers to the *emotional effect* which the sensation excites, whether agreeable or disagreeable.

The Conditions of Sensation.—Each of these characteristics depends partly upon (1) *physical* and partly upon (2) *physiological* conditions. These should now be studied.

(1) The Physical Factor.—The ultimate *physical occasion* of sensation is always some form of *motion*. Of taste and smell the sensory stimulus is molecular motions not well understood; of touch, the stimulus is motion in the form of vibration of masses and visible particles; of hearing, it is motion of air or some other substance having weight, while of sight, the stimulus is vibrations of an imponderable medium called ether. The intensity, and, to a certain degree, the quality of sensations, correspond to properties of the motions occasioning them. Imagine a ball hung by a string to be struck a blow; the harder the blow the wider will be the swing of the ball. That is, the amplitude of a vibration depends upon the impetus of the moving particle. Now if we imagine the swinging ball to come in contact with a drum head, it is evident that the harder the ball is moving (or the greater its amplitude) the greater will be the shock of the contact. From this illustration it may be gathered that the intensity of a sensation depends upon the strength of the motion which stimulates it, and, if this motion is in the form of a vibration, upon the amplitude of the vibration.

Sound and Color.—In the cases of sound and color, at all events, the quality of the sensation corresponds to the *velocity* and *form* of the vibration exciting them. By velocity is meant the number of swings that occur in a given time, whatever the width or amplitude of the swing. The lowest musical tones are produced by a rate of from twelve to twenty vibrations per second; the highest tone, by vibrations at the rate of about forty thousand per second. Between these two extremes come the various octaves of pitch. There is also a scale of *color* in which red corresponds to the slowest rate, which is, however, almost infinitely more rapid than those of sound, being four hundred and fifty-one billions per second; violet corresponds to the most rapid, seven hundred and eighty five billions per second, while the five other spectral colors occupy the interval.

Mixed Sounds and Colors.—So far we have been speaking only of pure or unmixed tones and colors. But if the vibrations are complex in form, composed, not of a single regular series of waves, but by the superimposition of a number of series, we have mixed or composite sounds and colors. In the sphere of hearing there is produced what is called *timbre* or *tone-color*. This is that quality in sound which distinguishes an organ tone from a piano or violin tone of exactly the same pitch and intensity, or from a human voice, or one voice from another. In the sphere of colors, this union of various systems of vibrations produces the mixed or impure colors which we call *shades;* for example, in red, we have scarlet, crimson, rose, pink, etc. The proper intermixture of the vibrations corresponding to the seven spectral colors forms white. This is, perhaps, all that need be said about the relation of the external stimulus to the sensation.

(2) The Physiological Factor.—We turn now to the physiological side of the sensation. Here there are three points to be taken into account, *first*, the nerve organ that receives the physical stimulus, *second*, the nerve conveying the stimulus from the organ to the brain, and *third*, the change in the brain itself. The organs that are exposed to stimulation are classified as *special* and *general* sensory organs. The special organs are those whose function is to receive some specific stimulus to which it is especially adapted, as the eye, for example, is fitted to receive and react upon the waves of ether. The *general* organs are those the main business of which is not the reception of sensory stimuli at all, but the regulation of some organic process, like breathing, digestion, or circulation. The nerves found in the lungs, stomach, etc., are not there for the express purpose of giving sensations, but secondarily and incidentally they do give rise to sensations which tell us how the respiratory or the digestive process is going on.

Differences between General and Special Sensations.—This difference in organs leads to a corresponding division of sensations into *general* or *organic,* and *specific.* The main distinctions are the following :

1. In the specific sensations, as touch, hearing and vision, *quality* is the prominent·constituent ; in the organic, as digestion, etc., *tone.* Taste and smell, although specific senses, have so much emotional accompaniment that they are intermediate.

2. From the above difference, it results that the specific sensations are *clear* and their contents easily distinguishable, while the organic are almost indescribable in their *vagueness.* So too, while the specific sensations are sharply defined in the order of both co-existence and sequence, the organic shade into one another by indistinct blendings.

3. The organic sensations report to us the *condition of our own bodily systems,* their health, comfort or the reverse, and serve along with taste and smell to direct our bodily processes properly, while the specific mainly report to us objects *outside of our own body,* and subserve the theoretical end of knowledge. On this account, the two classes are sometimes termed, the *subjective* and the *objective.*

4. One of the most important differences, from the teacher's standpoint, is that in the order of their development. At birth and in early infancy, sensations in which the factor of *tone* prevails are the predominating, but they gradually give way in importance to sensations in which *quality* is more important. The infant is at first taken up almost wholly with organic

sensations of hunger and thirst, comfort, or fatigue and pain, etc. Even taste and smell do not seem to convey much idea about the quality of the substance tasted, but only of its emotional effect. But in time sounds and colors are observed, at first the brighter and more intense. For a long time after colors are noticed, the child has no distinct idea of the difference between various color qualities—between green and red, yellow and blue, etc. The development begins, in other words, with the *emotional and the vague*, and advances towards the *definite and the intellectual.*

The senses in which quality predominates, particularly sight, hearing and touch, since they are the senses which give the most information about the surrounding world, are those of most importance to the teacher.

The Sensation as a Psychical State.—But, although the intensity and quality of sensation depend largely upon external and physiological circumstances , the sensation in itself is psychical ; it is a state of consciousness. The changes in the nervous system are all physical ; they are only changes of matter and of motion. They are objective and have no conscious existence for themselves. But the sensation is not material nor spatial. It has no right nor left, no quick or slow motion. It simply exists as a psychical occurrence. Materialism attempts to regard the sensation as only nerve force changed into another form, just as heat may be changed into light, this into electricity and so on. But heat, light and electricity may all be considered as forms of motion, and hence as convertible into one another ; while sensation is not a form of motion. Even the materialist is obliged to confess that the change from one to the other is unaccountable, mysterious, unthinkable.

Nervous Change is not Cause, but Stimulus. We cannot regard the change in the brain therefore, as sufficient explanation of a sensation. There is required something which may co-operate with the motion. This is the soul itself. The motion acts as an excitation ; a stimulus to call the soul into activity. The soul, thus incited, responds with a sensation. The true cause of a sensation is, therefore, the activity of the soul, while the affection of the sense and the change in the nerve and brain are necessary to set this cause in action. Sensation may thus be regarded as the meeting place of the physical and the psychical ; the transition from one to the other. It is in sensation that nature gains qualities, and is transformed into color, sound, shape, etc., instead of remaining a monotonous repetition of motions. And in sensation the soul comes in connection with mechanical law, with physical stimulus, so as to be itself mechanically controlled.

Touch, the Foundation Sense.—Touch is important because it is the foundation sense, and because it is most closely connected with the organ for the expression of the will—*the muscular system.* It may be called the foundation sense for two reasons—*First,* because the other senses appear to be developed from it; since biologically considered, they are differentations of it; and, *secondly,* because the other senses rest upon it for assistance and confirmation. Touch gives the most intimate and detailed knowledge of any sense. To be in contact with anything is synonymous with having relations of closest acquaintance with it. We also attribute a superior reality to the reports of this sense, for after feeling that our eyes and ears may deceive us, on account of their remoteness from the object, we attempt to grasp the object, and by handling it, to get a sense of certainty. It is characteristic of ghosts that while they can be seen and heard they cannot be touched. The other reason given for the educational importance of this sense is its close connection with the organ of motor activity,—the muscular system. Touch is pre-eminently an active sense. Touching is almost identical with the exercise of energy. Contact is not passive reception of impressions, but is grasping and exploring. The hand, that most mobile of organs, is the peculiar organ of touch. A child is never contented until he has the object he perceives in his hands, and turns it over and over, and "tries" it for himself. The *first real education of the senses comes through touch,* and wherever the senses are largely concerned, the teacher must continue to rely upon it.

Importance of Sight and Hearing.—The importance of sight and hearing in knowledge is such a commonplace that it is unnecessary to call attention to more than two or three points. One of these points is the complex and varied apparatus which each sense possesses for making discriminations. There is almost no limit to the *fineness* of culture of which these senses are susceptible. They give the clearest and most definite of all sensations. It is further to be noted that the eye is, in a certain way, the *sense* for *space*, and that it follows from this that whatever exists as a whole made up of co-existent parts should be presented to the eye in order to be apprehended most readily and thoroughly. The *range* also of this sense is so great that its capacity for simultaneous impressions makes it a fit organ for grasping the relations of a complex subject. Hence the use of maps, chronological charts, number-tables, and all graphic representations. The *ear*, on the other hand, is the sense for time and of events that follow one another, and hence should be appealed to wherever a subject is to be learned in which the relation of sequence predominates.

Individual Differences in Sense-Organs. —Atten tion however, should be called to the fact that individual differences may make necessary a departure from the rules just laid down. There are always some children in whom one sense predominates to such a degree that it is the natural organ for learning and for recalling. This prominence may occur in such a way that the child is of the *motor*, the *visual* or the *auditory* type. In the visual type, the eye is the leading sense, impressions being received most easily and retained most permanently through this organ. Such persons note readily all the details which they see, and can picture them vividly to themselves afterwards. Draughtsmen, geometers and chess players of unusual ability are generally pronounced visualists. Artists have been known to paint accurately portraits from the vividness of their mental vision without the presence of the person represented. Persons of this type when repeating memorized matter seem to see the written or printed page before their eyes and to read from it.

*Memory exists in terms of the sense through which the impression
is most easily received.*

The same is to be said of the *auditory* and *motor types*,
excepting that in these cases the ear or else muscular activity
with touch takes the lead. Those of the auditory type memorize most easily by reading the matter aloud. Upon repeating
it they seem to hear a voice reading to them. Those of the
motor type will articulate to themselves when reading, studying,
or engaged in reflection ; and when recalling they depend upon
a repetition of this silent articulation. They often assist themselves with a kind of suppressed movement of the fingers, as if
writing. While an excessively one-sided development of any
sense is to be avoided, the teachers can often be of great service
to the pupil by discovering to what type the pupil belongs, and
appealing to him through that sense.

Educational Principles.—We may conclude this study
by summing up certain educational principles flowing from the
psychology of sensation.

1. The teacher should remember that it is *impossible to have
knowledge where there has been no basis in presentation.* There
can no more be an idea of anything external not derived in
some way from sensation than a blind man can tell how colors
look. Hence the necessity of constant appeal to the pupil's
own sense-activity, instead of talking about or representing the
thing to be known. Seeing is more than believing in primary-
education ; it is the beginning of knowledge. This does not
imply that no knowledge can be had excepting knowledge of
just that which has been presented to the senses. On the contrary, the *imagination and reasoning* powers are capable of
erecting large and real superstructures upon a very slight basis
of sensation ; but it is meant that there must be *some* sensory
basis. Furthermore, a constant activity of the senses in early
years is necessary in order to develop the imagination and

thought to the point where they may be able to widen the reports of the senses.

2. The teacher should also keep in mind the *limitations* of sensation. *Sensation is not knowledge*, but only a stimulus to it, and material for it. The mental processes must act upon the sense-material. It must not be forgotten, therefore, that the *ultimate end* of appealing to the senses is the *development of the self-activity* of the pupil in putting into motion those processes of the pupil's mind which will apprehend the sensations, and in strengthening the processes so that they will grow naturally into memory, imagination and thought.

3. The teacher should remember the necessity of a proper *adaptation* of teaching, *first*, to the *stage of development* of sense-activity reached by the pupil, *secondly*, to the *proper sense* for taking in the particular subject taught, and *thirdly*, to any *peculiarities* that may exist in the senses of the individual under instruction.

NOTE.—Regarding the details of sensation, see Dewey's Psychology, chapter III.

§ 2. THE INTERESTS.

We have been dealing with sensation as the basis of information about objects and events—with the beginnings of *knowledge*. But we have had occasion to notice that sensations possess 'TONE' in greater or less degree, that is, that they have a certain agreeable or disagreeable emotional effect. This is not any part of the information conveyed by the sensation, but is a part of the relation of the presentation to the mind. It arises because of the interest which the presentation has for the mind. It is the matter of INTEREST which is now to be discussed.

Interest cannot be described, it can only be felt. But every one knows what he means by saying that something interests him ; he means that it bears such a relation to him as renders it attractive, and draws and fixes the mind's attention. While an analytic description cannot be given, certain differences between the *interesting* side of a presentation and that which affords *knowledge* may be pointed out.

1. Interest is *emotional* rather than intellectual. That is to say, it does not give information about anything in the external world, but arises from the state of the mind itself. It is usually accompanied with pain or pleasure, but cannot be said to be identical with them.

2. Interest is *subjective*, while knowledge is *objective*. The term objective means having to do with the world, with objects, events and their laws ; while the term subjective means belonging to the subject, to the mind without regard to the world outside.

3. Interest is *individual*, while knowledge is *universal*. By universal we mean belonging to a world which is open to all minds alike. That seven and nine make sixteen is a universal fact ; it holds for all minds under all circumstances. By individual we mean being the unique and peculiar possession of some one mind. Others may have an interest similar to mine in, say, the subject of arithmetic, but none can share in *my* interest. They cannot even know that it exists unless I speak of it, or, by some other external act, make it known. In itself it is wholly *internal*, and not a fact in the world, but a fact belonging to me, or to thee, to some individual.

Interest is as much a spontaneous capacity of the mind as sensation is. It is an ultimate and irreducible fact, and, like sensation, an indispensable basis for higher development. While it may be cultivated and transferred from subject to subject in such a way as to make interesting what was previously indifferent or repulsive, it can no more be originally created than a new sense can be created.

Importance of Interest.—The psychological importance

of interest is found in the fact that it is the means by which the mind is drawn to any subject, and led to exercise itself upon it. Whatever does not interest the mind, that the mind is indifferent to ; and whatever is indifferent is for that mind as if it had no existence. The problem of teaching an intelligent savage some technical scientific matter would not be chiefly a problem of how to give him sensations regarding it, nor how to give him mental capacity enough to understand it, but how to arouse his *interest* in such a way that he would set his mind to work upon it. Interest is, therefore, as much a necessary source of knowledge as is sensation. Sensations might have all the objective qualities that they now possess and yet if they failed to interest, the mind would pass them over and they would never enter into the structure of our knowledge.

Educational Principle.—The resulting educational principle is clear. While it is not necessary that learning should be made a matter of *play;* while, indeed, education as the direction of the mind by methods supplied from without, is opposed to the very idea of play, it *is* necessary that teaching should always appeal to some *interest*, and, if the subject is not intrinsically interesting, that interest should be made to gather about it That is, the subject should also be connected with something that does possess this intrinsic interest. In teaching children there is but little difficulty in ma .ing *interesting* sensations into elements of knowledge. The chief problem is how to invest the *indifferent* with *interest*. By no observance of rules can this be done ; it is matter of personal power in the teacher—a power almost wholly due to *sympathy* which is, in the emotional world, what *attention* is in the intellectual world. Under the influence of this power the teacher is interested in the subject for the sake of the pupil ; interest begets interest, and the pupil often becomes interested in the indifferent for the sake of the teacher. The teacher should also keep in mind the individual and subjective character of interest as a reason why his mode of presenting a subject should be varied sufficiently to catch the differing interests of different minds.

NOTE.—On this subject see Dewey's Psychology, pp. 16 and 246, *et seq.*

§ 3. IMPULSE.

Having studied the intellectual and emotional basis of the psychical life, we have to take up IMPULSE as *the volitional basis*. Impulses are *activities which arise from some feeling of want and which, guided by interest in the satisfaction of that want, lead to some physical change.* For illustration, we may take the impulse for food. This arises from the organic feeling, hunger, a feeling of lack and of desire for something to satisfy this lack, and it manifests itself in certain movements of the body, those necessary to supply the lack. Impulse reverses the order of sensation. The latter begins in outward physical motion which traverses the sensory nerves to the brain, and then becomes a psychical state. But impulses begin in a psychical state, and this, by means of the brain and motor nerves, is transformed into outward motion. Sensation moves inward and impulse outwards.

Importance of Impulse.—To be convinced of the importance of impulse we need but watch any sentient being from the lowest to the highest, and call to mind that all their actions, excepting the purely physiological, are only the outward expressions of impulse. Impulse, in short, is the basis of will. It is *only* the basis, however, for it requires to be regulated, and its various forms harmonized with one another before it becomes a true act of will ; the growth of will begins with the acquisition of power over bodily movements ; the *will less* activities of impulse are isolated and co-ordinated into movements in which *purpose* is clearly displayed : thus the child begins to seize an object, to hold the head erect, to sit alone, to stand, to walk, to talk, etc. Impulses, like sensations, have to be acted upon by higher psychical processes in order to be changed into finished products.

Impulse and Instinct.—Impulses are closely connected with instincts.   Indeed, an instinct may be defined as an impulse which takes at once, without being taught by experience, the channel necessary to reach its proper end.   Instinct, in other words, is an impulse which leads one to do, without any knowledge of the reason why, just what one would do, if he had complete knowledge of the circumstances.   The impulse for food, for example is, in most animals and in man in his infancy, an instinct, because the organism of each, as soon as it feels the want of food, takes just the measures needed to secure it, and does this without being guided by previous experience.

Impulses Classified.—Impulses may be classified, according to the stimulus which arouses the sense of want, as impulses of *sensation*, of *perception*, of *imitation*, and of *expression*.

1. *Impulses of Sensation.*—A sensation not only reports something external to the organism, but it excites a tendency to act with regard to that something, to appropriate it.   Thus the *appetites*, which are regularly recurring tendencies to lay hold of something external and to make it a part of the organism, arise in needs which are excited by organic affections, that is by *general sensations*.   But the *special senses* have also corresponding impulses.   There is a hunger of the sense of touch for contact with bodies, of the sense of hearing for sounds, etc.   Any one who has been shut off, as by sickness, from his accustomed quota of sensations, knows that the pleasure of recovery consists largely in the satisfaction of the hunger of these senses.   The impulses are now permitted to act freely.   There is such a thing as *starving the mind* by not satisfying the sense-impulses, as well as starving the body by not satisfying its hunger-impulse.

2. *Impulses of Perception.*—These are such as arise directly from the mere perception of an object. They come under the head of impulses to grasp something or, in some way, to continue the exploration of it. An infant begins to reach for things as soon as he begins definitely to perceive them. This impulse is one of the chief foundations of the *play* impulse. The child not only grasps the objects, but handles them, moves them here and there, tests their various qualities for himself, and tries to see what he can do with them.

3. *Impulses to Imitation.*—As soon as an infant clearly sees the actions of others, there is an instinctive impulse to reproduce them in himself. He does not understand the original intention of the action, nor why he endeavors to repeat it, but the very perception of the action renders the child, for the time being, an automaton. A baby "reads" when he takes a newspaper or book, marks when he gets hold of a pencil, brushes with a broom, strikes with a whip, and so on indefinitely. This tendency to imitation is an exceedingly *important factor* in early education, enabling the child to learn easily what would otherwise be effected, if at all, only by very laborious training.

4. *Impulses to Expression.*—These begin with the expres sion of emotion or of inward states. Thus the infant cries, smiles, laughs, draws back in fright, etc. These outward acts are not originally intended to manifest the emotions, but are their involuntary results. Finally, however, they may be used as signs for denoting the mental states which formerly produced them. After the expression of inward feeling comes the manifestation of impressions produced by external objects. The child points to and makes noises at any object that interests him, and thus there gradually arises the whole class of gestures. Among those in whom articulate speech does not render it unnecessary there is produced a *gesture language.* This is

found among deaf mutes and among savage tribes who are in close relations with other tribes, speaking different dialects. So instinctive and unconventional is this mode of expression that it has been found that North American Indians and deaf-mutes have no difficulty in understanding one another when they come together, even for the first time. The highest class of impulses of expression is that of the communication of ideas. This manifests itself, for the most part, in *spoken language*. In civilized mankind, at least, there is an impulse towards speech as strong and as instinctive as that towards locomotion.

Educational Principles.—The educational bearing of what has been said regarding the impulses is evident.

(1) The teacher should keep in mind the close connection of the senses as source of *knowledge* with the senses as active *tendencies*. It is not enough merely to put things before the senses, care must be taken to see that the senses are directed upon the things. Education of the senses comes through use of the senses, and *training in the use of senses is training of the will*,—of the regulation and co-ordination of impulses. An infant does not *see*, at first, not because the objects are not reflected on its retina, but because there is no fixity of gaze, no control over vision, but only a wandering, aimles glance directed by any chance impulses. The baby learns to see, as afterwards it learns to walk, by regulating and combining such impulses. The teacher's work in training the senses must be an extension and refining of this spontaneous learning.

(2) The teacher should bear in mind the great importance of the *instincts*. It is of the highest import that teaching should *appeal* to some *natural instinct already existing* and that it should draw out and develop this instinct. It is of equal importance that the order of instruction in subjects should correspond to the *natural order* of the appearance of instincts in

the child. It has been well said that the pedagogical equivalent of " strike while the iron is hot " is " seize every instinct at the height of its development." In early life, each instinct as it appears is so imperious that it is almost impossible that it should not meet satisfaction. This constitutes the self taught, or rather the unconsciously taught period, during which the child learns to talk, to walk, etc. Afterwards as the instincts are more subtle and involved, there is greater need of the teacher's tact and control. Before an instinct in a given direction has shown itself, it is hopeless to educate a child in that direction ; after that instinct has given way to another, *interest dies out* and the teacher, instead of availing himself of the tide of energy setting naturally in that direction, has to evoke activity by artificial aids.

(3) Let the teacher, then, make the most of the impulses that have been described. It follows from the *perception*-impulses that the child must be *doing* something ; under a judicious teacher this impulse can be gratified and at the same time *directed*. In rural schools a great deal of time is wasted, or more than wasted, which the child should occupy in gratifying his instinct for activity. He can be led—unless the teacher is quite without power—to take an interest in many so-called kindergarten operations, in writing, drawing, etc., by which he is sure to gain quickness of eye and deftness of hand.

In such occupations, too, the impulse of *imitation* finds play : the child likes to imitate the things that are pleasing to the eye, and skilful imitation soon leads to the desire and the power to *invent* beautiful forms. But more especially this impulse is a powerful co-factor with the " environment " in educating the child. At first he unconsciously imitates the actions, the tones, the gestures, the whole demeanor of those about him ; but unconscious imitation gives place to, or rather is strengthened by voluntary imitation. When the bond of sympathy has been formed between his teacher and himself, the child makes a conscious *effort* to grow like the teacher. There is an intense charm in imitating him to whom, as posessed of superior powers, he looks up with reverence—fear blended with love. He feels that he is growing in strength, in wisdom, in all manly qualities, when he is growing like his teacher whom he regards with so much deference. Thus it is that the characteristics of the teacher, his personal habits (neatness, etc.) his tones of voice, his gestures, his self-control, his energy, etc., have a powerful influence in forming the character of the pupil.

The impulse of *expression* is equally important and equally neglected. Let not the teacher thwart, but rather gratify the impulse ; through genuine sympathy let him gain the confidence of the child, who will then be able to lay aside his timidity and will take pleasure in trying to express his simple thoughts and feelings. Every lesson should be a lesson in *expression* as well as a lesson in *thinking*; in fact, a lesson in expression *because* it is a lesson in thinking.

Note.—Regarding the impulses, see Dewey's Psychology, Chapter XVII.

CHAPTER III.

THE PSYCHICAL PROCESSES.

Three Ways in which Elements are Connected. —We have now to take up the processes by which the raw material—sensations, interests and impulses—are worked up into the forms of actual experience. If we examine what makes up the contents of our minds, we shall see that the complex forms whose mode of production we have to discover, may be roughly grouped into *three* classes.

(1) In the first place, there are wholes made up of coexistent members. For example, as I look out of my window I

do not get disconnected and fragmentary color sensations, but I see a diversified landscape with its many features, and all are present at about the same instant of time. The first group is thus that which comprehends ideas composed of *simultaneous* or *coexistent* parts.

(2) But obviously not all our mental experience will come under this head. The sight of the landscape may suggest something that I have read in Wordsworth's poetry, this in turn may call up Tennyson, this the subject of the House of Lords, and so on indefinitely. Here we have a *train* of ideas, and its members are connected *successively*, not simultaneously.

(3) Finally we might be led from the idea of the House of Lords to consider the advantages and disadvantages of an aristocracy. In this case, we would compare the history of different nations, examine political causes and effects, weigh and sift evidence, reject all that did not seem to bear upon the case in hand, and arrange the remaining facts to meet the desired end. Here the result, as in the second case, would be a train of ideas, consisting of successive members, but yet differing from the second group. It is not a series whose parts suggest one another at haphazard, but a *controlled* and *regulated* series. The order is not one of time merely, but of an underlying idea or end with reference to which the ideas are connected. In other words, the second group comprises those trains of successive members in which one idea is allowed to suggest others just as may happen, while the third group includes those trains whose successive parts are *intentionally controlled* so as to lead up to some end.

The Processes which Produce these Groups.—We have now to study the processes by which the elements are united into these three groups. Still speaking in a rough and general way, we may say that *Non voluntary Attention* is the power active in producing what we may call the simultaneous group ; *Association*, that in producing the group of successive uncontrolled parts, and *Voluntary Attention*, the source of the group of successive parts purposely controlled and arranged.

§1. NON-VOLUNTARY ATTENTION.

Meaning of the Expression.—By attention is mean simply the dwelling of the mind upon some presentation or some factor of a presentation so as to give it prominence. The term 'non-voluntary,' implies that the mind is turned upon this subject-matter simply on account of the attractiveness of the matter, not by reason of any intervention on the part of the will. It is an act of attention when a student keeps his mind fixed upon his lessons in spite of all distracting circumstances; of *voluntary* attention if it requires a definite resolve of the will to effect it, of *non-voluntary* if the subject naturally arouses and absorbs his mind. It is evident that non-voluntary attention must always precede voluntary. A baby 'notices' (and this 'noticing' is precisely what is meant by attention) not because any appeal is made to his reason and will to keep his mind directed that one way, but because what is noticed interests and excites him. We have to study the *conditions* and the *effects* of non-voluntary attention.

1. **Conditions.**—The condition under which any presentation awakens non-voluntary attention is that it be *interesting*. The attention is aroused, awakened, drawn, attracted by some intrinsic interests in the presentation. We may possibly give attention to what does not interest us, but only if we force ourselves by power of will to do so; and such an act of volition is, of course, not *non-voluntary* attention. Interest may, however, be either natural or acquired.

(1) **Natural Interest.**—By this we mean the value which the presentation has in itself, apart from all connection with other factors of mind. For example, the color of an orange may interest a child either because the color is pleasing in itself, or because it suggested the pleasant taste of the fruit. In the former case only is it natural or spontaneous interest.

Quantity and Tone.—The constituent elements of natural interest are *quantity* and *tone* of sensation, including under quantity what we have previously classed as intensity and extensity. If there are presented at the same time, two colors or two sounds, the infant mind will always listen to the loudest sound and look at the brightest color. In the early development of intelligence, the impression that beats upon the doors of consciousness with the greatest force is the one admitted. The tone of a sensation we have already explained to mean the agreeable or disagreeable property which accompanies it. The organic sensations, hunger, thirst, fatigue, satisfaction, etc., possess the greatest amount of emotional accompaniment, and hence, as the most interesting, absorb attention almost wholly in the early life of the infant. To say that a baby knows when he is hungry, when he knows nothing else, is simply to say that the sensation of hunger will attract his attention when nothing else will do so. Gradually the mind is freed from its bondage to organic affections. The pleasures that go along with tastes, smells, muscular activity, and finally with hearing and sight, attract the mind to notice all the elements which are admitted through the "five gateways of knowledge."

(2) **Acquired Interest.**—As suggested, a presentation may acquire value in virtue of its surroundings. The sight of the cup from which a baby takes his food has at first perhaps not nearly so much interest for him as other more brightly colored objects about him, but its association with the satisfaction of his appetite gradually lends it an attractiveness of its own. We may reduce the conditions which lead to the acquisition of interest to two heads—*familiarity* and *novelty*.

Familiarity.—Originally all experiences aside from the influence of quantity and tone stand upon the same level, all are equally noticed and hence equally unnoticed. There is no perspective, no foreground and no background. We have a somewhat similar experience when we are thrown into surroundings wholly new.   Everything looks alike to us ; even the faces about us seem all made from one pattern.   "We do not know where to begin," we say.   That is, nothing stands out so as to attract our attention to itself.   We have to get our bearings. Nothing aids us so much in this process as the constant recurrence of certain features.   Those factors which are repeated stand out more prominently.   The familiar occurrences are separated from their surroundings, and become interesting from this very fact.   Similarly we may suppose that the fog which surrounds the intellectual life of an infant lifts from about those persons and objects which are always recurring in his experience, his parents, brothers and sisters, nurse, cradle, articles used in connection with his food, etc.   They become centres of interest, and in acquiring this interest they fix the mind's attention and gain *distinctness*.

Novelty.—While in general it is the familiar that interests and draws us to itself, yet familiarity may be carried to the point where it ceases to call out the mind's activity.   Those who live near a cataract or in a mill cease to pay attention to the noise. It has nothing to interest them.   Similarly, we do not notice the familiar ticking of the clock in our room, the pressure of clothing upon our body, or an even temperature about us. Qualities which are the first to strike a stranger we never notice in our most intimate friends.   It is a common proverb that familiarity deadens and dulls.   Now in these cases nothing arouses the sleepy attention so soon as *change*.   Let the water-fall change its noise, let the mill stop, let the clock cease ticking, let the unnoticed feature of our friend alter, and at once we are all attention.

Familiarity and Novelty in Connection.—The truth of the matter seems to be that it is neither the familiar nor the novel which interests in itself, but one in connection with the other.   It is the old in the midst of the new—as when a traveller hears his own language in a foreign country—or the novel in the midst of the customary—as when we hear a strange tongue spoken in our own country—that attracts attention. That which is *wholly novel* has no points of connection with our experience and hence cannot interest, while we have become so habituated to the *wholly familiar* that we find nothing in it which seems worth dwelling upon.

2. Effects of Non-Voluntary Attention.—Attention is both positive and negative in its workings. That is to say, the mind dwells upon some presentations only because it draws away from others. Imagine a light equally diffused over a room, then imagine all the light focussed in some one point. It is evident that the rest of the room will grow dark as this one point grows bright. So it is with attention. Attention has its aspect of exclusion as well as of inclusion.

Effects of Withdrawal of Attention.—It follows that what is not attended to is not brought into consciousness. Not everything that comes before the senses, or even that affects them strongly, comes to be knowledge. There is an indefinite throng of stimuli — sights, sounds, pressures, etc., knocking for entrance into consciousness, which never come within its gates, because, the mind not attending to them, no mental activity is brought to bear upon them. We are almost always unaware of our organic sensations, of the contact of our clothing with our bodies, of the surrounding temperature, etc., because these things do not interest us enough to attract our minds. One may sit before an open window and have the scenes of a busy street pictured upon the retina of one's eye, and yet be conscious of nothing that is going on. The withdrawal of attention may go so far that the mind can almost bid defiance to external stimulus. Soldiers, wounded in battle, but not aware of pain, Archimedes so engaged in geometrical study as to be unconscious of the battle at his very doors, will serve as illustrations.

Positive Effects of Attention.—On the other hand, to

attend to a presentation is to hold it before the mind, to get it within the range of psychical activity and thus to bring into consciousness what would otherwise remain outside. There is no fact of which we are aware, that would not serve as illustration of this principle, but perhaps instances of unusual ability in various directions show it in clearest light. Workers in steel are said to distinguish half-a dozen shades of color in what appears to one non-expert as a uniform glow. That is to say, by the cultivation of attention they are enabled to bring to consciousness what entirely escapes others. Similarly, tea-tasters, etc., perceive a great number of differences, where others would get only one impression. A trained botanist will see more in a casual glánce through a microscope than one untrained would discover by careful searching. The power of attending, in other words, is equivalent to the power of *being conscious*.

The Uniting Power of Attention.—Not only does attention distinguish what were otherwise unperceived, but it *unites*. Its general law, the basis of all mental progress whatever, is that *all elements attended to by one and the same act of mind become members of one idea.*

Consequently all elements *not* taken in by this act, must be grasped by another movement of attention, and hence become another idea. In other words, a single idea—a single concrete state of consciousness—means whatever has been laid hold of by one act of attention. It makes no difference to this one idea whether its parts are many or few, whether they are naturally coherent or the reverse. Here then we have the first process by which the mass of sensations pouring in upon us is given form and unity.

1. *Illustration that a Number of Elements are Capable of Union in One Idea.*—We may best begin with a simple example. Suppose twenty dots placed before the eye but arranged very irregularly. The mind in order to take them in may be

obliged to pay attention to one at a time—to count them. In this case, there will be twenty separate ideas involved. Now suppose them rearranged into four groups of five dots each, each group being regular in itself, but not symmetrical with the others. Here we shall have just the same amount apprehended by *four* acts of attention, and hence with four resulting ideas. If these four groups are now formed into one symmetrical whole the mind will apprehend all in one idea, although there is really just as much there to be seen, as when the act of apprehension involves twenty ideas. This illustrates the fact that it makes no difference to the unity of an idea, how much there is in it, provided only it can all be taken in by one act of attention.

Application of this Illustration.—This abstract illustration may be made more definite by supposing a fact substituted for each dot, and relations between these facts for the spatial arrangement of the dots. Twenty isolated facts will require as many acts of attention to apprehend them and hence will produce as many distinct ideas. But group the facts under one law—as various astronomical facts are connected in the law of gravitation—and the mind at once binds them together into the *unity of one idea* grasped and carried in one act. The same result occurs when no law is known, if any kind of connection can be made out between the various facts. Just as the mind, for the sake of ease in apprehending and economy in carrying impressions, will attempt to form some kind of grouping among the twenty dots, even where none is apparent, so it will strive to unite separate ideas by *making* connections, even if none exist upon the surface. This brings us to the second fact mentioned, that elements having no actual coherence will form parts of one idea, if they can be attended to at once.

2. *Illustration that Unlike Elements are Capable of Union in one idea.*—It may be said indeed that for the union of various elements in one idea, it is sufficient for these elements to exist

at the same time, without there being *any real* connection whatever among them.   This is without doubt the original source of union of the elements presented in sensation, simple co-existence in time.   At a later period, the mind, of course, reviews the connections which it has formed earlier in life, and rejects those whose parts do not seem really to belong together.   For example, an infant originally connects the smell, taste and sight of an orange, not because he sees that these qualities are really component parts of the orange (on the contrary, it is only *by* connecting them that he gets the idea of the orange at all) but simply because these sensations are given to him at the same time.   Afterwards he finds that there is more than a mere connection of time between these sensations, that they are what we call *really* connected, and he confirms his original act of union, while in other cases, he may reverse his first act of connection.   The important thing to notice here is that whenever there is no obstacle offered, the mind connects whatever it can connect, even upon so slight a basis as occurrence at the same point of time.   Many of the popular fallacies and superstitions have arisen from a tendency to give a *real* connection to events which are only *casually* connected; in this we have an explanation of the common fallacies described by the Latin phrase *post hoc ergo propter hoc*—" after this, therefore in consequence of this "—With the new moon a change in the weather has occurred, *therefore* the moon influences the weather ; with the appearance of a comet, a war or a pestilence has broken out, therefore comets portend disaster, etc.   For many generations the people of St. Kilda believed that the arrival of a ship in the harbour caused an epidemic of influenza, and clever men assigned many ingenious reasons why the ship should produce " colds in the head " among the population.   At last it occurred to some bold thinker that the arrival of the ship might not be the cause of the distemper, but that *both* might be the effect of a common cause, and then it was remembered that a ship could enter the harbour *only when a strong north-east wind was blowing.*

Further Illustrations.—Two or three simple examples may make the principles clearer. A French psychologist tells of a little boy who when going under a railway bridge happened to think of a toy horse which had been given him, and said "my horse." For a long time after that he never went under anything whatever without saying "my horse." Although there was absolutely no real connection between the two facts, they were connected for him in one idea simply because he had attended to both at the same time. Another example : a child who once noticed that a railway train stopped just as some one moved the catch in a window of the car, supposed for a long time after, that all trains were stopped by means of the window catch. These examples, trivial as they are, serve none the less to illustrate the law upon which all mental acquisition is originally founded—namely, that whatever sensations occur at the same time can be attended to by one and the same act unless there is some actual opposition between them, and, since they are grasped in one act of attention, they become members of one idea. Thus it is that sensations in themselves fragmentary and separate become united into the simultaneous wholes of co-existent parts, which constitute so large a part of our actual experience.

Educational Principles.

(1) *The Necessity of Activity.*—Perhaps the chief point for the teacher to keep in mind is the necessity of some activity of *attention* on the part of the child from the very first and in every operation. No amount of presentation, however skillful ; no amount of repetition, however persistent ; no amount of explanation, however clear—is of any avail, unless the child's *attention*, the one condition of learning which cannot be dispensed with, is secured. That there is attention, simply means that the child's mind is working upon the subject attended to ; and that the child is non-attentive, simply means that there is no connection between his mind and the subject. In the latter case, the teacher and pupil might as well be in different worlds so far as any educational relation between them is concerned.

(2) *Possible Errors.*—There is a tendency at present to emphasize the need of sense presentation, of intuition and of object lessons in teaching. This is well ; the need cannot be

C

over-emphasized, provided it be remembered that placing the objects before the senses, no more insures their being apprehended, to say nothing of their right apprehension, than putting food before one insures its being eaten, to say nothing of its being digested and assimilated. There must be an *activity proceeding from the mind;* this may be stimulated but cannot be produced by another. Here, we have occasion to renew the caution referred to in the first chapter against the error of over-estimating the part—important as it undoubtedly is—which the teacher can play in education. There is a disposition on the part of some teachers to substitute the work of presentation and explanation of material for the more difficult, because less mechanical and more *personal* task, of getting the pupils' mind at work upon the material.

3. *Non-voluntary Attention must be Secured Indirectly.*—This attention cannot be gained however by the mere directing of the child "to pay attention." Such an injunction, at the stage of development now considered, must be meaningless. Attention must be *attracted*, not forced. The subject matter, in other words, must be made of interest. This interest once obtained, attention follows naturally and even inevitably. The teacher therefore can hardly overestimate the importance of *Interest:* it is the beginning of non-voluntary attention, this leads to discrimination and association, this to *voluntary attention*, and this again is the test and condition of intellectual development.

4. It can hardly need repeating that interesting does not mean *amusing.* It does not mean that the subject must be surrounded with factitious attractions in order to appeal to some individual taste of the pupil. Such a conception wrongs and belittles the intelligence of the child. Every child, not actually stupid, takes delight in the activity of his mind as he does in the activity of his body, and to render a subject interesting means only to make it capable of calling forth this natural activity. To rely upon such sources of interest, as are directed, not to the native and simple delight in mental activity, but to awakening various outside pleasures, is like thinking that a child's natural hunger cannot be trusted to make him eat appropriate food, but that his palate must be artifically stimulated and tickled.

Two wrongs are thus committed. The child's true intellectual powers are left in abeyance, and an abnormal faculty, requiring constantly increasing artificial stimulus, is created.

5. *Use of the Play-impulse.*—On the other hand, in early training good use may be made of the "play-impulse" by a proper selection of work which the child will take delight in—for example, some of the *gifts* and *occupations* of the kindergarten. Between such work and the play-impulse there is an *available* relation, as the success of kindergarten methods clearly proves. The principles of the kindergarten, and some of its methods—or at least modified forms of them—may be applied in all primary education. Why not awaken attention by gratifying *the hunger of the senses*—of the eye for seeing, of the ear for hearing, of the hand for doing? There is scarcely a child that will not become deeply *interested* in Building, Folding, Pricking, Stick-laying, Drawing, etc. He will therefore give the best of non-voluntary *attention* to what he is doing, and thus will begin to form habits both mental and physical which must prove of high value in his future development.

6. *Methods of Awakening Normal Interest.*—Normal attraction is such as naturally calls forth in some degree the attention of *every* healthy mind. No specified rules for creating it can here be given. That belongs partly to pedagogy, in a narrow sense, and still more *to the personal power of the teacher.* But notice may again be called to the fact that interest depends largely upon *familiarity* and *novelty* and their intermixture in due proportion. To thrust something new upon a child, and take no pains to bring out points of likeness between this new subject and those already somewhat familiar, is to *repel* attention. To continue to dwell upon a topic or illustration worn threadbare will give the same result. Connections should be made between matters and interests familiar outside of school, and those taken up within, as well as between various school subjects. A boy may sometimes be interested in arithmetic by connecting

a problem with his father's business, etc.   Interest in history or in geography may be called forth in connection with contemporaneous events in which the pupils have or may be made to have a lively interest.   It is a great mistake in all ways, but in none more than in this matter of attention, to shut off the school from the outside world.

(7) *Further Suggestions.*—(*a*) The *negative* aspect of attention, the shutting out of impressions which would call away the mind from the matter in hand, should be looked after.   Before the development of voluntary attention the mind follows the greater of two interests, and if this should happen not to be connected with the study, the latter will suffer.   (*b*) In this connection there may be noticed certain physical conditions of attention, depending on the child's health and vigour, and on his *surroundings.*   Attention, even in its early stage, means mind-tension, and this, again, means a severe demand on nervous energy; it cannot therefore be expected that a sick or weary child can show much activity of attention even for a usually interesting topic.   Again, when there is a feeling of discomfort (or very often something worse) arising from bad *lighting, heating, ventilation, seating, etc.*, it is extremely difficult to arouse the attention of the child and keep it fixed in a definite direction.   (*c*) The *unifying* aspect of attention must also be kept in mind.   To present too many subjects in succession, to use too many illustrations, too many explanations, to hurry from one point to another is a successful mode of producing the habit of mind-wandering.   (*d*) Again, since the young mind is apt to connect things occurring at the same time, whether they should be united or not, great pains must be taken to select just the points which are important, and to present them in their *proper relation.*   (*e*) Finally, it may be mentioned that while *questioning* has a certain justification as a necessary means of reaching important ends in education, its chief justification is in its power of *arousing attention* and

keeping it rightly directed. A question is a challenge to attention. And, while disconnected, mechanical, unprepared questions gradually weaken what power of attention originally exists, orderly, progressive and suggestive questions infallibly strengthen it. The chief thing to be aimed at, in fact, is to cultivate in the pupil the habit of *asking himself questions*. This ensured, the power of holding and controlling attention from within (voluntary attention in other words) is secured. With the remark, therefore, that the end of the training of non-voluntary attention is to lead up to voluntary attention, we may leave this subject.

§2. ASSOCIATION.

What is meant by Succession of Ideas.—It has already been stated, that Association is the means by which a successive train of ideas arises. But, by succession, is not meant simply that presentations follow after one another. Successive acts of attention would produce a succession of ideas, on the principle already explained, that each act of attention results in a distinct idea. What is meant, is rather that there grows out of some presentation or idea, another idea, and out of this a third, and so on, the whole process going on without the intervention of any new presentation. This is generally called the *association of ideas*. A standard illustration is that of Hobbes, (born 1588) one of the first to call attention to the subject. In a company, when the conversation turned upon the subject of the civil war in England between the Stuarts and the Puritans, some one asked the value of a Roman Denarius. This question, he says, appeared abrupt, but upon reflection, he traced the following thread of associations : Civil war, the king, the treachery of those who surrendered him, the treachery of Judas Iscariot, the sum of money received, its *value*. We shall take up : First, the *conditions* of Association ; second, its *varieties* ; and third, its *results*.

(1) *Conditions of Association.*—Why is it that ideas enter into successive trains, each suggesting the next? The answer in a general way is that *ideas which have been once connected together have the power of calling one another up.* Association is thus seen to depend upon non-voluntary attention. In the latter, as we have learned, as many parts as possible are made one. Now, if one of these parts is presented, there is a tendency for it to complete itself by suggesting the parts not actually presented. These parts are said to be re-presented. Suppose, to take a very simple example, that I have heard a celebrated orator deliver a speech; by my acts of attention at the time, the speech and the speaker became indissolubly united into one idea. Now, years afterward, I read this oration and there recurs to my mind the idea of the speaker as he delivered it. The reason is evident; the speech is not an independent idea in my mind; it is only one part of a larger idea, and it completes itself by suggesting its other member.

Integration and Red-integration.—The two acts of presentation and of representation are sometimes called integration and red-integration. The term integration signifies as the etymology implies, that the original presentation was a whole formed out of parts; red-integration is a second act of integration based upon the first. Thus, when the sight of a flower recalls the place where it was picked, when the perception of some token suggests the person who gave it, when a Latin word calls up its English equivalent—in all these cases we have instances of one part of a whole idea completing itself by calling up the part with which it was formerly connected. It may be said, therefore, that the conditions of association are, *first*, original union in one idea by an act of attention, and *second*, the occurrence of one part of this idea, which then completes itself by calling up the other parts.

2. *Varieties of Association.*—There are two kinds of association, know as association by the principle of *contiguity*, and by the principle of *similarity*. They are also known as *external* and *internal* association. By the principle of *contiguity* is meant that whatever ideas or objects have been conjoined in *space* or in *time* have the power of redintegrating one another.

In other words, objects existing by the side of one another, events following one another, will become so associated that one calls up another. By *similarity* is meant that whatever ideas or objects are like one another, whether this likeness be in appearance, in meaning, in mode of use, in sound, or in any other respect, have the power of recalling one another.

Examples of Contiguity.—An instance of contiguity in space is the following: If I think of the post office, I may be lead to think of the adjoining building, this may suggest the next and so on. Were I sufficiently familiar with the whole city, this process of suggestion might go on till I had called before me all its buildings. Contiguity in time is illustrated by the fact that a note of music will suggest a bar, the bar the air, the air the entire tune, etc. One letter of an alphabet suggests the next and so on; a line of a familiar poem suggests the succeeding line, this the next until the whole poem is repeated. We think of something that occurred yesterday, and at once there arises in succession the entire day's doings. A visiting friend once asked a little Irish boy his age, he replied, "I was seven years old, the day the pig died;" evidently what to him were two important events had been associated because they had occurred at the same time.

Examples of Similarity.—Seeing a portrait calls up the original. One face suggests another which it resembles. The apple-blossom calls up the rose; the locust flower the pea, etc. Napoleon the Great may suggest Julius Cæsar; while Cicero calls up Demosthenes. The idea of a straight line may suggest rectitude; a hammer call up a hatchet. The word *frater* will call up the words *Bruder* and brother, etc. In some of these cases, there is similarity in appearance, in others, of meaning, or use, or sound, or of mere analogy. No limits can be put to the use of the principle. Wherever there is perceived to be the slightest similarity between two ideas, then one idea has the power of summoning the other into consciousness.

Association by Contrast.—A remarkable extension of the principle of similarity is seen in the fact that *opposites* call each other up; so vice suggests virtue, night day, joy sorrow, a dwarf a giant, a valley a mountain, etc., etc. It may seem absurd to call this mutual suggestion of each other by opposites a case of similarity, but such it clearly is. Vice and virtue are simply the extremes of moral conduct, night and day of the whole astronomical day, dwarf and giant of human stature, etc. That is, there is a common underlying basis, and the contrast only emphasizes this identity of basis.

External and Internal Association.—As already mentioned, association by contiguity is sometimes called *external*, that by similarity *internal*. The reason is as follows. In contiguous association both the suggesting and the suggested idea have been parts of one idea, but the bond of union was an external one, *i.e.*, it did not arise from any *essential* connection between them. When, *e.g.*, a certain idea brings into consciousness the place in the page where first I read it, the idea and place are connected, but only outwardly. Each would be unchanged if this connection had not occurred. The union does not affect the internal structure of either. Not so in association by similarity. When the sight of a portrait is followed in consciousness by the idea of its original, the bond of union is just the internal quality of likeness, and without this quality, neither the face nor its copy would be what it is. The connecting tie enters therefore into the very make-up of the ideas.

3. *Results of Association.*—**Mental Order and Freedom.**—The first result has already been remarked upon. It is the formation of a train of ideas, each member of which grows from the preceding member by some rule. Continuity, sequence, some semblance, at least, of order and of regularity thus come into psychical life. Ideas are no longer isolated, but shaped into sequences having some common bearing, some unity. While in non-voluntary attention the mind is always called into action from *without* and thus is subject to whatever is presented, in *association*, the mind forms a series of ideas from *within*. The succession of ideas does not depend any longer upon the order in which external objects affect us, but upon the internal

train of suggestion. It may fairly be said, therefore, that another result of association is to *free the mind* from bondage to its sensations, impulses, etc., and to allow it a certain independence of its own.

Superiority of Association by Similarity.—Association based upon internal similarity assists the development of mental power and freedom much more than that based upon accidental conjunction in space or time. One might associate for example, a dog with a wolf because he had seen both together, or because their pictures or names had been conjoined in a book. Or, he might associate them because of some common principle which he recognized to be involved in the structure of both. It is evident that in the first case (association by contiguity) there is no *reason* in the association; it might just as well have happened between other ideas; while in the latter case (association by similarity) there is *meaning* in the association and it may lead to something beyond itself—to a scientific comprehension of the relation of the two animals. Similarly an historical event may be associated with some part of a page or chart (spatial contiguity) or it may be associated with other events of a like kind. The former association has no significance the latter stimulates the mind to reflect and possibly to discover some historical law.

Formation of Habits.—The point made thus far is that the occurrence of an association tends to give the mind an *order and freedom in its ideas and activities* independent of the sense-impressions which are constantly beating upon consciousness. This is especially true if an association of ideas or actions is so often repeated that a *habit* is formed. By a habit is meant *such a thoroughly formed train of associations that if one member of the train comes into consciousness the other members follow almost inevitably, and without any intervention on the part of will or of consciousness.* For example, we now have the habit of standing erect and of walking. We do not need to pay careful attention to every detail and stage of the complex movements involved in these acts. It is enough that we begin the movement, the rest goes on of itself. But it was not always so. One need only watch a young child learning to walk in order to see that he has to form the associations between all successive movements of his muscles; that he has to repeat these successive associations carefully and an indefinite number of times. But these associations repeated often enough make habit, and the once difficult acts are performed automatically, *i.e.*, without the special intervention of the *will*.

Active and Passive Habits.—Habits are distinguished as active and as passive. By passive habit is meant simply that we are *habituated* or accustomed to anything. It implies no more than ability to hold our own so that we are not conquered by external impressions or activities. Active habit is more than this. It implies ability to react against the external impression, to make it of use to ourselves. It is skill, capacity, trained ability in some direction. Passive habit is illustrated by the binding force of a custom upon us; active habit, by the dexterity, quickness and accuracy of a well-trained mechanic.

Function of Habit.—Habit serves a two-fold purpose in mental life. In the *first place*, it forms a psychical mechanism or piece of machinery by means of which the soul both holds its own and asserts itself against the pressure of surrounding circumstances; and, in the *second place*, it allows the Intelligence and the Will time and opportunity to apply themselves to the mastery of new and higher acts.

First End.—In the early period of psychical existence, the mind is at the mercy of its impressions. It can understand nothing of its surroundings, and can execute no purposes, indeed, it is not capable of forming purposes. It is the *formation of habits* more than anything else that lifts the infant from this state of subjection. If he forms an intellectual habit— say that of noticing the circumstances under which his food is given him—there is at least one respect in which he stands above the chaos which in other regards overpowers him. If he forms a habit of will—say of walking, of controlling the movements of his hands, of putting sounds together into articulate speech—he is in these respects, the master of his impulses instead of being mastered by them.

Habit is Self-Control.—A habit, in other words, is a mode of self-control in some definite direction. It is, as is often said, *second nature*, that is, it is a mode of self-control so thoroughly acquired that it asserts itself spontaneously and without effort whenever there is any occasion for its use. It is by habit that the body becomes a fit and accurate instrument for the soul. It is through habit that the soul impresses itself upon the body, and trains it into a servant which is ever working for useful ends, without waiting for special instructions from its master. Thus, when the mind is thinking about other things, the required act is still executed—as when one talks, or walks, or reads, or plays a musical instrument, while occupied with some problem. The influence of habit is seen most clearly in the capacity of the body to perform certain complicated acts without any direction from the mind except in initiating the process, but there are also purely *mental* habits—*ways* of thinking or of feeling, as we ordinarily call them. The artist has one mental habit, the scientific man another, the teacher another, the statesman another, and so on. Each has certain kinds of mental trains into which the mind falls naturally and spontaneously and in which it is little or no effort to keep thinking, because the lines of association are so well established.

Second End.—If, as suggested, a habit may be fairly said to execute itself, requiring intelligence and will merely to start it, then clearly, the formation of habits relieves the mind from the necessity of any supervision of such actions and leaves it free to devote itself to other matters. For example, when a child is learning to walk (that is, when he is forming an association between certain impulses) he must give his entire mind to it; his mental processes cannot occupy themselves with anything else. But the habit once formed, it seems to be taken entirely out of the mental sphere ; the mind can think of other things as much as if the walking were not going on at all ; and so with every other habit in the degree of its perfection. If one counts the time given to purely mechanical acts, like dressing, eating, walking, the articulation of sounds, etc., and then supposes that the mind had to give itself specially to such acts — to the exclusion of all else—one can see what a boon to us is the power of forming habits which regulate themselves.

Educational Principles.—Following the idea originally laid down that the teacher's work is to assist and regulate the normal psychical processes of the learner's mind, it is evident that the associative activities demand the closest attention and wisest care of the educator. Their use is fundamental in *every stage of mental growth* and hence they may be helpfully discussed with reference to their employment in three stages, the *primary*, the *secondary* and the *higher*.

1. *The First Stage is Mechanical.*—It should be kept in mind by the teacher that in the earlier years it is chiefly the *mechanical* aspects of association that come into play. That is to say, the association is made, for the most part, by the mind acting as a machine would act, without consciousness of any reason for making the association, while the result is mainly to give the mind a machine-like power of performing the same operation in the future. The child who learns to read, for example, can have no clear conception of what he is really doing, of the mental processes called into activity, or of the ultimate value of what he is acquiring. From his standpoint, there is merely a mechanical putting together or associating of words, sentences, etc., And of course, the result is not, at this stage, the truly culturing effect that comes from later reading ; it is simply the

acquisition of a new capacity or habit, making it more easy to form similar associations in the future.

2. *Repetition the Principle of the Mechanical Stage.*—The mechanism, the capacity for performing the act spontaneously and without effort, is built up through *repetition.* There is in primary education absolutely no substitute for going over a thing again and again. The processes of *ideal* assimilation, much more those of rational comprehension, are undeveloped. The principal way of appeal to the mind is, therefore, the systematic repetition of an association, of a connection of facts, ideas or words, until a capacity, a habit is acquired in this direction. There is one dictum of modern pedagogy which, *under proper limitations,* finds its application here: *Learn to do by doing.* This principle is by no means co-extensive with the whole of education, and is in fact much abused by some educational "reformers," but it is the *basis* of all *early* training. Reading can be learned only by reading; spelling only by spelling; writing only by writing; the fundamental operations of number only by performing them, and so on. The teacher must aim, therefore, at thoroughness and continuity of repetition, and while having constantly in view the *dawning intelligence* of the child, must avoid *undue* reliance upon the *rationale* of the subject-matter, and undue appeal to a reason as yet undeveloped.

3. *Discipline the Object of the Mechanical Stage.*—The teacher must remember, however, that no piece of machinery has its end-in-itself; its value is in what it can do. To make even early mental training *purely mechanical* is as if a weaver were to regard it as his sole business to keep his loom in motion wholly irrespective of making any cloth. While the process of early education must be largely mechanical, its spirit must be *intelligent* and *rational.* There is a temptation in the practical work of teaching to forget this, and to allow the whole work to become one of dead routine. How shall the teacher avoid this and yet not make premature appeal to an immature reason?

By remembering that the end of the mechanical training is *discipline*.

What is Meant by Discipline.—Discipline, like habit, has its active and its passive side. It aims to make the mind at once capable of *resistance* and capable of *positive effort*. A mind is disciplined just in the degree in which it can hold its own against both the pressure and the distracting solicitations of sensations and impulses, and in the degree in which it has the power of systematically acting upon them, so as to shape them for its own ends. The effect of discipline, in short, is to give the mind *the capacity of acting steadily, easily and efficiently to the accomplishment of some definite work, while at the same time it gives power to act in new and untried ways.* The object of teaching elementary arithmetic, for example, is to give ability to ascertain the simpler relations of number easily, quickly and accurately, and at the same time, to enable the mind to act with greater strength and efficiency in all directions. Now, if this end is kept in mind, there is no danger that a mechanical spirit will pervade the teaching, no matter how mechanical the processes in themselves.

4. *Learn to do by Knowing.*—It may be well to warn the teacher against the present tendency to misapply the maxim quoted in the foregoing paragraph—"learn to do by doing.' It is true under certain conditions and is chiefly applicable in the primary stage of learning, but there have arisen educational evangelists who preach it as a universal principle. And thus, what is but a partial truth even in primary education, becomes a positive error in advanced stages. "Learn to speak by speaking"—*therefore* no formal grammar. "Learn to cypher by cyphering"—therefore, no science of arithmetic. "Learn to teach by teaching"—therefore no science of education and no professional training of teachers, and so on through a long list of "practical" inferences, which are plainly at variance with a sound philosophy of education. "Let eye, and ear, and hand, be thoroughly trained," by all means; but is there not Something behind these organs that *makes* the seeing eye, the hearing ear and the forming hand? Is the process from *without* inward—first the hand, then the brain, then the mind? Or is it from *within* outward—mind, brain, hand? Even in

the elementary work of what we have called the mechanical stage, *thinking precedes doing* ; in writing, for example, the child must have an *idea* of the form of a letter before the hand can reproduce it. It may be true that the making of the outward forms aids the mind to more definite conceptions; but from the elementary to the highest stages, the *ideal* is *before the actual.* " In aiming at a new construction," says Professor Bain, " *we must clearly conceive what is aimed at.*" And so, as we have already intimated, the teacher must constantly keep in view the growing *intelligence* of the child, helping him to form clear ideas of the new " constructions " aimed at, and teaching him how these constructions—manual or otherwise—can be mastered with the least waste of power. " Where we have a very distinct and intelligible model before us, we are in a fair way to succeed : in proportion as the ideal is dim and wavering, we stagger and miscarry." It appears, then, that the maxim, " learn to do by doing," is, after all, but the complement of a wider and profounder principle *learn to do by knowing.*

5. *The Secondary Stage is one of Forming Connections.*— While in the primary stage of reading (for example) there is rather association of the *activities* involved in reading than of the *ideas* read, in the secondary stage there is obvious and conscious connection of ideas. This is what constitutes "learning lessons" in the narrower sense of that term. When a pupil sets himself to learn a geography or history lesson so as to be able to recite upon it, he is intentionally forming certain connections of ideas. The work of teaching now changes its aspect somewhat and the main emphasis should be put upon *presenting* the *proper connections of ideas,* and upon assisting the pupil to re-make them in his own mind.

6. *The Associations in this Stage may be Sensuous or Ideal.* —As a pupil studies his lessons he may be forming associations of either of two kinds. He may connect the successive visible

appearances of the words, or their successive sounds. This is *sensuous association,* since it is only the auditory or visual sensations that are thus formed into a series. Or, he may connect the *ideas* conveyed by the sights and sounds ; this is *ideal association.* Of course it is almost impossible to form one kind of association without somewhat of the other also. Idiots have been known to learn pages of matter in a language of which they knew nothing, but no child of ordinary intelligence could form such a string of purely sensuous associations. On the other hand, one would hardly remember the ideas of a book which one had read without some knowledge of the look and sound of the successive sentences.

7. *Sensuous Associations should be Subsidiary.*—When a teacher compels pupils to recite lessons *verbatim* and calls upon one to stop in the middle of a sentence and the next to take it up at that point, he is doing his utmost to induce the pupil to form only sensuous associations. In such cases there is no proper activity of intelligence, and this fact alone condemns the method. Children's sense-organs are exceedingly *sensitive ;* they are plastic to mere sights and sounds, apart from what they mean, in a way that can be rivalled by no adult. The teacher should, of course, appeal to this ready receptiveness of sense, but it should be used only as an instrument or organ for forming connections between ideas.

8. " *Teach only What is Understood.*"--It is in this second stage of the development of association that the precept " A child should learn only what he understands " has its application. In the earlier, mechanical stage, it cannot be said to be true at all ; and in this second stage, its true meaning should be carefully noted. It does *not* mean what it literally says : that a child should learn only what he comprehends. To understand implies to know scientifically ; to grasp the *relations* of a subject, and it is absurd to demand this of one whose reason is yet undeveloped. In fact, the learning of a very large number of facts whose relations are not understood is the sole condition of understanding them at a later time. What the dictum really means is that the pupil should learn only that which has some *mean-*

ing—which appeals to him, which conveys something to him. It means that he should connect ideas, the significance of things, rather than associate meaningless sounds or sights. When a child learns, for example, that arithmetic is "the science of the relations of numbers," it is impossible that he should fully understand what this means. But it is possible that the definition should be something more then a mere association of words—that it should carry some significance with it. And this it does, if there be associations of *ideas*, instead of sounds or of sights alone.

9. *Importance of Habit.*—The teacher can hardly exaggerate the importance of the law of habit. Rousseau's saying "Émile must be allowed to learn no habits save that of having none," is substantially false as a general principle of education. It is much nearer the truth to say that *education consists in the formation of good habits*—good habits of body and of mind. The *first act*, mental or bodily is the starting point of habit; it leaves a tendency or disposition to recur, so that the second act is easier than the first, the third easier then the second, and so on, till the performance of the act becomes a *seeond nature*. In other words *the power and tendency to follow any course of action are measured by the frequency with which the acts involved have been repeated.* This law, from which there is no escape, works in all education—intellectual, moral, physical, and it works with special power during the impressionable period of childhood. Assuming that the teacher is possessed of a living personality, that in his little kingdom those great psychic forces, *sympathy and imitation*, hold sway, it seems impossible to unduly exalt the greatness of his work. Such a man will teach not by precept alone, nor by example alone, *but also by action :* laziness, fickleness, disorder, uncouthness, slovenliness, irreverence, etc., are not to be found in his pupils *because they are not to be found in him.* On the other hand, dilligence, neatness, cleanliness, order, politness, self-sacrifice, etc., become *habits* with the pupils, because they are *habits of the teacher.*

10. *The Third Stage is One of Culture.*—As the first stage is one of discipline, and the second of learning in the narrower

sense of the word, the third is one of *culture*. Associations are formed on the principle of *similarity*, and thus ideas are grouped about a common centre. The tie in the case of association by similarity is natural and intrinsic. While ideas associated by *contiguity* may be in themselves so foreign to each other as to require a constant effort of mind to hold them together, ideas united by *similarity* naturally grow into each other and strengthen the mind. Ideas externally associated have been compared to a bundle of food strapped upon the back; ideas internally associated to food eaten and digested, and wrought over into blood, bones and muscles; the one may be a strain upon mental fibre, the other adds to it. Rational comprehension grows naturally from the habit of forming associations by similarity ; the *common principle* constantly gains in distinctness and is finally seen in its relations to all the facts united by it.

NOTE.—Further upon Association, see Dewey's Psychology, pp. 90-117.

§ 3. VOLUNTARY ATTENTION.

Relations to Non-Voluntary.—Voluntary attention is based upon non-voluntary, but differs from it as a mental movement directed with fixed purpose to attaining some fnture end, differs from one which moves here and there stimulated simply by the chance attraction of the moment. For example, we may suppose a botanist's attention called spontaneously to a flower by its vivid colouring. He may be attracted the next moment to the contrasting colour of the foliage, and so on. Or, he may observe something peculiar—say an apparatus for catching insects. Now he has an end in view. He will examine the plant scientifically to see the mechanism and its mode of operation. He observes the structure of the flower ; compares it with others of the same genus ; with other plants that attract insects. He notices the insects that are already caught and speculates upon the mode and purpose of their capture. He sets himself to watch the plant and see the exact method by which some insect is entangled. *Non-volun tary attention has passed into voluntary ;* he no longer notices because of some attractive trait in the flower, but because of some *end* he wishes to reach, something which he desires to find out. Voluntary attention, in other words, is directed in its movements with a view to getting at something, with *reference to an end*, while non-voluntary is based upon agreeable qualities of the presentation.

Relation to Association.—Voluntary attention can create no new material. It can deal only with the presentations afforded by non-voluntary attention and the representations given by association. But while association by itself goes on at hap hazard, one idea suggesting another according to any accidental bond of contiguity or of similarity, voluntary attention lays hold of this train and manipulates, controls it for its own end. It compels the train in one direction ; it shuts off all suggested ideas which do not appear to lead towards the desired end. Ideas which the mind feels to be helpful towards the end are selected and emphasized. Association passes into voluntary attention when the ideas that form the train suggest one another not by any accidental bond, but by some fundamental characteristic, some unity which gives them a common bearing and end.

Example.—Take again the botanist who has noticed the apparatus for catching insects. Following association alone he might then think of some former time when he had seen a similar plant ; then of the swamp where he saw it ; then of some luxuriant marsh in South America ; then of the wonderful vegetation of the carboniferous era; then of the making of coal ; then of the present price of coal, and so on till he had thought of any number of topics apparently disconnected, yet each naturally growing out of the preceding. Thus one often finds himself wondering how he comes to be thinking of something so foreign to what his mind was occupied with a few minutes before. The train of associations has led him on. But voluntary attention prevents a succession of ideas having no common significance. It keeps the suggested ideas of our botanist, e.g. in harmony with *the end desired*—knowledge of the structure of such an apparatus, and of the process of its development. Voluntary attention is a *train of associations confined to some channel leading up to an unified result.*

Early Forms of Voluntary Attention.—Voluntary attention arises as soon as the mind becomes capable of forming the conception of an *end* which it finds interesting. Ideas no longer come and go at random, but with reference to this end. At first, voluntary attention is simply attraction of the mind by a *remote* instead of a *present* interest. For example, a boy forms the idea of making a kite. As soon as he has this idea, his thoughts and activities at once get a certain unity. They are controlled by the end which he desires to reach, and the end suffices of itself to suggest those ideas which lead to it, and to expel others. So, too, a boy may wish to find how a story "turns out," and the interest in this end will keep his mental processes engaged in reading, while otherwise they would be straying here and there. There is simply an extension of non-voluntary attention by interest in some future occurrences.

Higher Forms.—But cases occur in which the end interests but yet does not suffice of itself to control the train of ideas. The boy, for example, who has made a kite, afterwards sets himself to making a steam-engine. Here the matter is so complicated that the intermediate steps must be separately studied and their relations to one another and to the whole, made out. The end is forgotten for the time being, and attention is given to all the steps leading up to it. So with a pupil solving a problem in algebra. While the whole process is directed with a view to reaching the end (finding the value of x), yet it is the *successive* operations to be gone through that absorb attention. In the earlier stages the end "takes care of itself," so to speak; the mind need only be fixed upon the end and the means to it naturally suggest themselves. But in the higher forms, the laborious concentration of attention upon each step is required. As the power of attention grows, the end becomes more and more comprehensive until it requires the cooperation of almost every process of the intellectual life. Thus we may imagine Newton's attention to have been absorbed while he was engaged with the discovery of the law of gravitation.

Activities Involved in Attention.—Attention may, therefore, be defined *as a movement of ideas unified and controlled by the conception of some end.* There are various activities involved in this movement, of which three may be particularly mentioned. Attention is (1) an *adjusting*, (2) a *selecting* and (3) a *relating* activity.

1. *Attention as Adjusting Activity.*—In *association* the mind is, in one sense, passive. It seems to be a spectator before whom ideas come and go. Its extreme form is *reverie;* the mind drifts on from one topic to another. If we ask why this happens, we see that it is because the mind *lets* ideas take their course. It is not filled before-hand with some idea by which it tests, and with reference to which it directs, other ideas. But in *attention*, the mind comes to the train of ideas *prepared.* It is not indifferent; it is hardly impartial. It has a controlling and compelling interest in a given direction. It has a predisposition, a trend, in favor of certain ideas. Hence it is watchful, alert for everything favouring these ideas, while everything not connected with this interest is passed over.

Illustration.—By way of illustration, consider a biologist engaged in studying the life history of an animal under a microscope. He cannot allow his mind to follow up any train of ideas that suggests itself; he must be indifferent to all sights and sounds unconnected with the animal observed. He must notice the slightest change there; must connect this with what goes before, and what comes after. It is evident, therefore, that whatever corresponding ideas he has already in mind must be held prepared, even in tension, to go out and meet whatever corresponds to them in the object. The mind *at-tends*, is stretched towards what is coming, to anticipate it, to meet it more than half-way. Hence the fatigue accompanying any prolonged activity of attention. Ideas are not allowed to follow their own course; but a certain group of ideas must be held to the front by a *special mental effort*, to react on the new presentations.

Why Called Adjusting?—It is clear, therefore, why the activity is called an *adjusting* one. An empty mind cannot attend to anything; a mind empty in a given direction cannot attend in that direction. It must have some idea, however vague and general, of what is coming, of what is to be looked for. The more a mind knows of a certain subject, the more quickly and accurately it can pay attention to anything new in that subject. Attention is thus the bringing to bear, the *adjusting*, of what already is in the mind, to the presentation without. Attention is not the fixing of the mind *in general* but the fixing of a *definite* group of ideas upon presentations having points of community with the group. The adjusting power of attention consists in getting to the foreground of the mind and holding there, those ideas allied to the object-matter attended to. A pupil attends to a problem in arithmetic only as he brings to the foreground of consciousness that knowledge of numbers which he already possesses, and applies it to the new case.

Illustration.—The nature of mental life may be illustrated as follows : An individual is in a dark room with which he is unacquainted. This room is lighted up at brief intervals by an electric spark. Now, previous to the first illumination there can be no preparatory activity of the mind. It does not know what to look for, and hence cannot get ready. But at the first spark, it obtains some dim idea of the room, and this makes a basis for attention at the second lighting up. Being slightly prepared, it now sees more in the second flash. This gives greater power to adjust the next time, and so on. Finally, some flash, though not lasting any longer than the first flash during which nothing was seen, reveals almost the entire contents of the room. In other words, the more perfectly the mind can make a *preparatory adjustment* of its internal ideas to the outward presentation, the better it can attend, and, of course, the more it can become conscious of.

Attention and Past Experience.—It is furthermore evident that the power of voluntary attention in any direction depends largely upon past experience in that direction. We cannot bring ideas to bear, cannot form adjustments, where we *have* no ideas. In every fact learned, in every process of knowing, therefore, we are deciding our future knowledge as well as our present, for we are deciding in what directions we may be able to form adjustments, to pay attention. The difference between a child and a man, between an uncultured and an educated man, is largely that one has definite groups of ideas, or instruments of adjustment, ready to bring to bear upon presentations, while the other has not.

2. *Attention as Selecting Activity.*—Thus far we have been considering the attitude of the mind in attention ; the *preparation* necessary in order to give attention. Now we shall suppose that adjustment has been secured, and ask what is the effect upon the subject-matter attended to. The primary effect is *selective*. The mind emphasizes and slurs, brightens and dims, according to the end it wishes to reach. Attention has the same effect upon any mental content that a lens has upon light: the point focussed stands out with brilliancy, while the surroundings are dull and indistinct. Attention, as adjustment, has been called " asking questions of the future," and the question once asked, the mind must select material fitted to answer it.

Basis of Selection.—The mind when attending is in a *cross-examining* attitude. It does not take presentations as they come, but inquires into their value, and makes use of them accordingly. The basis on which some are chosen and others are rejected is the *end in view* and the interest the mind takes in it. A flower will produce the same *sensations* in the mind of an artist, a farmer and a man of science; but the artist will notice the qualities that make for beauty, the farmer's attention will select those that refer to use, that seem to testify to a weed or to a useful plant, while the botanist may neglect both use and beauty in an examination of the scientific relations of the flower. In a certain sense, no two of them see the same flower. One perceives, or selects, one thing, and this is invisible to the others who neglect it. And in any case, it is the *end* which the mind wishes to reach, the prevailing interest which it brings with it, that decides the selection.

Variable and Permanent Ends of Selection.—Different persons and different classes of persons, since they have different occupations and interests in life, will, as just illustrated, select varying things. But all minds, since they are minds, have a common interest in *knowledge*, and a common end in noticing these universal features, at least, without which there would be no knowledge. Thus we may suppose a thousand persons reading a book and each underlining what especially strikes him. A large number of the passages underlined would vary according to the various ages, tastes, stages of culture, etc., of the readers. But there might be a number of passages in the book which would appeal to all, and which all would emphasize. So with the book which the world presents to be read by every mind.

The Law of Common Selection.—While no rule can be laid down for the selective activity when it varies, excepting that it follows the prevailing interest whatever that may be, there is a law for the selections in which minds agree. *The mind always selects those sensations and impulses*

that are signs of something else ; that point to something beyond themselves.
Elements having no meaning outside their own occurrence, are neglected.
For example, although muscular sensations are of great importance to us,
we are never conscious of them in themselves, unless it be when we are
tired. We notice only what the sensations are signs of—what they *signify*
We move the hand through the air and are not conscious of the muscular
strain, but only of the *space* which is measured by it. There are instances
of persons who became blind in one eye and yet did not know it for
years. Their knowledge of objects, of what the sensations pointed to,
being unchanged, they never noticed the change in the sensations themselves. Each of us has a multitude of sensations which he neglects entirely either because they have no reference to objects, or because this
reference is so much more important than the sensations, that he attends to
that alone.

3. Attention as Relating Activity.—As we have previously
noticed, ideas may be connected externally or internally, *i.e.*, because they occur at the same *time* or because there is something
in their *meaning* which connects them. The relations which
form the internal connection are those of similarity and contrast. And it is the chief characteristic of voluntary attention
that it aims at penetrating below the accidental, superficial, connections of ideas, and at discovering the hidden relations which
unite and which distinguish them. Ordinary experience,
chance contact with objects, presents us with no arrangement,
no classification. Objects might forever thrust themselves
upon the mind, and if the mind did not react upon them with
the idea of a system according to which they might be grouped, a
system based upon points of internal likeness and difference,
experience would remain an accidental juxtaposition of ideas,
without true order or law.

Example.—If we depended simply upon the order in
which our ideas present themselves or suggest one another,
what kind of Zoology, for example, should we have ? It would
consist simply of a continuous description of animals taken in
any chance order of arrangement, with no law of subordina-

tion and co-ordination, no principle of classification. Association by similarity would suffice, doubtless, to give some larger divisions—birds, insects, quadrupeds, etc., might fall into groups by themselves. But here, without further action of voluntary attention, there would be no standard which could be used to test even such a rough classification ; bats would be called birds, and whales fishes. Finer classification and knowledge of the *relations* of various groups would be almost wholly lacking. For zoological classification consists in this, that we examine into our presentations instead of taking them just as they come, that we search for some hidden unity, some common principle or cause among facts the most diverse in appearance, and then, in accordance with this principle, rearrange the accidental connections which experience provides.

Comparison.—This act of voluntary attention by which we search for identities and distinctions is termed *comparison*. We compare when *we hold two ideas together in the mind, and then let our thoughts move from one to the other in order to see in what points they agree or differ*. It is association, without doubt, which originally brings the two ideas together ; but attention is required to hold the ideas before the mind, to keep them from being displaced by further suggestions, and attention,—the idea of an end, and the direction of our thought by it—is required to seize upon the points of likeness in apparent difference, or of diversity in apparent similarity. Comparison holds together and holds apart at the same time ; it unifies and it discriminates.

Unification.—When we say that attention aims at unifying ideas, it must not be thought that two ideas are *fused* into one. The two ideas still remain separate in their existence, it is only their *meaning* that is identified. Both are seen to signify the same thing. Thus the fall of the apple, the path of the cannon ball in the air, the revolution of the moon, the rise of the tide, facts separate in themselves, are unified by the law of gravitation. Voluntary attention, then, sets out with the idea of a law, a relation, a principle common to different facts, and it controls the flow of ideas with reference to this one idea ; it seeks for it everywhere ; it tries this and that experience to see if it contains this one idea. Consider, for example, the procedure of a scientific man, endeavoring to discover or to verify a law ; it is the idea of this law which compels his experiences to assume unity.

Discrimination.—When speaking of non-voluntary attention, we noticed that one of its effects is to bring whatever receives attention more clearly into consciousness. In voluntary attention we have an extension of the same principle. The mind sets itself intentionally to distinguish between one object and another, between one feature or quality of the object and another property. It is through this process that knowledge ceases to be vague, and gains clearness. For example, a child recognizes a tree before he recognizes any particular kind of tree. The elm, the oak, the maple, are all simply trees to him. But he notices, say, the difference in the leaves of two trees ; he then compares the two trees with a view to ascertaining in what other respects they differ. Each difference as it is noticed makes knowledge of the tree known more distinct, or definite. Thus, also, the child begins with a vague idea of meat, which by noticed differences, becomes discriminated into ideas of beef, veal, mutton, etc. The undefined in every case precedes the distinct, and the vague becomes the definite by the activity of attention in fixing upon differences.

The Goal of Attention.—Through the double act of identifying and discriminating, knowledge becomes at once *unified* and *definite*. While, at first, attention can grasp only a small idea, one with few details in it, and these few vague, with growing culture it takes in larger and larger wholes, and the *details* of these larger wholes are better and better defined. The mind takes in more at one grasp, and the details stand out more clearly. For example, a child just learning to read has before him a printed page ; the unit of attention is necessarily small ; say the single word, or at most the sentence. And the members of this unit are not clearly defined ; the child will hardly discriminate 'mop' from 'map'; 'apply' from 'apple ;' or, if he can recognize the meaning of a *sentence* at one act of attention, he will not know the relations of the different parts of the sentence, the value of each of its members. But ten years after, he will be able to take in a paragraph in one mental act, and at the same time he will have a more definite idea of each of its factors, than he had when he was obliged to go through them laboriously one at a time. The goal of the development of attention is, therefore, *ability to grasp in one act large wholes*, and at the same time, give *distinctness to every part of this whole* In the degree in which this goal is reached, there is economy and facility in the expenditure of mental power.

Educational Principles.—The work of securing attention from any individual pupil is something, of course, which depends upon the patience, tact, interest and skill of the teacher. But there are certain psychological principles upon which he must build either consciously or unconsciously, if even his best energies and sympathies are to be of any avail.

1. *Voluntary Attention Demands Mental Effort.*—The train of ideas, if left to itself, will go on by the principle of association. And when all successions of ideas are occasioned wholly by mere suggestion we have *mind-wandering*. It requires, therefore, a certain mental energy to interfere, as it were, with the sequences of association and to control them, to compel them to take a certain course. It requires no positive effort or training to let the mind wander; we have simply to allow it to follow its own course. This is easy, and so mental laziness becomes one of the greatest hindrances of the teacher's work. There is a certain strain or stress involved in attention, and the student must be awakened from the inertia natural to the association of ideas, and made to *exercise* his mental powers, and to assume an active, energetic habit of mind.

2. *Voluntary Attention Demands Unity and Permanence of Interest.*—Dissipation of interest is, next to sheer mental laziness, the great foe of attention. Watch an inattentive school-boy; one moment he studies one lesson, the next moment, another lesson, then he must write upon his slate, then sharpen his pencil, then speak to a fellow-pupil, and so on in a con-

stantly interrupted round of disconnected doings. There is no one and lasting interest which runs through his operations. This dissipation of interests results inevitably in *discontinuity* of attention. The pupil may have had good powers of non-voluntary attention, that is to say, objects may have attracted him readily and kept his attention fixed as long as the attraction endured, but if the successive attractions were never welded into a series, if they were given no underlying unity, the result is necessarily a skipping, jerky, disconnected habit of mind. *Whatever secures unity of interest in diverse subjects works in and of itself to secure continuous attention.*

3. *Voluntary Attention demands that there be already in the Mind some Store of ideas akin to the Subject to be attended to.*— Attention, as we have seen, is not bringing the *mind in general*, that is an *empty* mind, to bear upon a subject, it is focussing upon the subject ideas already had, knowledge already obtained. To require a young student, for example, to pay attention to abstract statements about the form, position, mode of revolution and subdivisions of the earth, without ascertaining whether he has any analogous ideas, any acquired knowledge, which may serve to fix and interpret the new statements, is to commit a pedagogical blunder. A certain superficial attention of the eye or the ear may be secured, but no truly *mental* attention. To demand a merely *formal* attention from a student, that is, to ask him to fix his psychical processes in general upon a subject, is to demand an impossibility. That there may be real assimilation, attention must be paid to *something in particular*, and requires the presence in the mind of ideas somewhat similar— having some relation to the subject taught.

4. *Voluntary Attention requires that this Store of similar Ideas be not latent in the Mind, but Actively brought into Play.* It is not enough that the mind should have experiences analogous to the topic in hand stored away, it must bring them to the surface ;

it must have them ready to seize upon whatever is presented. If mental effort and unity of interest exist, and yet there is failure of attention, it is, nine times out of ten, because this preparatory work has not been done. Of course, training in holding attention in *any* subject gives self-control, and makes attention easier in other directions, and yet it is, for example, no great help when attention is required in historical study, to have just been absorbed in mathematics. Indeed, it may be at first a hindrance; the circle of historical ideas must be brought to the surface of the mind. Historical conceptions and interests must be fresh and active ; then attention—the conjunction of the inner mental acquisition with the outer object to be acquired —is easily secured.

5.—*Counterfeit Attention.*—It follows from this, that there may be the outward form and attitude of attention—the apparently hearing ear and seeing eye—while the mind is utterly out of connection with the subject. There are, also, other forms of such spurious attention which are, as already intimated, all but equally futile. Some attention may be paid to a lesson ; its facts and principles may be *severally* apprehended while the underlying *unity* is never grasped. A pupil, for example, may give sufficient attention to a reading lesson to enable him to understand the separate sentences, . and yet fail to acquire a clear conception of the lesson as a whole ; the higher activity of attention, the *relating* power is wanting ; there are disconnected acts of attention but no perception of relations, no unifying power. Similarly, a pupil may comprehend each of the successive steps in a demonstration and yet fail to master it, through not giving the higher power of attention necessary to such mastery. Or, again, a student may grasp the connections of the several points of a topic and still fail to assimilate the new knowledge with the old ; he does not revive and hold in readiness the groups of ideas bearing on the subject ; he fails in the *adjusting* power of attention, and the result is neither permanent increase of knowledge nor development of mind-function.

6. *Voluntary Attention requires that the Mind move along Related or connected Points.* Contradictory as the statement may sound, *attention can be kept fixed only as it is kept moving.* Let us suppose that the preceding conditions have been met; the mind is aroused to active effort, it has continuous interest; it has had knowledge of matters analogous to that to be attended to, and this knowledge has been stirred up and called to the surface. And now the subject is put before the pupil, and he is told by the teacher to pay attention. A most lame and impotent conclusion! The pupil is now waiting and anxious to pay attention; *how* to pay it is the essential point, and the point on which he is too apt to get no help. If he tries to keep his mind resting, to keep it literally *fixed*, one result is inevitable: the mind *must move* in one way or another; it cannot rest without consciousness ceasing; some association suggests itself, this suggests another, and so on. So, with the firm purpose to pay attention, the pupil finds his mind wandering.

How then shall the attention be kept fixed? Attention is the movement of ideas controlled by the relations of identity and difference. The process of paying attention is, therefore, one *of noticing and discovering these relations.* In the early stages, this work must, of course, be performed largely by the teacher; he must *arrange* the material, he must arrange his questions so as to make the relations, the connections of a subject, prominent. Unimportant and irrelevant features must be excluded; the points of connection must be made salient; they must be emphasized and reiterated until the pupil's mind forms the *habit* of following their connections, to the neglect of all else. This habit once formed, there grows, almost naturally and of itself in higher stages, the habit of picking out and forming the connections without help. When this point is reached, no attention need be paid to attention. Attention takes care of itself, for this power of observing and creating relations *is* Attention.

7. *Further Suggestions.*—(*a*) In infancy and childhood attention must be secured indirectly, that is, it must be *attracted* by some interest in the subject, or secured by the personality of the teacher ; his tact, earnestness, sympathy, patience, will power, etc. But as non-voluntary attention grows into voluntary, and the creature of impulse becomes capable of self-control, *rational motives* may be effectively appealed to. Thus, a subject unattractive or even repulsive in itself, commands attention through its association with " pleasure in prospect " of some desired *end*. (*b*) As in the earlier years something must be given the child to *do*, so in the later years something must be left to his *thinking;* the *child* delights in doing with the hand, the *youth* delights in *doing* with the mind—in conquering difficulties for himself. (*c*) The different tastes and and abilities of pupils must be taken into account. A pupil may have little native capacity for a subject, or, through irrational teaching, he may have acquired a thorough dislike for it. In either case, true attention on his part is extremely difficult. He cannot *attend* in the specific direction, because he has nothing *to attend with* —no groups of ideas which are related to the new subject and without which he cannot seize upon it ; for, once more, a *mind* empty in a given direction, cannot attend in that direction. In such a case, if the teacher is without sympathy and the kindly insight that flows from it—a servile follower of pedagogic rule and formula, he draws the sweeping inference : Stupid in *one*, stupid in *all*. Thus, many a youth of fine ability has been grossly wronged because of his inability to make progress in a pathway along which his blind guide would force him. (*d*) Not only is attention the prime condition and the measure of intellectual

development, it is of perhaps equal importance in the moral sphere. "The boy is father of the man;" if, in the school, the *habit* of attention is formed, the power of *concentrated* thought developed, there will be thoughtfulness and steadiness of pur·pose in the character of the man. But the *habit* of inattention and the incapacity for steady thinking, are the chief factors in a character infirm of purpose, "unstable as water." Defective attention in practical life, (says Compayré) is the synonym of thoughtlessness and heedlessness. To be habitually attentive is not only the best means of learning and progressing in the sciences, and the most effective prayer we can address to the truth in order that it may bestow itself upon us; but it is also one of the most precious means of moral perfection, the surest means of shunning mistakes and faults, and one of the most necessary elements of virtue. See Dewey's Psychology, pp. 132-148.

§ 4. APPERCEPTION AND RETENTION.

We have finished our study of the processes—attention, voluntary and non-voluntary, and association—which elaborate the raw material of psychical life, previously studied, into the concrete forms yet to be taken up. Before taking them up, it is necessary to notice that these processes have a double refer-ence or aspect. They affect both the *material acted* upon, and the *mind which acts*—they look towards both the object and the subject. For example, certain sensations are occasioned by an object; the processes of attention and association work-ing upon them, form the idea of a flower. This is the outward *objective* effect. But the mind now has knowledge of this flower; its own store of ideas is increased; its structure is en-larged in this direction. This is the inner, *subjective* effect.

Retention and Apperception.—This latter effect is

E

known as *retention*, the former as *apperception*. Apperception may be defined as the *action of the mind upon the material presented to it.* Retention is the *action upon the mind of this material when apprehended.* Apperception is, thus, the process of taking anything into the mind (*ap-prehending*), of giving it psychical position and meaning. Retention is the effect which the material, when taken into the mind, has upon the mind itself.

Illustrations.—These abstract definitions may be made clearer by examples. An infant, a savage, an ignorant man, and a skilled mechanic are before a steam-locomotive. It produces the same effect upon all, so far as *sensat'ons* are concerned, supposing that all have their senses intact. And yet the baby *apprehends* nothing; there is no result except the mingled feelings of curiosity and terror. The savage also has these feelings, and in addition recognizes some qualities; its immense size, the peculiarities of its form, some analogies of appearance and of movement with those of animals that he has known; perhaps he calls it an "iron-horse." The ordinary man perceives the *locomotive*—that is, he knows the purpose of this object, knows that it is propelled by steam, and knows some details of its structure. The mechanic perceives, in addition, the precise purpose of each part; the 'bearing' and relation of it. He perceives the adjustment of means to an end; the exact significance not only of the whole locomotive but of each member of it. Whence come these differences of ideas in the four cases? Not from the engine; not from the sensations; but from the *attitude of the mind* towards the sensations—in short, from *Apperceiving* power—from the different ways in which the mind acts upon the sensations.

On the other hand, certain results flow from the apperception. The baby, it may be, will not be so frightened the next time he sees a locomotive; he will have a dim sense of familiarity, of recognition. The structure of his mind, in other words, has been changed in a slight degree. The savage watches the locomotive; he notices how it moves upon the rails; how it is governed by levers, etc. The next time he sees a locomotive he does not have to observe these things in order to know that they are there; his mind supplies them from his previous experience. This experience, therefore, after vanishing, left some *trace*, some relic of itself. Let us now suppose that the mechanic shows the unlearned man the details of the engine; that he imparts to him, as far as possible, his own knowledge. It is evident that, from this time forward, the attitude of mind of the latter toward locomotives, has entirely changed. He has not simply had some new facts told him, but these facts have entered into his mind and enlarged its powers. Knowledge is not a temporary occurrence, but is a permanent possession. In these instances, we have the fact of *Retention* illustrated.

Mutual Relations.—It is evident that each of these processes depends upon the other. We can retain only what we have once apprehended, so much, at least, is clear. Furthermore, what we retain from one experience is that *with which* we apprehend ever afterwards. If the baby, or the savage, or the ignorant man apperceives more the second time he sees a locomotive than he did the first, it is because of what he has retained from that former experience. If every experience were "writ in water," if it left no trace of itself behind; in other words, if there were no such thing as retention; the result would be that we should always remain infants intellectually, for there would be no growth in apperceiving power.

The Nature of Retention.—The student is not to infer that the experience itself is stored up in the mind, as grains of corn are stored in a bin. The mind is sometimes spoken of as a store-house, or as a magazine or granary, but such metaphors are misleading. The idea, as an idea, ceases to exist the moment that it leaves consciousness. Nor can we say in strict truth that a copy, or image, or trace of it is left behind. What then is retained, if it is neither the idea itself nor a copy of it? The reply is that the *effect* which the experience makes upon the mind is retained. The apprehending activity of the mind may be compared to the reception and assimilation of food by a living organism. As the tree, for example, does not absorb surrounding gases, moisture and mineral substances and "store them up" unaltered, but as these act and react upon the living tissues of the tree until they themselves are changed into living tissues; so the mind deals with its experiences. They are not passively received into the mind, to be preserved there unchanged, but they are worked over into the strengthening of old powers and tendencies and into the germination of new ones.

Educational Illustration.—Suppose a child has to add a column of figures. If he has added columns before and if he has "retained" something from the mental action involved in the operations, he will be able to do this without assistance. But it is not the preservation in his mind of the figures which he has added before, nor of their copies, that enables him to add. These former experiences have acted upon his mind, however, so as to give him the power to control its action in a certain direction, and to perceive and to construct relations in this direction. A child should not learn the multiplication table so that its exact image recurs to him when he has to multiply two numbers, but in order that he may form *the habit*, gain *the power*, of dealing with numerical combinations.

Dynamical Associations.—What is retained is sometimes called a "dynamical association." By this is meant that retention consists in an active tendency to form connections.

The mind which has joined objects or ideas by attention or by association, has not only the *capacity* of making similar connections more easily in the future, but it has a *tendency*, a predisposition, to make them. Long before a child has conscious memory or recollection, he retains something from each of his experiences and it is by this retention that his mind grows in power, that it develops and matures. If we examine what is retained before memory exists, we see that it is the ability and the impulse to form associations like those formerly experienced.

Nature of Apperception.—We are now prepared to see more clearly what constitutes apperception. *It is bringing to bear what has been retained of past experiences in such a way as to interpret, to give meaning to, the new experience.* Without this act of bringing to bear what is retained in the mind, there is no knowledge of what is presented. It may be said, therefore, that in a certain sense all cognition is re-cognition. Knowledge of what is perceived depends for its meaning upon relations to what the mind *brings with it* to the perception.

An Objection Considered.—It may be objected that if this were the case, there would be no such thing as growth or, advance in mental life. The objecter might say that, on this theory, if a new fruit, a guava, for instance, were presented to a person, he would not know it at all, since he could not recognize it. But this objection may be met so as to bring out the very point desired. The person tastes the fruit; his mind from its previous experiences, recognizes a taste; by similar acts of recognition he gets its odor, size, color and other properties. By its relations to his past experiences he thus judges the object to be a kind of *fruit*. In relating it to similar things he has known, he recognizes differences, as well as similarities, and thus enlarges his past experiences. He reorganizes qualities into new combinations, into a new objects. From the united similarities and differences he gets his knowledge of something hitherto unknown. On the basis of the *likeness* he recognizes what sort of an object is presented to him, *i. e.*, he *identifies* the object; on the basis of the *differences*, he enlarges his past experiences into a *distinct* idea, an idea of something different from what was previously known. And in either case, it is only by the results of his past experiences that there is actual knowledge of the thing examined.

Educational Principles.

1. *As to Retention.*—If the teacher will keep in mind that the retention of what is learned consists not in preserving it unchanged, but in working it over into mental capacities and tendencies, he will see that the end of instruction is not so much the acquisition of a given amount of information as the production of powers and tendencies, of abilities and tastes. Not what is perceived so much as power to perceive and interest which impels to perception, is the end of " object lessons." Not what is remembered so much as capacity to remember, and a fixed tendency to seize upon the salient points of *every* experience, are the objects of memory lessons; not what is thought about so much as the habit of thinking, is the end to be sought in the instruction of reason. Knowledge of the real nature of retention affords the psychological basis of what it often stated as an empirical truth, viz., that *education consists not in the imparting and acquiring of mere facts, but in the development of the whole personality.*

Yet, it is to be observed, there is often too broad a contrast made between knowledge and mental power as ends of education. The fact is, that the mind gains power in the act of acquiring knowledge. The two processes are necessarily correlative. For organizing mental faculty, there is no other means than organized knowledge. Still, if the mental power

is made the true aim, it is likely that the elements of knowledge will be *more logically* presented, and so both results will
be.more thoroughly attained.

2. *As to Apperception.*—The psychogical equivalent of apperception is precisely " learning." The student learns what
he apperceives. Since apperception consists in bringing the
mind (with its past experiences organized into its structure)
to bear upon material, it is evident that learning *depends
upon the relation of the mind to what is presented.* The
teacher's office, therefore, in relation to learning is, on the one
hand, to secure the presentation of material *of such a kind* and
in such a manner that the mind can be brought into relation
with it ; and on the other hand, to secure such a preparation and
attitude of mind that it may easily be brought to bear upon
what is presented. *Proper presentation of material* on the one
side, *proper preparation of mind* on the other are the two conditions of learning. Further details regarding these conditions
we shall meet with in our next chapter in discussing the principles of intellectual development.

3. *Organization of Faculty.*—The mind of the infant, while
inheriting certain tendencies and abilities which act instinctively, does not possess powers and faculties ready for action in
definite directions. There are no apperceptive organs formed,
no groups of ideas ready to seize upon and assimilate new
material. There is simply a bundle of dormant capacities which
must be stimulated into activity and organized into faculty by
the presentation of material from without, and by the mind's
reaction from within. Every mental experience leaves behind
it a *trace*—called by some *residuum*—an *effect*, which tends to
reproduce the experience, and the accumulation of such *traces*
creates special power and tendency—mind-function of a
definite kind. Moreover, from the known connection of
mind with brain, there is no doubt that such experiences are

accompanied by some modification in groups of brain cells, and that their growth into special organs of apperception is attended with nervous growths which actually modify the structure of the brain. It is not strange, therefore, that *habit* becomes a *second* nature so strong and active as sometimes to be mistaken for the *first*. This power, bent, facility to act—right or wrong, good or evil—in a definite direction, has *entered into the structure* of both body and mind, and will give a coloring to all future thoughts and actions, just as the food-elements absorbed by the tree, become part of its living tissue and affect the assimilation ˙of all material afterwards absorbed. Now, the teacher is not wholly responsible for such development of faculty—the powerful influence of environment must be taken into account—but there can be no doubt that, under conceivably favourable circumstances, he is, in no small degree, responsible. He can make the child love what he himself loves, and hate what he hates. It is difficult to over-rate the far-reaching influence of a teacher of strong personality. Under the teaching of such a man, the child once thinks certain thoughts and is stirred with certain emotions; *from that moment he will never again be exactly what he was before;* it is, indeed, possible that he will have acquired a bent which will determine his character forever.

In this law of retention and apperception, the teacher holds in his hand the principle which underlies all educational processes, moral, physical and intellectual; the law that exercise strengthens faculty, develops faculty, and almost literally *creates* faculty. A child, e.g., of volatile disposition comes into his hands; he gets from the child one act of attention suitable to his feeble capacity, then a second act, then a third, and so on till a fair habit of attention and a moderate power of concentration are formed, and the whole psychical life thereby influenced. Or, the child is found to possess no "faculty" for literature, or mathematics, or science, or art; but the *teacher* has power to develop faculty, ability, taste for one or more of them, according to the special apperceptive " organs " which have been developed in his own mental life. On the moral side, the law is equally effective. If a teacher finds that a child is of a selfish disposition—" a wretch concentred all in self"—does he leave him to the workings of this meanest of all passions ? No, he watches for a favorable occasion to excite a generous sentiment in the selfish heart, and to make this effective in a kindly act ; he now occupies a higher vantage-ground ; it will be easier to excite a second generous emotion, and to lead to a second kindly act ; and thus the process goes on—the selfish principle becoming feebler with each successive act—till by the accumulation of the *right* experiences, a noble self-sacrificing *character* is formed—a new creation over which something higher than "the morning stars" may sing : for, "to make some human hearts a little wiser, manfuller, happier, more blessed, less accursed, is a work for a God."

NOTE.—Further on Apperception and Retention, see Dewey's Psychology, pp. 81-90 ; 148-153.

CHAPTER IV.

FORMS OF INTELLECTUAL DEVELOPMENT.

We have studied the Raw Material of psychical life, and the Processes which elaborate the material. We have now briefly to study the Finished Products. As stated in Chap. I., p. 6, these may be arranged in three classes, the *Intellectual* (matter of knowledge), the *Emotional* (matter of feeling), and the *Volitional* (matter of will). In this chapter we shall discuss Intellectual Development, taking up in the first section its general principles, and afterwards the concrete stages, particularly in their educational relations.

§ 1. PRINCIPLES OF INTELLECTUAL DE-VELOPMENT.

1. *The Development of Intelligence is from the Presentative to the Representative.*—Sensation, pure and simple, cannot be said to *stand for*, or *symbolize*, or *represent* anything beyond its own occurrence. But the test of value of a sensation is its power to merge its own existence in what it represents. A sensation of hunger fills the mind with itself; it thrusts out of consciousness everything but its own quality, all but its own imperious demands and hence gives next to no knowledge. A sensation of color, on the other hand, leads the mind beyond its own existence, to associations with other sensations, those of touch, of sound, etc. It suggests these sensations when they are not present, and thus becomes a sign or symbol of them—it *represents* them. As I look at a rose, for example, all I *see*, strictly speaking, is certain shades of color. Were my knowledge to stop short with this presentative factor, it would never occur to me that a rose was before me. But these shades of color *stand for* a certain size and shape, etc. They call up other sensations not now present, but experienced in the past ; they call up also associated sensations of touch, of smell, etc. And from all these factors—the most of them being now only *representative* in character—I get the idea of a rose.

Further Illustration.—Or, suppose I hear a strain of music which I recognize as, say, part of the song of " Robin Adair."   All that is present is a certain auditory sensation ; as such, it is not Robin Adair, it is not a song, it is not music ; it is not even significant language. It is *sound*. But by what the sound stands for, what it symbolizes, it gains successively all its meaning.

2. *The Development of Intelligence is from the Sensuous to the Ideal.*—This, indeed, follows at once from the principle

already laid down. The presented element is sensation ; the represented element can only be images, ideas. Not being supplied from the senses, the representative factor must be supplied from within the mind itself, and is thus called " ideal." Consider the perception, for example, of some particular object, this pen, this paper, this book, as now present in space. It might seem at first as if, in the perception of this book, there were no ideal element, because the entire book is actually present. But if we simply look at the book, the only elements presented to the *mind* are the color-sensations with which the mind is affected. The color-sensations do not make up an idea of the book. This contains not only color-element, but also those ot weight, size, forms, and also the notion of a number of pages, printed with type, containing information and meant to be read. Now, of all these elements, the only one that can be seen, as matter of *sensation*, is color. The other qualities, therefore, are *ideal* —are supplied to the perception by the mind itself.

Idealizing Activity.—Since the ideal factor, which is also equivalent to the representative factor, is of so much importance, it will repay further study. The ideal factor is due to *retention*. It is what the mind has preserved from its former experiences and supplies to the sensuous presentation. The development of knowledge from the presentative and sensuous to the representative and ideal, *is due*, therefore, *to the results of past experience that are brought to bear upon new experiences.* The sensation produced by the object as it affects the senses is all that in strictness can be said to be presented. Whether this sensation comes to mean or signify anything beyond its occurrence, depends *first*, upon whether the mind has had similar experiences in the past ; *secondly*, upon whether these experiences have taken root in the mind and produced fruit there, and *thirdly*, upon whether they are brought to bear upon the new presentation. Certain principles of great educational importance flow from what has been laid down.

Educational Principles.

1. *The development of knowledge is the result of an interpreting process.* The sensation, the presentative factor, must be interpreted in order to become representative, symbolic, or ideal; in a word, in order to become significant, and upon the degree of interpretation depends the degree of significance. It is not enough to present a lesson to a pupil to be learnt, to show him natural objects which he is to understand, to lecture to him upon laws and relations. From the point of view of the pupil, the important thing is whether he can *interpret* the lesson, the object, the lectures. If he has no *organs of interpretation*, the material, however true and well arranged in itself, is so much mere sensation to him, sound and color signifying nothing.

2. *It is the result of an assimilating process.* The interpretation must occur through what the mind has *within itself*. The past store of knowledge, not held mechanically in mind, but wrought over into mental structure, capacity and tendency, is that through which the interpretation occurs. The process of interpreting is a process of assimilating what is presented with what is already contained in the mind. It is of great importance, therefore, that the instructor should carry on his work in such a way as

a. Not to load the mind with information, but *to develop tendencies, organs, which may receive and elaborate new material.*

b. To create centres of interests and of ideas which shall be on the alert for new material, so that whatever is presented shall gravitate naturally to these centres, and be appropriated and assimilated by them.

c. To be as careful, upon presenting new material, *to arouse preparatory interest and the activity of the mental organs which are to interpret and assimilate the material,* as to have the material itself well chosen and arranged.

d. Always to utilize past knowledge in acquiring new. There is no greater educational blunder than disconnected, dispersive instruction. In the primary stages, not only should lessons in the same subject be closely connected by proper grading, by overlapping of ideas, etc., but *different* subjects should gather about some *common centre*. In proper instruction, reading, writing, construction of sentences, arithmetic and geography, should have a certain amount of interconnection and unity, so as mutually to co-operate with and aid one another, instead of calling into play diverse and separate groups of interests and ideas. To present four subjects isolated from one another is to treat the pupil as having *four minds ;* it is almost to quadruple the required expenditure of energy. One subject is out of relation to another, and can give no aid in apprehending it.

3. *The Development of Intelligence is from the Vague to the Definite, and from the Particular to the Universal. Its End is, therefore, to be both Specific and General.*—Knowledge, in its first stages, is both indefinite or vague, and limited or non-general in character. A child's knowledge of, say, a horse, as compared with a man's, possesses no sharply defined features or qualities, and is lacking in recognition of the relations which this horse has in common with others. The child neither discriminates *this* horse carefully from all other horses, nor from other animals somewhat similar. If the horse is the animal with which he is most familiar, the dog will be to him a small horse, the elephant a large horse. Taine tells of a child who had often been shown an infant in a picture and told that it was a baby ; for a long time that child called every picture, no matter of what, a baby. And this example is typical of the beginning of intelligence. There is no *definiteness*, no recognition of specific qualities ; all is vague, and, as it were, massed, not individualized.

It is evident that early knowledge has a *certain* kind of generality—the generality of vagueness. The word " mamma," may mean every woman, the word "dog," every animal, and so on. This is not a true universality, however, for there is no recognition of any general relation as such. The child may call every round object, from a circle drawn on his slate to the moon, "plate," but this is not because he grasps the identity of relation (in the matter of *form*) in these various objects. It is simply because he sees one salient quality and ignores differences. Knowledge is general only in the sense that it is not individualized. In reality, the child's knowledge is *limited*, not general. Immature intelligence always takes facts in their isolation; each is taken to be what it appears to be on its surface, a separate fact without connection with others. Dependencies of one fact upon another, internal relations, reasons and laws, do not appeal to a young child; in fact, he cannot be made to see them. Since each fact stands alone, knowledge is necessarily limited or particular. With the recognition of internal connections, of ways in which one fact depends upon another, or is the reason for some third fact, limitation is removed.

Generality.—An idea is general, in the degree in which it stands for, represents, or symbolizes, ideas not contained in its own existence. It becomes general just in the degree in which it is taken out of its separation, its isolation, from other facts and is connected with them through some bond of like meaning. To a child, for example, a pebble may be simply what it appears to be in itself, one object, separate from all others, with an individuality of its own. But a scientific man *generalizes* the pebble. He sees it connected with other objects through the law of gravitation, through physical forces, through chemical actions and reactions. He may finally rise, through the discovery of the law of interdependence of all things, to the statement that if the pebble were otherwise than as it is, the whole structure of the Universe would have to be different. In other words, the qualities of the pebble have now become *significant* of *wide relations*, instead of being just what they seem to be in themselves.

From the Unrelated to the Related.—The principle of the development of intelligence may be otherwise worded :—The development of knowledge is from the *unrelated* to the *related*. Relations, as we saw when studying attention, are either of identity or of difference. Now, the mind has only a very limited capacity of relating its first experiences ; it has almost nothing with which it may compare any presentation ; hence, as the relation of *difference* is not noticed, knowledge is vague, and, as the relation of *identity* is not recognized, knowledge is limited. The *discriminating*, or *analytic*, activity develops relations of difference, and hence, clearly discriminates one thing from another, and gives each an individuality of its own. The *identifying*, or *synthetic*, activity develops relations of unity between various facts and then takes them out of their isolated. separate character, into the generality of their common law or aspect. Every fact, as soon as it is connected with another fact, *widens* its meaning, for it has added to it the significance of this other fact. On the other hand, every fact, as it is distinguished from another fact, *defines* its meaning, for it is seen to signify something slightly different from the other fact.

Illustration.—If we return to the child who confuses a plate, a circle and the moon, we shall find him, as he grows older, seeing differences. He will notice the brightness, etc. of the moon ; the solid, useful character of the plate ; the abstract character of the circle. Each object thus gains in *individuality*. But, as time goes on, he learns that the circle is a geometrical figure, a surface, curvilinear, etc. He identifies it with these other figures—the plate, etc.,—and learns that it has certain qualities in common with them ; thus his knowledge of it becomes wider, more general. He learns also to know the moon as a heavenly body, as not a fixed star, as a satellite, etc. In other words, he identifies it with each of these classes of objects, and in identifying it with them, adds to it the qualities which they possess. Then too, he recognizes the laws which connect the moon with other heavenly bodies; the moon ceases to be an isolated body in the heavens, and 'becomes a member of a vast system, connected with every other member by permanent and universal laws. Knowledge of the moon is now both *definite* (in that its *differences* from other bodies, similar in some respects, are recognized) and *general*, in that its *connections* with other bodies, however different in appearance they may be, are recognized.

Educational Principles.—The princip'es just laid down are important as suggesting both the ends aimed at in the education of intelligence, namely, *definiteness* and *generality*, and the means by which these ends are to be reached, namely, *analysis* and *synthesis*.

1. *The Teacher has to make Knowledge Definite.*—It is sometimes said that knowledge begins with the concrete and advances to the abstract, and from this principle the rule is deduced that particular, definite, objects, should first be presented to the pupil, and afterwards his mind be led to consider abstract qualities. However true the principle may be, if it is rightly interpreted, it is thoroughly false if it is meant to imply that *knowledge* is at first concrete, and that this concrete, definite knowledge may be used as the basis for further knowledge. So far ought the teacher to be from assuming that objects have the same concreteness and definiteness to a pupil that they have to him, that his rule should be to *make knowledge definite and concrete.*

Illustrations.—It is an extremely common error to suppose that, because an object, *in itself*, is definite and concrete, it is so to *the mind*. A triangle, for example, is in itself, perfectly definite; it has just such and such properties and no others. But a child's idea of it has no such concreteness. Indeed, the process by which he learns about the triangle is simply the process by which his idea gains definiteness. If his idea were already definite, his knowledge would be complete, whereas it is only beginning. A triangle is *not* a triangle to the child in the sense of a definite figure; it has to be *made* a triangle, as he learns that it has three sides, in distinction from a square, that it is bounded by straight instead of curved lines, as a circle, etc. Primary object lessons, in the same way, are not to lead the mind on from some definite idea which the pupil already has, but to *give him* definite ideas, corresponding to the concrete individual character of the object.

2. *The Teacher should present, first, Wholes, then Parts: first Outlines, then Details.*—The growth of knowledge in a child's mind has been well compared to the growth of his representation of, say, a man. The child, at first draws upon his slate two circles, one for the head, another for the body, and puts under the body two lines for legs. After a time, arms are added, perhaps a neck; then the face begins to gain features, first eyes and mouth, then nose and ears; the arms are endowed with hands; the legs are given feet. Then the same process is repeated for each organ. The eye gains eye-brows, lashes and ball; the arms have joints; the hands, fingers, etc. Then perhaps the child undertakes to draw different individuals, and delineates the characteristic features that distinguish one person from another. So it is with our idea of any object; it exists first in *vague outline* rude and typical in character. Gradually *parts*, members, are recognized, the most interesting first, then these again, are, subdivided. Various objects of the same general kind are examined with a view to seeing individual differences, and thus knowledge becomes gradually spe-

F

cific and concrete. The teacher should follow this natural psychological order.*

3. *The Teacher must rely on the Mind's Analytic Power.*— To reach his end, the educator must be able to excite the distinguishing capacity of the student's mind. He cannot present the differences, the details directly to another; but he can *call attention* to these qualities. That is to say, he can set the pupil's mind working in such ways that the latter will naturally *produce for himself* the required distinctions. This process of recognizing differences is native to the mind, and goes on, therefore, spontaneously and largely unconsciously. The teacher has rather to incite it and rely upon it, than to create or consciously manipulate it. If suitable material is presented, the pupil's mind will be almost as sure to act upon it properly, without specific guidance, as his digestive organs will be sure to digest wholesome food without being told how to do it.

The awakening and developing of mental appetites or interests, and preparing apt material for them to work upon, give wide enough scope to the teacher's ability without his attempting to show the pupil's mind just how it must work. The right use of object lessons, of definite and precise statements in text-books, of talks and lectures by the teacher, etc., etc., are all covered by the three heads of *arousing interest*, of *presenting material properly arranged* and of *preparatory mental activity*. The native, distinguishing capacities of the mind must be trusted for the rest, and if the teacher succeeds in securing the conditions just mentioned, he need have no doubt about the result. The mind is always seizing upon whatever is

---

* The term "whole," however, is here used in a psychological not in a spatial sense. Because the world is really the whole of which geography treats, it does not follow that it is the whole with which the child's mind naturally begins. Or because the sentence is a grammatical whole, it does not follow that it is the psychological outline first in a child's mind.

presented, noticing differences, subdividing, comparing, and producing new distinctions. It cannot work at all without going through these operations. *Discrimination is a fundamental mental capacity.*

4. *The Teacher must depend, similarly, upon the Synthetic Function of Mind.*—The mind naturally works towards unity, as it does towards definiteness. If the teacher awakens a genuine appetite for facts and reasons, and by all methods at his command, presents material so that this appetite is *fed*, and not *pampered* on the one hand, or *repressed* on the other, the pupil's mind will instinctively work towards the underlying relations of things. Ideas *grow together* in the mind ; centres of psychical gravitation are formed about which ideas of a like kind gather ; and these centres become organs for the apperception of like ideas in the future. If the mind works upon facts of like kind and along the lines which connect them, the time will surely come when it will *notice* these connections and the similarities. *First, unconscious growth towards unifying or grouping facts, then conscious recognition of the unities, classes and laws, is the order of nature.*

5. *Neither Facts alone, nor Relations alone, but Related Facts should be Taught.*—It is now generally recognized in theory, at least, that it is an educational blunder to cram the mind with a mass of isolated facts, regarded simply as facts, apart from their reasons. It may be questioned whether there has not been, in some quarters, a reaction to the opposite extreme, and whether *reasons, relations, causes,* are not presented at too early a period. For example, many teachers require pupils that are little more than beginners in arithmetic, to write out examples in addition, subtraction, etc., with a statement of the exact reason for every operation performed. Teachers have been known to explain to children beginning technical grammar, the difference between a percept and a concept, in order to make them understand the

difference between a common and a proper noun !   If a florist were not content with supplying a plant with all necessary material for its growth, and with then allowing it to produce fruit naturally, but should insist upon analyzing the flower in order to find the seed within it, he would be acting on precisely the same principle.

Facts, in and of themselves, *have* relations to one another, or *explain*, that is, *furnish reasons* for one another.   The mind also has an *instinctive tendency to connect* facts and search for reasons.   Now, if facts be taught according to the relation which unites them, and if interest be awakened in the mind in assimilating the facts, the mind can hardly help, even if it would, a final discovery of the relation.   The teacher must have the greatest confidence in the *rationality of facts*, when they are rightly connected, and in the native tendency of the mind to develop itself through, first. *unconscious appropriation* of this rationality, and, second, *conscious recognition* of it.   If the teacher will but have confidence in facts and in intelligence, he will not try himself to take the place both of the facts and of the pupil's mind.

6. *The so-called Faculties of Mind are Successive Stages in the Development of Intelligence.*—These faculties are Perception, Memory, Imagination, and Thinking.   They are sometimes treated as independent powers of mind, having no connection with one another, excepting that they all happen to belong to the same being.   But, in reality, they are the results of the progressive growth of intelligence in representative, ideal and related character.   The same activities, the same principles run through all, but in various degrees of development.

1. **Perception.** This may be defined as the *recognition of some particular object now present in space*, as, for example, this particular tree, this particular blade of grass, this particular pebble, etc., such knowledge is

(1) *Both presentative and representative.*—It is presentative, because based on actual sensation. It is representative, because this sensation does not constitute the perception excepting in connection with what it stands for. Take, for example, the perception of this tree. As I stand here, I see it at a distance of twenty feet. The only sensations that I get from it now are, therefore, those of color and the muscular sensations which I have as my eye turns from one point of light to another. The *representative* elements are the form, size, height and distance of the tree ; the feeling it would give if I had power to touch it ; its wider, unseen, structure and arrangement ; the kind of tree, as *e. g.* a maple, and all the scientific knowledge that I have of its modes of growth and reproduction, etc., etc. The very few sensations, which I have, *symbolize all the qualities which are not actively (that is sensibly) present.*

(2) *It is Largely Ideal.*—These representative factors are ideal. They are supplied from the mind, not given in the actual affection of sense. All the meaning, the significance, that the present perception has, is supplied from what the mind has preserved of former experience. The mind, on the basis of its own content, thus idealizes the given sensation, into the complex *idea of the tree.*

(3) *It is Largely made up of Relations.*—The relations which are most prominent in perception are those of *space.* The object is at a certain distance, has a certain position, form, surface and bulk. Each of these qualities is relative. Distance is measured from my body or from some other object ; position is the place of the object with reference to other objects; its form is its relation to bodies that bound it, etc. We perceive an object, therefore, only by relating it to other. objects. A body absolutely isolated cannot be perceived at all. Such relations, (that is spatial ones) are, however, largely external

The relation of one body to another in space may be changed without changing its own nature.

2. Memory.—This, in its most complete sense, may be defined as the *reproduction of some event or idea once present to mind but not now so, with a reference of it to its proper place in time.* My remembrance of a railway accident, for example, is complete when I can reproduce all its details, and also tell *when* it occurred, that is, place or date it with reference to preceding and to succeeding events. Such reproductions are

(1) *Largely Representative.*—The representative element is greater than in perception, for, in the latter, the sensation which is present, say of color, represents other sensations of weight, contact, taste, etc., which might be made present, if only we applied our other senses. But in memory, both the remembered event and the time in which it occurred have vanished, and we could not make them present if we wished. We represent not what we could experience, but what we *have* experienced.

(2) *It is Largely Ideal.*—The memory of pain is not itself a pain ; the memory of the sun does not shine ; the memory of an apple does not taste, etc. etc. Memory, in other words, is largely divested of sensible qualities, and is mental or ideal in nature.

(3) *It Consists of Relations.*—In memory, we extend the sphere of relations beyond those of space to those of time. We fix the object or event not only with reference to co-existing objects, but with reference to those that go before and those that come after. An event can no more be fixed in absolute time, independent of relation to other events, than an object can be located in absolute space. It is the extent of relations involved that makes it so difficult for young children to have any idea of the duration of experiences, or of the times when they occurred.

3. Imagination.—*Imagination is the power of producing ideas without any reference to our own past experience.*—Suppose that instead of recalling some railway accident which we ourselves have experienced, we attempt to picture it to ourselves. We frame mental pictures of the moving trains, of their collision, of the crash, of the escaping steam, etc. etc.,—and all this without ever having experienced any such combination of incidents. Here we have *imagination.* It is evidently closely allied to memory in two ways. *In the first place*, we must even in memory, picture or image, what is not present, and thus use a kind of imagination. *In the second place*, we very rarely recall events just as they happened ; we leave out unimportant details, we re-arrange the details according to some plan or system, we gradually and unconsciously shift the relations of facts, and even sometimes transform the facts themselves. In so doing, we are virtually making new combinations, we are *imagining.*

Persons who have formed decided recollections of important events that happened years before, are often startled upon coming upon an actual description of the experience (perhaps even written by themselves) at the time it occurred, to see the difference between the fact and their recollection of it. The latter has become a work of fancy, and this has happened simply by the natural laws of the development of reproduction, without any intention on the part of the person concerned to alter or distort. *Re*-production always tends to bring out the universal, the typical, to neglect the accidental and insignificant, and thus passes gradually into *production.* Imagination might be called idealized memory—memory which has lost its personal reference to our own experience and become generalized. Thus art, the product of imagination, has been termed " the world's memory of things." In the same sense poetry has been pronounced truer than history.

The productions of imagination are thus—

(1) *Both Representative and Ideal.*—The image which we make for ourselves need not correspond to anything now present, or ever present, either to ourselves or to another. Or, it may correspond to what indeed is not present, but to what *would* be present if our senses were greatly enlarged and our vision into things deepened. In the latter case, it represents real but unperceived and unremembered facts. Professor Tyndall thus gives to imagination a very high place in the development of science. It may also represent not what is capable of being present, but what we should *like* to be present, if we could have our way, if we could reconstruct affairs about us. Imagination thus reshapes the *actual* order and under the influence of love and desire gives birth to *ideals*, which in turn become guides to conduct.

(2) *It Involves Wide Relations.*—Imagination, as it is more representative and ideal, deals with wider relations than memory and perception. Its relations are not confined to space and time. Indeed, it frees its images from the limitations of place and of time, and contemplates them in their universal significance. Take the old story of Sir Isaac Newton and the fall of the apple. As a matter of perception he saw the fall of this particular apple; in memory he could call up the falling of many material bodies, of all he had ever experienced. By imagination he grasped the fall of this apple as significant of *relations of all material bodies to one another ;* he saw embodied in it, relations as wide as the material universe. This illustrates the usual working of imagination in its higher forms. It idealizes some particular fact or idea, and makes it typical of a whole group of facts ; it *universalizes* the fact or idea.

4. Thinking.—This may be defined *as the recognition of universal factors or of relations in their connections with one another and with particular facts.* While we perceive, or remember, or imagine something *particular*, some given object, or event, or person, we *think* what is *general*. In thinking, we do not deal, for example, with any particular rose or geranium, but with the *class* of roses or of geraniums ; with the relations that make the rose what it is as a rose, independent of the peculiarities which any one individual rose may happen to possess. So, while the mathematician may have before him a particular triangle drawn on a certain blackboard, yet his demonstrations do not concern *this* triangle, but deal with triangles in general, when he proves that the three interior angles are together equal to two right angles. In thinking, the particular is degraded to be simply a sign, or instance, or illustration of the general law or relation. It is of no value in itself, but simply as standing for a universal.

Thinking deals accordingly with *representative, ideal* and *related* factors.

(1) They are *representative*, for, as just said, the presentation has no value of its own ; its worth is entirely in its capacity to stand for a law or a class. It is a sign like the x of the algebraist, having *per se* no value ; and having its value finally determined by what it is discovered to stand for.

(2) That which is thus signified is *ideal*. The universal has no existence as a separate thing in time or space. It is the significance or meaning which is general, and meaning is ideal. When we speak of having a general idea of a rose, for example, this does not mean that we think of some object somewhere existing, which is a universal rose. Nor does it mean that we are able to frame an idea of a rose in general, that is of qualities common to all roses, and excluding all qualities peculiar to each. Any idea we frame must be of a rose of certain size, color, form, etc. ; it must be particular. It is just like the triangle drawn on the board ; we can make only some particular triangle, not triangle in general. What is general is the power which the particular has of standing for, or symbolizing, a

relation or group of relations. In other words, the general factor lies neither in some one actual object, nor in an actual idea, but in the *relations* of a particular object—in the *significance* of a particular idea.

(3) *Thinking is an Explicit Process of Grasping Relations.* Relations are *implied, involved* in perception, memory and imagination, but thinking deals expressly and openly with the relations and with nothing else. The mind discriminates and identifies in those earlier stages, and in thinking it simply aims consciously at discovering unities and differences; the whole process is one of conscious analysis and synthesis.

Educational Principle.--*The Teacher should always keep in Mind that Perception, Memory, Imagination and Thinking are Stages of Mental Development, and that one grows naturally out of another.*—Much harm has resulted in pedagogy from treating these stages of development as if they were independent faculties, having no connection with one another. When this is laid down as a fundamental principle of psychology, unity of education is lost; each " faculty " is then trained by separate methods. There is one process to train perception, another to train memory, another for thinking, etc. The inevitable result is so great a number of " methods " that both teacher and pupil are burdened. Again, this separation is abnormal, not corresponding to any psychological fact. The methods employed are, therefore, artificial as well as too numerous. Spontaneity and interest are thus killed. Above all, the multiplication of separate and artificial methods is wasteful of mental energies, and inefficient in results. But in reality each " faculty " is but a stage in the increasing growth of knowledge in symbolic or representative character, in meaning or significance, in generality and in definiteness. No arbitrary line separates one from another; much less does each have an independent and isolated principle of activity. It follows that the right education of *perception* is at the same time a training of *memory*, and the proper education of memory insures the correct development of *imagination* and of *thought. Any right method trains intellectual function and, thereby, trains each faculty.* These topics will now occupy us in more detail.

§ 2. PERCEPTION.

The training of perception should be considered by the teacher both (1) in itself, and, (2) in its reference to other stages, a preparation for them.

Perception is the most immediate and presentative of all the stages of knowledge, and hence is the closest to sensation. There can be no perception except when there is an object affecting the senses, and the richness of the perception will depend on the degree in which the senses are exercised. What has been said regarding sensation should, therefore, be again refered to.

(1) The Training of Perception in Itself.—This should be of such a character as : (1) To render the percept — what is perceived—accurate and complete; (2) To render the perception independent, and (3) To form the habit of observation.

1. *Accuracy and Fullness.*—Very few persons see just what is before them, or see it in its fullness, for seeing is using the mind, not opening the eyes or staring with them. To avoid hazy perceptions, those which slur over the object and report it in a dim way, or only partially, the mind must be active. There must be mental alertness instead of indolence and inertia. In the earlier stages of life, this alertness and the corresponding degree of definiteness of perception, are ensured by the child's physical activity—the attempts to reproduce the object, to imitate it, to get hold of it, to do something with it ; and in carrying out any course of action, in making anything, there is necessarily a process of *taking apart and putting together,* which is the best possible preparation for future *mental* analysis and synthesis. These activities, as previously sug-

gested. may be carried into the school. Folding, weaving, drawing, modelling, etc., all of them make perception accurate, because all of them require an unconscious analysis, at least, of the features of the object, and then a recombination of them into a new whole. Such activities exercise the mind as well as the senses.

Principle further Applied.—The teacher should strive to have the pupil carry the same spirit of enquiry into subjects where chiefly mental analysis and synthesis are required. The student's mind should always be in a questioning attitude ; what features has this object, this event ? How do they go together to make the whole ? What have I known like it ? What of the same kind, and yet different ? and so on. It is a mistake to carry on a recitation simply as a test of memory : its primary end should be to test the original perception ; to discover what the student has grasped, and should (without confusing him) leave him with such a sense of imper. fect perception as to stimulate him to renewed perceptive activity.

2. *Independence.*—In the higher grades of education, fresh. ness and originality should be aimed at. This does not mean necessarily that the student should make original discoveries, that he should see what no one else has ever seen. But it does mean that he is to observe *for himself;* that, so far as he is concerned, what he perceives is to be a discovery, whether it is for other people or not. Every teacher knows that there is a tendency on the part of the pupil to fall into the habit of seeing only what he is expected to see, of seeing what is *repre- sented* by others to be before him, rather than what is actually presented. Perception thus becomes barren and conventional.

Agassiz was accustomed to put his pupils at a microscope, and giving them no idea of what was to be seen, compel them to look for themselves until they had observed everything possible. Whether this is the best method of accomplishing the result or not, there is no doubt about the de- sirability of the pupil's using his own mental powers in perception, rather than following the reports of others.

3. *Habit of Observation.*—Far more important than the per- ception of any object or number of objects, no matter how ac-

curate and comprehensive the percepts may be, is the formation of a *habit* of observation. A pupil who leaves school on the look-out, with his senses wide awake and keen for whatever is presented, and with a knowledge of how to employ them, has the most perfect equipment the teacher can provide him with, so far as perception is concerned. The *training* of *the power* to observe should be the prime object, rather than the actual observation of a certain number of things. This power involves three elements: (1) An interest in natural objects amounting to sympathy with and love for them; (2) An attention which is both alert and under control; and (3) Ability to use the sense-organs, especially the eye, the ear and the hand, as *instruments*, just as one would use the microscope or the pencil.

(2) Perception in its Relation to other Stages.—

The other stages of knowledge *are developed from perception* by a natural process of growth. It is their germ. Unless, therefore, perception is rightly educated, memory suffers, not merely because it is not supplied with sufficient *material* to remember, but because the functions which enter into memory itself are feeble and imperfectly developed. So, too, there will not only be less material for imagination and reason to work upon, but the mental activities which are necessary for imagination and reason will be defective. A training of perception is, therefore, necessary not only for knowledge of things which are and may be perceived, but for the sake of knowledge of what may never be, or perhaps cannot be, under actual observation. For example, a child will learn about many things in his geography and history lessons which, from the nature of the case, he cannot perceive; foreign countries and their productions; past epochs and their customs. Now, these things will either mean nothing to the pupil, or will be thought of in analogy with what he *does* perceive. The pupil will extend and combine his own past perceptions till they seem to convey to him the required idea. We thus derive the important principle :

All that a child hears or reads about, if not itself matter of perception, will be translated into perceptions already familiar, and only as so translated will it have any meaning. The teacher must absolutely see, therefore,

(a) That the child has a sufficiently wide store of actual perceptions before he goes into fields which demand representative ideas, and

(b) That the child connects ideas which are given to him in a representative way (from the teacher or from the text book) with some actual perception, and with the perception best fitted to render the representative idea significant ; that is, there must be *illustrative* teaching, and the teacher must take care that the illustrations appeal to clear and adequate perceptions.

Possible Errors.—It is easy to blame a pupil for ideas that seem ridiculous and absurd, when really his having such ideas shows that he is doing his best to translate unknown topics into what is familiar and significant. That his translation is inadequate or erroneous, is rather the fault of the teacher than of the pupil. It should also be remembered that to put constantly before pupils representative ideas which they cannot make over into perceptions previously experienced, is to burden the mind with what is *meaningless.* And the evil does not stop with loading the mind with this mass of dead matter. In the meaningless, the mind cannot take any *interest.* It is interested only in what has some connection with itself; interest has even been defined as the relation of an impression to a group of ideas in the mind. If, therefore, there is no connection between what is given to the mind to learn, and its own store of experiences, interest is an impossibility. And, finally, with the loss of interest vanishes the power of paying *attention.*

The Cause of Dullness and Mind-Wandering.—It is a too common experience to find children who at five or six years old are keen and alert—interested in everything with which they come in contact, become after six or eight years schooling, dull and listless in all that concerns their studies. In the great number of cases, the reason undoubtedly is that so much matter has been put before them which they cannot "apperceive," that is, which thay cannot really bring their minds to bear upon. And the reason they cannot bring their minds to bear, cannot interpret and assimilate, is the *lack of previous experiences* into which the new material can be translated. Thus studies become unreal and artificial, belonging to a realm outside the significant experience of the pupil, and the mind can assume only a mechanical relation to what is learned.

§ 3. MEMORY.

For the teacher's purposes, memory may be defined as the *power of getting anything into the mind so that it can be got out again when wanted.* One factor then concerns the original *getting of a thing into the mind*, or *learning*, the other, the *getting of it out again*, or *recollecting*. Each of these factors depends chiefly upon attention and, of course, interest, since attention itself depends upon interest.

(1) **Learning.**—The chief thing for the teacher to keep in mind is that the training of memory is, to a very large degree, training in original apperception—in apprehension and assimilation of what is to be remembered. It may be laid down as a rule : **Do not aim at training memory directly, but indirectly, through the training of the apperceiving powers.** The attitude of the pupil's mind should be : I must *perceive* this just as it is and in all its bearings ; not, I must *remember* this. If the original perception, in other words, is what it should be, accurate, comprehensive and independent, memory may be left very largely to take care of itself. For the first step in remembering anything is to get it within the mind, and apperception is just this getting it within the mind. If this is thoroughly done, the first step in memory is already taken, and it needs no special training of its own. We may now apply this general rule so as to make it more specific.

1. *A certain amount of material which has, in itself, no meaning, always has to be memorized.*—This includes, to a large extent, the spelling of words, historical dates, names of countries, rivers and other geographical data, and, perhaps to a certain extent, in primary teaching, rudimentary arithmetical facts. Now, the wrong method of training, that which insists on the direct training of memory, would pay small attention, or none, to the original perception of these facts, but would endeavor by the force of repetition to get them impressed upon the mind. The correct method endeavours to see that the pupil's interest is aroused, that he pays keen attention, and that he forms a *lively* and *definite* idea of what he is to remember. If he is to learn to spell " deceive," he is not to do it by a mechanical repetition of the letters one after another till they are graven into his memory, but by a perception of them, based on interest in the form and structure of the the word, and by holding the mind in strong tension to see just what should be seen and nothing else. If the child performs this act of interested and lively perception, and if he is occasionally called upon to reproduce his knowledge, there is not much danger that he will forget the word. And so with memorizing the other classes of facts mentioned. The teacher thus best cultivates memory by arousing interest, keeping the senses sharp and tense, and by allowing memory to grow out of the resulting perception.

2. *There is also material to be memorized, which consists in the consecutive statement of matters of fact.*—It differs from what was included in the first class in that it has meaning of its own; but it consists of facts rather than of reasons for the facts. It includes the largest part of historical and of geographical studies, and of elementary physical science. Here again it is original apperception that needs most looking after. " Learning by heart," in the sense of impressing the facts upon the mind by the force of sheer repetition, should not be permitted. It may

be necessary to learn many of the *important statements* so that they can be *repeated exactly*, and it will probably be necessary to use repetition: but the literal memorizing should be accomplished through the ways in which the statements are apprehended, and repetition should be used as an *aid to the apprehension*, and not as the basis of the memory.

"**Learning by Heart.**"—This, as a process of memorizing by repeating the subject-matter over and over till it is fixed in mind, is faulty for four reasons.

(1) *It employs only sensuous association.* The mind has to form *some* associations, even in such memorizing, but it forms only associations between the *sounds* of the words, or their visible appearances. There is no association of the ideas involved.

(2) *It leaves the mind passive.* What is learned is *impressed upon* the mind, not produced by the mind's activity. The result of treating the mind as a wax-tablet is always that the various impressions blur and blot out one another, and that finally the wax is worn out, and there is left only a hard surface which will not receive impressions. The common complaint that memory fails with increase of years is largely due to this misuse of memory. In childhood there is without doubt a very great impressibility of the senses. The mind is plastic and sensations are vivid. The result is that sensuous associations are easily formed. But as impressions grow less vivid, and sensations become common place, this plasticity and the forming power of sensuous associations is greatly impaired.

(3) The mind being passive, only *receiving* impressions, *it is burdened by what it remembers.* This does not enter into the mental structure and is thus a load for it to carry. It may be laid down as an axiom that whatever does not help the mind hinders it ; whatever does not aid the mind to group new material is a strain on mental energy.

(4) *The senses, rather than the mind, being engaged, the habit of mind-wandering is produced.* One of the commonest sources of inability to *concentrate attention* and keep it fixed, is that the pupil has been accustomed to memorize by the mere repetition of sense impressions while his mind was really occupied with something else.

It is to be borne in mind that the foregoing remarks apply to learning-by-heart as a mechanical process in which only *verbal associations* are formed. If learning-by-heart includes—as it ought to include—an appeal to the *intelligence*, it becomes of high value in education ; it is accordingly to be

G

regretted that, in the just reaction against mere *rote* learning, there is a pernicious tendency to *disparage* the *memory* and especially to eliminate from "modern" methods the truly educating practice of *intelligently* learning by heart selections from the masterpieces of our literature.

Reliance upon Association and Attention.— What has been said should not be taken to mean that the senses are not to be employed to the utmost in memorizing. On the contrary, whatever vividness and plasticity the senses possess, should be utilised. But they should be employed in subordination to the mental functions. The senses are *good servants* but *poor masters*; they should be used in memorizing, just in the degree in which they are necessary to *clear*, *vivid* and *full apperception*, and no further.

Association of Ideas.—On the positive side, it may be said that memorizing should rest upon the association of *ideas*, not of *sensations*. That is, what the sensations mean, what they convey to the mind, should be connected; and, so far as possible, the kinds of connection, whether of contiguity or of similarity, should be noticed. It will be found a great aid, even in teaching young pupils, to point out the way in which facts are connected.

Analysis and Synthesis.—The constant employment of the functions of analysis and synthesis should be relied upon. The student may, for example, first read over the whole lesson, reading it with *attentive mind*, and not with his eyes alone; that is, interpreting it by his present store of knowledge, and assimilating it to that as far as possible. Thus he will gain a general idea of the whole; then let him go over the subject again, *making the various parts of the whole definite*, and *getting them in their relations to one another*. If the material is suited to the pupil's stage of development, that is, if he can grasp its bearing and properly apperceive it, then by the time he has apprehended the material as a whole and in its parts, it will generally be found that no special draft upon the specific capacity of memory is requisite; in taking it in, he *has* memorized it.

3. *There is material to be learned consisting in the relations of complex Ideas.*—This includes subjects like higher mathematics, political economy, psychology, the more advanced stages of natural science, etc. Such material has meaning in itself, and also states, either expressly or by implication, reasons for the facts, as well as the facts themselves. Here the main principle, that memory is a function dependent upon original apprehension, still holds good. Such material must be *understood* and the process of understanding it, of developing relations and tracing their connections with one another, is a process *of making it over into mental structure*, and, therefore, fulfils the first requisite of memory. To memory in this third and highest stage, the statement of a French author that memory should be the cradle and not the tomb of an idea, is particularly applicable. Such material when taken into the memory, should not lie dormant, but should be constantly assimilating material to itself, so as finally to re-appear in transformed and enriched shape.

Forgotten Knowledge.—It is on this ground that we are able to answer the question often asked as to the benefit of studies, such *e. g.,* as Greek Grammar and the Calculus, which] are often forgotten after leaving school, by one who never uses them. There is not only the *formal* benefit, the discipline of the mental powers employed in learning these subjects, but there is a *material* benefit. While the person may not be able to recall just what he learned, he yet *remembers* it in the sense that it has been transformed into new mental growths. It has been changed into assimilating power—into mental function. This accounts for the paradoxical statement sometimes made, that one never remembers till one has forgotten.

(2) **Recollection.**—Beside learning or getting the subject-matter into the mind, there is *recollecting*, or drawing it forth again when desired. Correct apprehension greatly aids ready and correct recalling, for correct apprehension takes hold of the connections of ideas in what is learnt, and thus makes it easy and almost necessary for the mind to pass from one idea already present to another which it wishes to make present. If the association is merely sensuous, however, there, is nothing inter-

nal to connect the facts or objects, and hence recollection may be broken off at any point. Aside from this, however, recollection depends upon (1) *Repetition* and (2) *Attention*.

1. *Repetition.*—If the original act of apprehension has been an interested and an attentive one, difficulty of recollection will generally be found to be due to the multiplicity of associations that arise. The idea that is already in the mind, instead of suggesting the idea desired, starts a number of allied ideas. Thus, it will be found that the reason why an illiterate man seems to have a better memory than an educated one, or a child than an adult, is that the child and the illiterate have, comparatively, so few experiences that there is less difficulty in passing from one to another. When there are a great number of associations clustered about the same idea, they run into and obstruct one another. The best means of obviating this is *fre quent repetition* of that association deemed most important, until the mind acts more easily along that line than along the lines of other associations. Each exercise of an associative activity strengthens capacity in that direction, and, makes subsequent exercise easier.

Reviews.—From what has been already said, it will be understood that repetition is not to be mechanical but active. That is, it is not to be a repetition of the impression upon the mind, but of the activity by which the impression is apprehended. In the great majority of cases it will be found that *mastery of a subject depends less upon its first reception into the mind than upon the frequent going over of what was then learned.* To use the com_ parison of a recent writer, just as a military officer must daily review his troops to see that they are in proper condition for battle, so a student must constantly review his ideas to keep them fresh and ready for use.

2. *Attention.*—In this connection, we do not refer to the use of attention in the original apprehension, but in the act of *recol- lection.* The machinery of recollection is as follows : There is an idea in the mind which has either been contiguous to the idea we wish to recall, or is similar to it. By the laws of asso-

ciation, therefore, the present idea will suggest what is wanted. When we say *we* recollect, it is really one idea or a group of ideas which recalls, or redintegrates, the other. But it may fail to suggest the other spontaneously. It is then necessary to pay attention to *all factors connected with what we wish to recall*, and thus stimulate them to suggest what is wanted. In other words, the will cannot aid directly in recollecting, but only indirectly by dwelling upon associated factors. It is these factors which, working by contiguity or similarity, bring about the recollection. If, for example, we wish to recall some one's name, we think of where we met him, who introduced him, what was said, etc.; we go over the letters of the alphabet, to try whether the name will be suggested by its initial letter. Thus we start by attention a number of *converging associations* to produce what is wanted. If the original act of apperception was one of mental connection, of analysis and synthesis, this production will easily occur.

§ 4. IMAGINATION.

Of all the stages of intelligence, Imagination *is the least capable of direct training.* As reasons for this fact, may be mentioned, (1) its *free* character, (2) its *individual* nature and (3) the *unconscious* mode of its growth.

1. *Imagination is free in that it is not bound down by any external laws.* It is not, like perception and memory, under constraint to actual experience ; nor to logical rules like thinking. Objects of perception may be put before a pupil and he can be directed as to what and how to see,—and the resulting perceptions can be tested by questioning. Lessons to memorize may be given the student, and he can be examined to find out what he remembers. But the pupil cannot be told to imagine, cannot have rules laid down for him to follow, cannot be examined on the results of his imaginings. The free nature of imagination puts it beyond such external direction and restraint.

2. *Imagination is personal, individual, taking its spring in feeling and desire* rather than from information or logical processes. Its birthplace is in what is most intimate to the soul itself; it is the reflex of hope, love, reverence and admiration. Thus it cannot be pried into from without; nor can it be greatly stimulated from without, excepting by awakening the feelings. A child's imagination is often so deeply personal that it cannot be treated with too great reserve; too close scrutiny or guidance is violation of the child's personality.

3. Imagination does not grow by the *conscious* following of certain methods, or from the formal study of certain subjects, *but by unconscious steps.* It grows with the development of the child in power of feeling and desiring; it grows by what it feeds upon, beautiful scenes, pictures, poems, ideas, characters. Its roots are in the underlying forces of human nature, fundamental instincts and feelings, which rarely come into consciousness, and which, if forced into consciousness, lose their spontaneity and value. Thus a child questioned about his imagination, will often conceal his real fancies entirely, or will produce an artificial product, either conventional or strained and mawkish in sentimentality.

The training of the imagination must, therefore, be largely indirect. This indirect training may come about (1) Through cultivation of its modes of expression; (2) Through cultivation of the feelings that find their outlet in imagination, and (3) Through presentation of material—scenes of nature, works of art, fine literature—fitted at once to awaken and guide imagination.

1. It is natural for the imagination to *project* itself; to attempt to embody its images in outward form. These outward modes of expression may be very largely guided and controlled without interfering unduly with the inward moods and dispositions whence they flow. Drawing, modelling, designing,

even plaiting, sticklaying and machine work, may be made, not only means of training the impulses, the sense-organs and the functions of intelligence, but also the imagination. Composition-work and essay-writing are means which should not be neglected; the choice of subjects and the mode of treatment, both being of importance.

2. The cultivation of the feelings, which shape the material provided by the senses and by memory, and which give rise to the ideals that the images try to express, may be treated under two heads.

(1) The Personal Influence of the Teacher.—It

is feelings of love, of admiration, and of desire for something not attained, that underlie imagination in all its higher forms. Imagination must be unselfish; one who is wholly interested in his own needs and appetites and in their satisfaction, will not be able to get outside of himself, and hence will not be able either to produce or to notice external beauty. The emotions and the mood, which predispose to imagination, must be left largely to the vital influence and personal sympathy of the teacher. The enthusiasm and the devotion of the teacher for whatever is worthy of admiration, will go further than any set methods.

(2) The Development of Religious Emotions.—

The imagination is an idealizing and universalizing power. It attempts to clothe all objects with beautiful forms; to find them significant of ideals. It takes the mind beyond its own experiences of perception and memory into what is general, what has no concern with private enjoyments. Imagination thus tends to take the mind beyond the present and the apparent. Hence its kinship to religious emotions and ideas. Early religious ideas are at once the product of the imagination and the most influential means of forming it. Religious emotions, reverence, and especially awe, the objects of religious worship, especially the great personalities of religion, if rightly presented to a child, call out imagination more than almost anything else.

3. Imagination must have material to feed upon. Imagination is the *outgrowth of perception and memory*, and unless these supply a rich and varied material, it will be defective or unhealthy. While originating in the emotions, imagination should not feed upon them, but upon outward objects, scenes and ideas ; imagination which both springs from and lives upon the emotions will be morbid and unhealthy. Material proper for imagination to work on may be classified as follows :

(1) **Natural Scenes.**—Taking children into the woods, to lakes and mountains, calling their attention to sunsets, clouds and all the forms of animate and inanimate nature, are highly important. The beautifying of the school-room with flowers, with works of art, etc., the inculcation of care for whatever is beautiful, are means that tell with great effect. An important step in the training of imagination is taken when a child realizes that a beautiful object, simply because it is beautiful, should not be destroyed, or *sacrificed to his own needs.*

(2) **Studies like Geography and History.**—These studies take the pupil beyond himself, one in the direction of space, the other of time. They should be taught almost as much as means of widening and deepening the imagination, as of furnishing the mind with information.

(3) **The Study of Literature.**—The products of the imagination of the race, as embodied in literature, are perhaps the most influential means of training the imagination. For young children, that literature is the best which is the unconscious product of races and of peoples rather than of the conscious invention of individuals. Fairy tales, folk-lore, myths, historic epics, and traditions are natural and healthy. There is a connection between the childhood of the race and of the

individual that makes such literature peculiarly appropriate for the imaginations of youthful minds. As the child grows older he should be introduced, of course, to more conscious literary products, the preference being given to such as are narrative rather than subjective. Sir Walter Scott will appeal to children whom Shelley or Wordsworth will leave untouched. Upon the whole, also, preference should be given to literature produced as literature, rather *than to works of imagination produced expressly for children.*

§ 5. THINKING.

The stage of intellectual development next higher than imagination is thinking. It is important for the teacher to notice that the training of thinking may be either *direct* or *indirect* ; that is, it may be by means whose specific end is the development of reasoning power, or it may be by methods, which in themselves, are directed toward the development of other powers, but which, nevertheless, tend towards the education of th ought.

1. Indirect Training.—Thinking, since it is not an isolated faculty, but a stage of mental development, must have implied within it the same mental processes (association and attention), the same mental functions (analysis and synthesis) as perception, memory and imagination. *Of necessity, therefore, any correct training of perception, etc., is at the same time a training of the power of thinking.* There is no abstract faculty of thinking, that is no faculty apart from what is thought about : there is simply the power of dealing with certain kinds of mental relations and products, and this is an outgrowth, a development of preceding powers. These statements may be illustrated in more detail by considering the relations of the various mental stages to (1) generalization, (2) relation, (3) retention.

(1) Generalization.—Thinking is, as previously shown, generalizing ; it is dealing with the universal factor. The general factor is implied or involved in the lower stages. It is a mistake to suppose that there are two *kinds* of knowledge, one particular, the other general. There are two *factors*, one particular, the other general, *in every kind of knowledge*, and thinking differs from perception only in the more explicit development and conscious recognition of the universal factor. When we perceive that this something now before us is a book, we generalize or classify. We bring this particular thing under a wider class or genus, and ascribe to the particular the relations which the genus or class possesses. There is involved, therefore, in the simplest perception an unconscious recognition at least, of the identity of the present experience with something else. This generalization is also a process of reasoning. We conclude, or infer, that this something is a book, *because* of certain similarities between what is presented and the general notion of book.

(2) **Relation.**—Thinking is comparison with a view to recognizing relations, identity and difference. It involves *conscious analysis and conscious synthesis*. These functions appear in thinking as induction and as deduction—*induction* being the recognition of the one common law, in the midst of diverse, particular facts; *deduction*, the application of the general law to some particular fact as a case coming under it. *Induction* begins with particulars and advances to the universal relation implied within them; as when Newton advanced from the study of particular heavenly bodies to the discovery of the law of gravitation. *Deduction* begins with the universal and brings some particular under it, as when we say that since the law of gravitation applies to all heavenly bodies, it *must* apply to some newly discovered comet, although we have not discovered as matter of observation, that it *does* apply. Now, since all knowledge requires the functions of discrimination and identification, and induction and deduction are only the higher developments of these functions, all knowledge is, to some degree, a preparation for reasoning.

(3) **Retention.**—There goes on, in retention, an unconscious assimilation which groups facts about some common centre and according to some common principle. Every one has had the experience of learning some branch of study, as algebra, without having comprehended all of it ; but a year or two later, upon returning to this subject, it appears clear and even simple. The facts seem to have fallen into their right relations, and to be just what they should be. In other words, the results of thinking have been obtained, and this without the conscious exercise of thought. This would not have occurred, indeed, had the algebraic knowledge lain inert in the mind, but the use of it, the employment of relations similar to those learned in algebra, have performed for us what thinking would perform. This result inevitably follows, whenever knowledge once *appropriated*, is afterwards *used*. The relations *implied* within it become *explicit ;* perception and memory, in other words, have grown into reason.

From the facts that knowledge retained and organically assimulated becomes thought ; from the facts that generalization and relation are involved in all mental stages, we gather this law : *The power of reasoning is a natural and necessary growth from the powers of perception, memory and imagination, provided these are trained rationally, that is according to true psychological principles.*

2. **Direct Training.**—Not all subjects, however, call forth, to the same extent, the processes of generalizing and relating, and the power of organic assimilation. Among the subjects which call them forth the most, and thus give the best training of thought, may be mentioned *language* and *science.*

1. *Language.*—There is a common educational precept that needs careful interpretation, namely, " *Teach things, not words.*" Its only proper meaning is that *mere* words, or sounds, should not be taught, but that *with* the word, the *meaning* for which

it stands should be taught. So far as the principle seems to imply that the development of language is not of the greatest importance, for the sake of the *knowledge of things*, as well as for its own account, the *principle* is *erroneous*. Proper training in words is, in and of itself, one of the most effective methods of training thought. This may be shown (1) with regard to the employment of words themselves, (2) with regard to their combination in sentences, and (3) with regard to the combination of sentences.

(1) *Words.*—Every common noun is *general;* it names a class and not an individual. Every adjective expresses quality, and quality is *general;* quality is the basis upon which classes are constructed. Every verb expresses a mode of action, or of being, and this again is general; 'to be,' 'to run,' 'to study,' are not particular things, but relations. When a child learns such words (not the *sounds*, but the *words*) he is necessarily performing, although only unconsciously, acts of generalization. When an infant learns the word 'dog,' not only does the object, the thing, become more definite, because he has now a means of specifying that object, but *he performs an act of classification.* He apprehends, however roughly, the properties possessed by all animals of this class.

(2) *Sentences.*—Grammar is the logic of language. Every structure in language is objectified thought. The unit of sructure is the sentence, and this corresponds to the unit of thought, the judgment. In a judgment a relation is affirmed, or an act of thought is completed, some connection between a universal and a particular is stated. A sentence but manifests this connection, and, if the meaning of the sentence is understood, it requires, however imperfectly, the action of the same functions of analysis and synthesis that are involved in judgment.

(3) *Combination of Sentences.*—Reasoning is termed, logically, *discourse.* This is the consecutive employment of sentences upon some subject, and *is*, in substance, a process of reasoning. While the statements of a book are not arranged in successive syllogisms, they are none the less arranged, if the book has any system or order, upon logical principles. There is *reason* in the presentation, that is, there is classification, grouping, selection, movement towards some end. If a pupil really reads, that is, if he appropriates the meaning, the thought in what he reads, he himself thinks, for he reproduces the connection, the order and the subordination of ideas.

2. Science.—Scientific knowledge is, of course, the most perfect expression of orderly thought. It is conscious and explicit statement of relations, of groups of relations, of reference of fact to law, and law to fact. In each step of science, *description, classification, explanation*, reasoning is concerned. If then the pupil studies science as he should, that is if he really reproduces what he learns so as to know what it means, he is training his thinking powers. Scientific study, therefore, should be not only the memorizing of facts, or even the training of observation, but the *development of thought.* If, on the one side, the scientific material is properly presented, and if, on the other side, the pupil really appropriates it, or makes it his own, the education of the thinking powers will surely be attained. Natural science gives the best training of the analytic or inductive powers, mathematical science of the synthetic or deductive.

CHAPTER V.

THE FORMS OF EMOTIONAL DEVELOPMENT.

We have completed our study of intellectual development, and turn now to the growth of Feeling. Since the same processes of attention and association underlie it, and since its development is analogous to that of the intellect, it may be treated with comparative brevity. It may also be mentioned at the outset that the training of feeling is so largely personal and indirect that the educator must be left for the most part to apply his own knowledge of the psychology of the subject without detailed suggestions as to *method*. The subject may be conveniently treated under the head of I., *Conditions of Interest, or of Emotional Development;* II. *The Principles of Growth;* III., *The Resulting Forms.*

I. Conditions of Interest.—The most general law of interest is that feeling accompanies *exercise* or *activity*. Feeling is excitation, and implies, accordingly, stimulation and response to stimulus in some activity. If the activity is free and unimpeded, if it results in increasing activity, the feeling is *pleasurable.* If the activity is hindered, either from internal defects, or from external obstacles, if it decreases the amount of energy that may be put forth, the feeling is *painful.* Since feeling accompanies activity, its traits are dependent upon the nature of the activity, and this dependence will now be discussed.

1. *Spontaneity.*—As just said, pleasure is the result of free activity. It is an ultimate law of *mind*, both in its higher aspects and in its connection with the body through the senses and the impulses, that it strives to express itself. It has an internal tendency towards action, and this is stimulated by every impression made upon it. Whatever calls forth this activity, or whatever increases it, *interests* by that very fact. Interest is

the *accompaniment of the spontaneous self-activity of the child.* This principle transcends almost all others in educational importance. The child's mind must be aroused from within and his own activity called upon, if he is to be interested in any subject.

2. *Strength of Activity.*—All materials of study, regarded from the standpoint of the pupil, are a stimulus, a challenge to his own powers The stimulus must, therefore, be properly adjusted to these powers. Too weak stimuli—that is, too easy material—do not call out enough activity to be interesting; too strong stimuli, the mind cannot respond to. Very slight stimuli often irritate the mind; each seems to call for activity, and yet it does not call loud enough to get an answer. Slight, repeated excitations have the effect of distracting mental activity, while intense ones fatigue and finally exhaust it. Strength of stimulus is thus a relative term, depending upon the mind's power of response. The stimulus which calls forth as much of the mind's activity as is possible without straining it, is of proper strength and awakens the most interest.

3. *Change of Activity.*—A stimulus which the mind has wholly responded to, ceases to be a stimulus, and calling forth no more activity, it awakens no more interest. Hence the need of change, of alternation in studies and in modes of present-ing them. That a subject is monotonous means that the mind has already exercised itself in that direction as far as is possible. When a teacher detects signs of monotony, it is time for him to vary something. He must appeal to the mind from a new side, and, awakening new activity, call out new interest. Constant activity in one direction, also, if the mind does *not* succeed in answering the challenge of the stimulus, produces mental fatigue, and thus lowering disposable energy, lowers interest. It is a well-known fact that if the eye gazes upon the color red for a time and then turns to green,

the green seems brighter than it otherwise would seem. The nerves being fatigued in one direction, give stronger impressions in another. This law prevails in education, and the teacher should avail himself of it by providing for due alternation of activities ; first an activity of the senses, then one of memory, then of bodily impulses, like gymnastics, etc., then an appeal to imagination, etc.

4. *Harmony of Activities.*—Activity is more permanent and wider in the degree in which it is harmonious. Harmony is defined as a unity made up of a variety. Variety which has no unity interrupts and distracts the mind ; unity which ha; no variety within it is, as just seen, monotonous and dead. But the co-operation of various factors, having some common end and meaning, calls forth one activity, and yet an activity which manifests itself in a great many directions. Each activity supports and stimulates every other. Hence there, arises a permanent and ever-growing interest. There is no more practical problem in the school-room than how to attain the due adjustment of unity in variety. The subjects must be brought into relation with one another, and the various facts and principles of the same subject must be united, but yet the mind must not be kept dwelling too long upon bare unity. The best method, in general, of solving the problem and thus keeping interest awake and increasing, is to start from some centre and then develop facts, principles, subjects from that. The common centre ensures unity of activity ; the various branches developed from it ensure variety and growth.

II. Principles of Emotional Growth.—The development of the interests from their original form into complex products, is analogous to the intellectual development already traced. It begins with immediate sensuous states, and advances by idealizing them into more universal, and at the same time more distinct forms. What has been said on the

principles of intellectual thus hold good very largely of emotional development. Instead of repeating these principles, we need only call attention to some of their aspects,

1. *The Widening of Feeling.*—Feeling is originally limited in scope and significance. The early feelings spring from the senses and do not extend their value beyond the time in which they are experienced, or beyond the individual who has them. A feeling of taste, or of smell, or of hunger, is *personal* in the narrowest and most exclusive sense of the term. But gradually emotions take a wider bearing and value.

(*a*) *Transference.*—This widening of feeling occurs first, through what may be called the transference of feeling. Feeling which intrinsically belongs to some one presentation passes over into whatever is associated with it. The pleasure which a child gets from his food is extended to the utensils used, formerly indifferent, and to the person who gives the food. The interest which a child has in gaining the approbation of a parent or a teacher, is widened into interest in the study or occupation which was at first simply a means of gaining approbation. The pleasure which a child takes in mere activity, physical and mental, becomes transferred to the objects upon which the activity is exercised.

(*b*) *Widening through Unconscious Sympathy.*—The widening appears oftentimes to be purely instinctive and reflex; a child becomes interested in matters simply because those about him are interested in them. The child unconsciously puts himself in the place of others, and thereby widens his interest to the horizon of others. A child's games generally follow the business of his parents. Almost all children play "keep house" and "school." These plays simply witness to the fact that the child's feelings are being colored by his contact with others, and that he is desirous of making their wider life his.

H

(*c*) *Widening through Conscious Sympathy or Love.*—The most important method (at least from the teacher's standpoint) of widening emotional life, is arousing personal sympathy and love. This is an outgrowth of the second principle. If a child really cares for his parent or his teacher, he is perforce interested in what he sees them to be interested in. This is not the result of desire to gain praise, but the result of an identification of feeling with them, so that whatever affects them affects him. The moulding and transforming influence some teachers possess, is due more largely to their power to make their pupils share their interests, than to anything else. And this power to communicate interest arises in the admiration and regard of the pupil for the teacher's personality. It is a vital and personal force.

2. *Deepening of Feeling.*—Interests at first are not only limited, but they are transitory and unstable. Their development consists in making them fixed, instead of fickle ; deep, instead of superficial.

(*a*) *Repetition.*—This deepening results very largely from *repetition*, coming under the general law that exercise strengthens function, while disuse weakens it. A feeling constantly restrained from expression is starved ; one always allowed to give itself outward form, is deepened. A feeling may be developed, first, by constantly presenting material that will evoke it, and, secondly, by allowing it to act upon this material whenever present. Thus, the sentiment for beauty is deepened when beautiful objects are always at hand to stimulate it, and when the sentiment is allowed and encouraged to re-act upon the stimulus. On the other hand, the disposition to anger dies out when persons and objects that would excite it, are kept away from the child, or when, although they are present, the child is not allowed to manifest anger.

(*b*) *Co-operation.*—Besides *repetition*, the teacher may rely upon *co-operation* of feelings. Feelings of similar kind strengthen one another; for example, to train one moral feeling, like truthfulness, will generally be found to deepen others, like reverence and purity. On the other hand, it is generally difficult to uproot any feeling by acting upon it alone. Another and antagonistic feeling must be called into play, which by superior strength shall drive away the feeling it is desired to displace. The habit of anger is more easily corrected by getting the child under the influence of motives of love, than by negative injunctions not to give way to anger.

The result of the deepening of feeling is the formation of *dispositions*, moods and emotional tendencies. There is such a thing as emotional character, manifesting itself in fixed capacities and active tendencies, as well as intellectual or volitional character. The principle of *retention* covers the life of feeling.

III. The Forms, or Stages, of Feeling.—These may be classified as *Intellectual*, *Aesthetic*, and *Personal*, according to the order of increasing significance (or representative character) and of increasing universality and definiteness.

1. *Intellectual Feelings.*—These are such as lead to the acquiring of knowledge, or as result from its positive acquisition. The intrinsic feelings that induce a child to intellectual activity are *wonder* and *curiosity*. A distinction may be made between these two terms : Wonder is the feeling the mind always has (or should have) in presence of the unknown. It is the feeling, that a universe of objects is before the mind calling upon it for action. It is the feeling that intelligence is challenged into activity to discover what is presented. It is thus a permanent feeling or back ground of emotion. It is an *active* feeling ; that is, it serves as a stimulus to the intellectual processes to put themselves forth and master what evokes wonder. It has been termed the " mother of science and philosophy."

It has been said that while the customary and the familiar cease to excite wonder in the ordinary mind, it is a mark of genius that it wonders at the familiar as well as at the novel. It should be one result of education to keep alive the feeling that there is, in every experience, something wonderful, something which demands attention and inquiry.

Curiosity.—This is not a feeling that can be awakened by every experience, but only by an occurrence which goes against what was expected. When the mind takes it for granted that something is thus and so, and then finds it to be otherwise, there is the feeling of *surprise.* This awakens *curiosity* to find an explanation for the puzzling fact. Curiosity has both a good and a bad sense. In the good sense, it is desire of investigation, to discover what the fact is. In the bad sense, it is desire of investigation in order to satisfy some personal or selfish interest. In its good sense, curiosity is one of the most potent allies of the teacher. The teacher should endeavor so to educate it that it may pass into openness and disinterestedness of mind. Some minds seem shut to all new ideas and hard and rigid in structure, others are flexible and open to new ideas, and hence never cease mental growth.

Feelings of Acquisition.—As the two relations implied in knowledge are identity and difference, there are two corresponding emotions which arise. Every *identification* of ideas apparently diverse, is accompanied by a peculiar thrill of satisfaction: a feeling of harmony and of expansion. Every *distinction* is accompanied by a feeling of clearness and light in place of confusion and darkness. These feelings together give a sense of self-command, of power and of intellectual freedom. It has been said that the great advantage of education is not so much the information it gives, as the sense it affords that we are not *deceived.* True education, in other words, gives a sense of control over ideas and objects, instead of a sense of being at their mercy. The educated mind feels that it has the power to deal with facts, to discover the relations of identity and difference among them ; in other words, to distinguish the reality from the appearance, and so avoid being deceived. The sense of power which the acquisition of knowledge awakens is one of the most potent allies of the teacher. It shows itself in the earliest stages.   The child who has learned to put together easy words, to make simple numerical combinations has gained a sense of capacity which rewards him for past effort and stimulates him to new activity.   Studies which are too difficult or which are meaningless do not permit the pupil to master them, and thus deprive the teacher of this ally.

II. Aesthetic Feelings.—These may be defined as *emotions arising from the apperception of an ideal element embodied in some form of reality.*   In the beautiful object there seems to be a balance, an equivalence of the real and the ideal.   There is presentation, some sensible object, and there is representation, for embodied in the presentation is an ideal value or significance.   It differs from an object of scientific knowledge because in the latter the presentation serves only as a *symbol to suggest* the idea ; while in the beautiful object, the idea is so *embodied* in the presentation that no distinction can be made between them.   It requires activity of the reasoning power to get at the ideal factor in science ; while the conscious activity of thinking must be excluded from a recognition of beauty.   The beautiful object, in other words, is an object of *perception*, not of *conception.*

Factors of the Beautiful Object.—It is impossible to tell beforehand just what particular qualities an object which awakens aesthetic feeling will possess, for the very reason that this object is an embodiment of imagination in perceptual form, and not of reasoning in a symbol.   But in *general* every beautiful object has adaptation, economy, harmony and freedom.

1. *Adaptation.*—By *adaptation* is meant such inter-relation of parts as expresses some one meaning, or serves some one end. There may be either external or internal adaptation.   In *external* adaptation, the arrangement of parts is such as to render the object useful for something beyond itself.   It serves an outside purpose ; thus a tool, a piece of machinery, is sub-

servient to something beyond itself. So, too, a poem which is meant to convey some moral lesson, is adapted to this extraneous end. In *internal* adaptation no outside purpose is subserved. In every living being, there is complete adaptation of parts to one another and to the whole. But this adaptation is for the sake of the living being itself; it is identical with its own structure; it serves its own purpose, and not anything outside. So far as adaptation is external, the object is useful but not beautiful; when it is internal, however useful it may be, the object is beautiful.

2. *Economy.*—There is another method of stating the same principle. Where some one end is reached by the co-operation of members and the members co-operate to bring about the richest end with the least waste and in the simplest way, there is beauty. Economy is not to be mistaken for poverty, or *sparseness.* It implies rather fullness, and abundance, but it implies that this fullness *means* something in *all its details*, that there is nothing superfluous. Grace, whether of existence or of action, always means that the result is reached with the slightest expenditure of means, with no perceptible effort; while clumsiness, awkwardness, always shows that the result is not easily and economically reached.

3. *Harmony.*—This signifies many members constituting a unity. A regular form, a picturesque landscape, a pleasing poem or statue or painting, always possesses proportion, harmonious adjustment of parts. In a beautiful object there is sub-ordination and co-ordination; there is a central figure about which others are grouped; there is a leading motive to which others are tributary; there is perspective, etc.

4. *Freedom.*—The very fact that the adjustment or harmony serves no external end, implies that it is free or unconstrained. Life is more beautiful than what is inanimate; indeed, when we find nature or some of its forms beautiful, it is because we

attribute to them a life of their own. There are law and order in the beautiful object ; even the most irregular and apparently capricious piece of music is based upon mathematical and physical laws ; but the law is internal ; the beautiful object appears as living law, not as a lifeless object obeying some law outside itself. On account of this freedom, aesthetic activity partakes of the nature of *play* ; it is activity which has its end in its own manifestation.

Factors of Aesthetic Feeling.—If we turn from the beautiful object to the feeling which it awakens, we find that aesthetic feeling has a certain *universality* and *ideality*. From these characteristics it follows that

(1) *The lower senses do not have any important place in art.*—Tasting and smelling may produce agreeable sensations, but not emotions of beauty. Such presentations have no universal value ; they are of worth only to the organism that has them, and only while it has them. They are *sensuous* and *particular*.

(2) *Aesthetic feeling must exclude the feeling of ownership.*—The beautiful *object* can be owned, but not its beauty. Every feeling that enters into aesthetic enjoyment must be *capable* of being shared by all who witness the object. Aesthetic feeling is unselfish.

III. Personal Feelings.—These may be defined to be *such as arise from the relations of self-conscious beings to one another.* They may be classified as Social, Moral and Religious, in the order of the increasing width of relations involved.

1. *Social Feelings.*—These come under the general heads : *regard for others and regard for self.* These are not necessarily exclusive, although, of course, they may become so. But regard for self is a *social* feeling, as much as regard for others, because the self has no meaning except in relation to others. An absolutely isolated self would be no self at all. The recognition of "me" and "mine" implies a related "thee" and "thine."

(a) *Feelings for Self.*—The root of all feelings that gather about one's own self is interest in one's own *existence*. Love of property, a desire for fame, regard for one's rights—or what one may demand from others—feelings of self-respect and humility—all personal emotions—have a common source in the desire to affirm or express the self. Interest may be taken in the self as physical, or as intellectual, as moral, as in relative union with or isolation from others, and from these various sides of self arise the various forms of personal feelings. The love of property, for example, arises from the desire to affirm one's being or will in control over material nature, and thus indirectly over others. The love of power and influence is the desire to extend personality beyond the limits of the body, and to realize it in the deeds and thoughts of others. In itself this desire to affirm or express one's own being is neither moral nor immoral. It may become the source of the highest and purest achievements of humanity, or of its most vicious and degraded acts, according to the direction which is given to it.

(*b*) *Feelings for Others.*—These, as they are friendly or hostile, are *sympathetic* or *antipathetic.* In both, there is an identification, conscious or unconscious, of the state of mind of others with our own ; in one case, we find this state repulsive, while in the other, if not agreeable, yet a *possible* state of our own.

Origin of Sympathy.—Sympathy has its origin in the contagious character of feeling. Laughing and crying are both "catching." A person is depressed, if he goes into an atmosphere of sorrow, even if the sorrow does not touch him personally, or even if he does not know the cause of the grief. Children are constantly manifesting such sympathy. Babies in their second year cry or "make believe" to cry when they see others grieved, while quite early in the first year there is a smile, that cannot be other than reflex, responsive to the mother's smile. This imitative sympathy is a factor which the teacher may largely rely upon, especially with younger pupils. It is also the psychological fact which lies back of *class*-work as opposed to individual treatment. The teacher knows that every school and even every class has its own peculiar atmosphere and coloring; and this results from the contagion of emotion. Many a child that has refused to study or learn when trained alone at home has "taken a start" as soon as he went to school through the influence of his fellow pupils upon him. This feeling possessed by *groups* of persons may be disciplined, and then it becomes *esprit de corps*—as important a help to the teacher as to the officer.

Development of Sympathy.—Higher than *reflex* sympathy, however, is active sympathy, which in addition to reproducing states of another, recognizes that *they belong to another*. We must first, indeed, make the feeling *our own*, but must then make it *another's*. To have true sympathy with a man suffering from poverty, for example, we must feel in ourselves somewhat as he feels, but we must also realize that *he* actually has those feelings, those sufferings, and the latter factor is *practically* much more important than the former. Many philanthropists appear very callous to the feelings of others, while persons who are most sensitive in reproducing feelings of others, are sometimes least ready in removing the causes of their sufferings. The fact that we have taken our illustrations from sympathy with *sorrows* should not mislead the student; sympathy is with *joy* as well as with grief, it is with every feeling of another.

2. *Moral Feelings.*—A complete account of these emotions belongs to ethics rather than to psychology, but a statement of their origin and contents is in place here. They are, psychologically, an *outgrowth* of social feelings, particularly of sympathy. They contain, *as factors*, feelings of rightness, of obligation, and of approval or disapproval. Reversing the natural order, we shall take up first the *contents* and then the *origin* of moral feelings.

Contents of Moral Feeling.—The feeling of *rightness* is the feeling that a certain act, say truth-telling, *is in harmony with the ideal of personality*, while its opposite contradicts, and in so far, destroys the true personality. It is a personal feeling, therefore, because it deals with the relations of states of mind and of acts to personality. An act felt to be right is also felt to be obligatory. Thus the feeling that one *ought* to be what ideally one may be. Something is *due* to the ideal personality; one is *bound* to do everything possible to make it real, and hence all acts contributing to its realization are felt as *duties*, something due or owed. A right act or character calls forth *approbation*; a wrong one, disapprobation, or, if the act is our own, remorse. Approbation is the pleasure which spontaneously arises upon feeling the harmony of real and ideal *character*, just as aesthetic pleasure spontaneously arises upon perceiving the harmony of real and ideal in an *object*.

Origin of Moral Feeling.—As already said, it grows out of social feeling. Sympathy in its highest form, is interest in everything which concerns the interests of personality; it is *unity of interest*, the realization that a group of persons has a common relation to a common good, and that this good is, therefore, to be shared by all. It thus becomes *love*, which not only feels the experience of others, but is actively interested in making those loved sharers in whatever is good. In this way, beginning with a sympathy which is purely natural, even having a physical basis, arises an *ethical* sympathy. Love becomes the source of moral groups or communities. The family, for example, while made up of distinct persons, parents and children, has a common good, and hence a common interest and purpose. A moral community is one in which there is felt to be some common end, or good, and where there is felt the need of realizing it in every member of the community.

Ethical Basis of the School.— *The school is*, both historically and philosophically, *the expansion, the continuation of the* *family*. It is the connecting link between the family and a higher ethical community, the general social order. Thus the school is, both historically and philosophically, *the preparation for the community and the state*.

These propositions give the ethical basis and function of the school, as a distinct organization having education in its charge. The school is a definite social and moral organization ; it aims, like the family, at the highest development or good of each of its members; like the family, it attempts to reach this end by definite training, authority and order imposed from without. It prepares each of its members for membership in a larger community, where each takes charge of his own development or training, and where he comes in contact with external authority only as a restraining, not as an educative or developing power. The school, therefore, while, *resting on the authority of the family, must train with reference to free citizenship in the state*. This is the principle which underlies, ethically, the disciplinary organization of the school.

Training of Moral Feeling.—A few specific principles may be mentioned. (1) It is generally useless to give abstract and didactic moral teaching. It should be connected either with something the pupil has actually done, or with social relations which he will have to meet in later life, and with which he is already somewhat familiar. It is not enough to exhort to do right; it should rather be shown, by examples coming within the range of the pupil's experience, *what* it is that is right. Failure of the pupil to do, what he should do, may be made the occasion of awakening his own sense of disapprobation and of obligation. His interest in business, in politics, may be appealed to, and thus he may be interested in the rights and duties that spring out of such relations. In other words. moral instruction should be *concrete* not abstract. (2) However it may be in the state, the object of punishment in the school is the development, the awakening and the strengthening of the pupil's own moral nature. Its ultimate aim is *the development of the sense of obligation, and capacity, through the formation of corresponding right habits, for self-control and self-government.* The thorough recognition and application of this principle would do more for our schools than any one can easily imagine. (3) The vital motives as interest, sympathy and love, are much more effective in securing right conduct than fear, regard for authority, or even reverence for abstract law. It has been well said that the worst of men probably *know* as much of what is right as the best of men can *do*. The practical problem is, therefore, the cultivation of feelings and dispositions which may be relied upon to impel the pupil to right action.

3. *Religious Feeling.*—As previously suggested, this is connected with the imagination. The feeling of a synthesis or connection of all natural objects with one another, and of the inmost nature of things with ourselves, is a factor contained, however, dimly and unconsciously, in religious sentiment. And this factor is supplied originally, at least, by the imagination. Fused with this, controlling and giving it meaning and content, should be factors supplied by moral motives. As the result of this fusion there come feelings of dependence, of peace, and of trust or faith. The feeling of *dependence* has as its intellectual element, the feeling that we are only a part of a whole, much wider, more powerful than ourselves. As its moral element, it contains the feeling that the source of all *good*, in ourselves and in the world, is a Being upon whom we are dependent for power to think and attain the good. The feeling of *peace*, as the factor supplied by imagination, has the idea of unity already referred to, the feeling that the heart of things is one with our nature. The moral factor adds the feeling that this peace can be attained only through unity with the Being who is perfect Goodness.

So of *faith*. Through the intellectual feeling of our oneness with the world, we feel that we can trust it, that we are borne along by it. The moral element is that the Being who is perfect Goodness is the only ultimate Reality and is the Ideal towards which we should strive. This Ideal cannot be seen or felt, or made known to the senses, but is to be apprehended by faith.

No specific methods of cultivating religious emotions can be laid down here. As a general principle the teacher should keep in mind that a vague form of the religious feeling of unity, is supplied by the imagination, although in very varying degrees of strength and intensity in different individuals. But to a certain degree this feeling of unity, and desire for it, exist in every child, and so far the teacher can assume it as a basis. His work is then to give this feeling a moral and personal turn and filling.

NOTE.—For the development of feeling in general see Dewey's Psychology, pp. 262-295; for intellectual feeling, pp. 296-308 for aesthetic, pp. 309-325; for personal, pp. 326-346.

CHAPTER VI.

FORMS OF VOLITIONAL DEVELOPMENT.

As already stated, in the second chapter, the beginning of will is impulse. Impulse becomes volition proper by the processes of attention and association working upon it. There are no new activities, no new functions, no new laws to be met with in the subject of will. Analysis and synthesis play as great part here as they do in the intellect; development is here, as there, from the immediate, the particular and the indefinite to the ideal, the general and the definite. From the fact, how·ever, that the development concerns a different material, the impulses, and not the sensations or the interests, certain new phases present themselves.

Contrast of Impulsive and Volitional Action.—The characteristics of an act of will may be seen by comparing it with an impulsive act. Action originating in impulse is *blind ;* that is it does not see its way clear to any end. It occurs *from* a tendency to act, but it does not know whither this tendency leads, *towards* what it is aiming. A bird builds its nest from impulse, without knowing the purpose to be reached ; a child when hurt strikes wildly about him without having any end in view. When we say that such and such a person acts from the impulse of the moment, we mean that that person is inclined to act out any impulse that occurs to him *without looking beyond the moment* in which the impulse takes him. Its end is not taken into consideration. Impulsive action is thus opposed to *intelligent* action, the latter being that which has an end in view.

Uncontrolled.—Another distinction is that impulsive action is *uncontrolled.* When we say that a person is a creature of impulse, we mean that his conduct is apparently unregulated; that it does not evince settled law or order. Action is uncontrolled when the impulse is not measured by some standard and its value fixed by the comparison. For example, there is an impulse towards speech, but unless this impulse is controlled by a standard, the speech will be mere meaningless babble. In strictly impulsive action, each impulse has its *own* value, and this intrinsic value is sufficient motive for action. Every impulse is followed, none is suppressed, none is checked, none is guided towards any end. Every impulse expresses itself, and only itself. But if the impulses are *directed towards an end* all this is changed. The impulse now is not valuable in itself, but only so far as it helps to reach the end. If it does not make towards the end it is suppressed ; if it does lead towards the end, it is connected with others with which it may co-operate ; it is thus nowhere allowed to express *itself*, but only the end, to whose law it is subjected. In other words, it is *controlled.*

The Conception of End.—It is evident, therefore, that what makes the difference between impulsive and volitional action is the *conception of an end.* Impulse is blind, because it has no purpose, no end in view; it is uncontrolled for the same reason. Volitional action has an end in view, and this end controls and subordinates all the steps of the activity Volition is *impulses controlled and harmonized by the conception of an end.* In studying will, we have to study *the development of the idea of an end, and the ways in which the idea becomes actual.*

Illustration.—Take as an example of volitional action, the building of a house. This is the end of action. In the first place, there must be an idea of this end, the builder or the architect must have a plan. The clearer and the more definite, the more detailed the plan, the more orderly and efficient will be the work. But at this stage, the end is *only* an idea. The idea must be changed into an actuality; it must be realized. The execution of a purpose, is as necessary, therefore, to complete volition as the formation of the purpose. We shall (1) take up the way in which the purpose, or the idea of an end is formed, and (2) the *process of its realization.*

1. *Beginning of Idea of End.*—While an impulsive action does not aim at an end, it none the less *reaches* an end. A child grasps after a bright-colored ball, not because he has any purpose, but because an impulse has been aroused by the excitation of the retina of his eye; but if he grasps the ball an idea of the ball, of its feeling, and especially of *what can be done with it,* is formed. The child sees that he can throw it, can bound it, etc. The next time he sees the ball, the idea of the action that he can perform is (by the law of association), part of his idea of the ball. The sight of the ball thus suggests or redintegrates the action, and this is accordingly performed.

Illustrations Continued.—No one can watch a baby of the age of from one to two years and not be convinced that, to the child's mind, the qualities of an object are mostly made up of what he can do with the object. A hat is something to be put upon the head; a whip something to strike with ; a drawer is something to be drawn out and pushed back, etc., etc. His own actions about or with the object constitute his ideas of the object ; his knowledge exists in terms of his actions with reference to the thing. The idea of an object accordingly always suggests—rather *is*—to him *that which he can do*, and so the idea of an object passes naturally, or even inevitably, into action.

Completion of Idea of End.—Here we have the transition to true volitional action. The action is no longer the mere expression of an impulse, but occurs as the *accompaniment* of an idea. The idea which an object awakens is the connecting link between the impulse and the action. It is not yet true volition, however, because the action does not occur for the *sake* of realizing the idea of an end. But when the child learns that there are a great many things which he can do with an object, and that some of these conflict with one another, when he learns (mainly through language) that the object has qualities *independent of his actions*, he comes to distinguish between the object and what he can do with it. Thus the idea of what he can do becomes a distinct idea to him, and so an end in itself. He learns that a whip is not something to strike with always and under all circumstances ; and he learns also that the act of striking is not necessarily connected with a whip. This act, therefore, becomes a distinct idea in his mind, and hence a distinct end ; while previous to this time it was only one quality always suggested by the object.

Summary.—At first, as Professor James very truly says, we do not know what we are going to do until after we have done it ; the true nature of the impulse is not revealed until it has executed itself. But the act once done the idea of the act is ever afterwards associated with the impulse, and hence there is an end supplied to that impulse for the future. Thus the impulses gradually and normally, if they are properly trained, pass into volitional action. It is to this point that we now come.

Training of Impulses.

1. *The development of the impulses depends upon the development of the intellect.*—There can be no volitional activity until there is an *idea of an end.* The child cannot *do* until he *knows.* To quote Professor James again, we might as well ask a man to give the Choctaw equivalent of some English word, as to ask him to perform some action corresponding to which he has no equivalent in the way of a mental notion. If, for example, a child is to pronounce the word 'cat,' or is to write the word, he must *first* have a mental image and *then* express it.

2. *Every development of the impulses results in a training of the intellect.*—While the foregoing principle is true, it is also true that the operation of an impulse, the reaching of an end is necessary to the idea of the end. The child will not have a *distinct* knowledge of the sound of ă, for example, until he has made it. At first he imitates the position of the vocal organs of his teacher, and by his own activities makes sounds resembling that of the teacher. Finally he hits the correct sound : he has the thrill of identification, and now for the first time he truly recognizes or knows the sound in the future, as well as know how to make it. And this but illustrates the general law. First, the manifestation of an impulse reaches an end and leaves behind the idea of the end ; then this idea is utilized as guiding and controlling the impulse. The impulse now manifests itself, under the control of an idea, in a more definite and complete way, and the idea is further enriched. This, in turn, supplies a still more definite end to impulse, and so on indefinitely. Thus the development of intellect and of impulse is reciprocal.

3. *Knowing and Doing must, therefore, be trained by the same processes, and correlatively to each other.*—We are now able to state the psychological principle which reconciles the two precepts already given (pp. 45 and 46), " Learn to do by doing,"

I

and "Learn to do by knowing."   The principles when rightly interpreted include rather than exclude each other.   Unless we *do*, we cannot *understand the ideas involved in action*, much less act.   And unless we *know*, we cannot act in a significant way, in a way which is really expressive of ideas.   Apply this to the teaching of arithmetic.   A child will never understand an abstract rule or principle until he has *acted* according to it : until he has embodied it in arithmetical operations ; he will never *fully* understand it until he has *repeatedly* acted upon it, so that he is thoroughly master of it.   But, on the other hand, his actions will be blind and meaningless, excepting he comes to see them *as* the manifestation of a principle.   He is, in other words, to "do sums," not for the sake of forming a blind habit of " doing sums," but in order to understand the rational ideas involved in the operations ; and he is to learn the rule and the principles, not for the sake of the abstract ideas themselves, but for the sake of power to act upon them, for the sake of mastery.   There is a similar relation between speech, and the laws of language found in grammar.   These laws cannot be understood apart from the action of which, indeed they are only the abstract statement. The child must "do," must speak and write in order to know the laws.   But on the other hand, unless the child is brought consciously to realize the laws involved in language, he not only has nothing by which to test speech, but has no idea of its rational basis.   Language to him will be a mere meaningless tool.

4. *Such a reciprocal training of the Impulses and the Intellect renders education Practical.*—There is no need of saying that practical does not merely mean commercial, or capable of being applied to money-making.   Nor does it mean that everything learned must be capable of *direct* application to action.   It is only in early childhood, while action is still largely impulsive, that all ideas are converted, upon the spot,

into action.   But no education is practical which does not, in training the intellect, train the will ; which does not, in giving knowledge, give *ability to act*.   No graver accusation can be brought against any course of education than that it is not practical, in the true sense of the term practical.   A course of school-training which does not fit one for his true life of action, is defective, regarded even as training of the intellect, for knowledge is not truly knowledge as long as it remains impersonal, remote from the activities of its possessor, and it is yet more defective on the moral side, for he who is not trained to rational activity has no preparation for a moral life.   We have now seen what is the goal of the training of the impulses—such a development of them as subordinates them to ideas, while ideas are, at the same time, employed to control impulses.   We may now briefly discuss the means at the command of the teacher for reaching the desired goal.

5. *Educational training should be based upon natural impulses and interests.*—The teacher does not have to create impulses, but to utilize those already existing.   School life is a *development* of the instinctive activities, not a creation of new and artificial ones.   This is a common-place, and yet it may be doubted whether any pedagogical precept is more frequently violated, or with more harmful results.   The artificial atmosphere of some schools, the dislike of pupils for their studies (and perhaps for their teachers), the stupidity of some children, and the feverish mental activity of others, are too often due to the fact that an unreal goal has been set up ; study has become something apart from the normal impulses of the pupils, and consequently factitious and unhealthy methods must be resorted to.

Pleasure in Training.—Since education is only a training of natural impulses, it follows, almost axiomatically, that, if the great mass of pupils do not delight in their training as they do in the expression of their natural impulses, there is something defective in the educational methods.   There are, of course, individual exceptions : some children through hereditary, home and other influences beyond the teacher's control, do not seem to have any tendencies worth mentioning towards knowledge and mental activity ; while others are morally so defective that any subjection of impulses to law and order is irksome and repulsive. But the statement regarding the " great mass " remains true.

6. *These natural impulses are to be subjected to discipline.*—This again is a normal process, as natural as the expression of the impulses. Every impulse tends to reach an end, and the end once reached it tends to subordinate itself in the future to the control of that end. The teacher simply utilizes this normal psychological principle. He employs it in a *systematic* way by overseeing the *end* towards which the impulses work, and by taking care that they work *regularly* toward these ends. The *spontaneous* self-discipline offered by the tendency of impulses to subject themselves to the law of their end, is defective, *first,* because there is nothing to ensure that the impulse reaches its *highest and fullest end*, and *secondly*, because there is nothing to ensure that it reaches the end so *regularly* that the tendency to work towards the end shall become a *law*. Surrounding influences preclude the impulse manifesting itself to its highest capacities, and they preclude anything more than a fitful and intermittent activity of it. **The teacher supplies ends which call out the fullest manifestation of the impulses, and he supplies regular and constant means for working towards these ends.** This may almost be said to exhaust the work of the teacher.

7. *A portion of this discipline consists in external arrangements.*—A child left to spontaneous self-discipline, is left to the natural *force* of the impulses and to *chance* for their expression. A child in school is surrounded with a multiplicity of special influences reinforcing the natural strength of the impulses and almost ensuring their regular expression. The child is to take and to keep a certain place in school : he is to be present at a certain hour : **to be doing fixed things at fixed times, etc., etc.**

Order is either of space or of time. *Punctuality* as to time-relations, and *regularity* as to place-relations are demanded of the pupil. All that comes under the head of the organization and administration of the school has for its purpose the ensuring of regularity and certainty in the manifestation of the impulses. This organization, with all it includes, is a good servant, but a bad master. Its true significance is to be tributary to the discipline of the pupil—it is a *mechanism* for a certain end, and the meaning of mechanical, real as well as etymological, is *instrumental.*

8. *A portion of the discipline is internal.*—The external means accompany and render efficient *instruction in certain subjects.* There is a regular recurrence of studies; a fixed order in the materials studied as well as in the arrangements that induce to study. The educator, through these studies, furnishes the ends best fitted to guide the impulses into complete activity, and he gives them orderly and regular exercise. To go into details upon the ways in which these studies afford discipline, would be to repeat all that has been said upon the training of association, attention and the various faculties, and to anticipate all that will be said in the next part upon educational praxis.

9. *Discipline accomplishes its purposes when it results in Self-control.*—The training, to which the impulses are subjected, is to become the law of the impulses; a law internal to them, which they manifest, not merely something external to which they must conform. The training is to result in a law inherent in the impulses, and when this is done there is self-control, that is, *freedom.* It must be repeated that the school-discipline is not *to repress* the impulses, nor to substitute something else for them, but to ensure to them their highest activity and development, and this not fitfully but regularly. When discipline has had this result, freedom takes the place of authority. The impulses have again, and in a true and lasting sense, become *a law unto themselves,* because they have embodied disci-

pline, *law within themselves.* The person acts both from *impulse* and from principle. This ideal may never be reached, but it is none the less the teacher's function and duty to aim at its realization. ˙

Idea and Desire.—Aristotle says that volition, or the power of originating action, constitutes a man, and that volition may be termed either reason that desires or desire that reasons. As impulse is blind action, so it is blind desire. It includes feeling of want or lack, but it does not know *what* is wanting ; the want thus aims blindly at its own satisfaction. Desire is intelligent impulse ; it is want that has become conscious of its own nature and of the end that satisfies. Thus volition is *desire that reasons ;* desire that takes account of itself. But, on the other hand, a mere idea does not constitute volition. The idea of an end will not move to action if the mind is satisfied with its present condition. This idea must stir the emotions, must influence the feelings – in a word, arouse desire—before there is any tendency for it to become more than a mere idea. Thus volition is also *reason that desires* : reason that has ceased to be abstract and impersonal, and become emotional and interested. So far we have studied only the rational side, the idea ; we must now take up the emotional side, the desire.

Origin of Desires.—In the impulse of a child to seek food, to grasp bright objects, to throw them and play with them, there is contained *a tendency to satisfy some want,* whether of food for the body or for the senses, or of physical activity. As soon as the impulse is manifested, some end is reached which satisfies the want to some extent. The child finds the food, he seizes the ball, etc. The child who has played with the ball finds that it satisfies his previous need of activity. From this time playing with it is an object of desire with him. If the child sees the ball and yet does not play with it, the *idea* conflicts with *reality*. The idea, moreover, as compared with the reality, is pleasurable ; in comparison with it, the present reality does not interest. The child would rather play with the ball than do what he is doing. As long as this state continues there is tension ; there is pleasure so far as the idea of the end is found satisfactory : there is pain, so far as the present reality is opposed to the idea. *This conflict of an idea felt to be satisfactory, with a reality which fails to satisfy, constitutes desire.*

The Object of Desire.—It is to be noticed that what is desired is not the thing or the activity, nor yet the pleasure afforded by them. *What is wanted is the satisfaction of the self.* The thing is desired only because through it the self is satisfied; pleasure is wanted only so far as it testifies to satisfaction. Pain is an object of desire when it is considered to satisfy self better than pleasure. The desires are developed, therefore, just in the degree in which the self is developed. When the self becomes complex, having many kinds of activities and many interests, desires are correspondingly complex. When the self becomes aware of its possession of any capacity—of a capacity for finding satisfaction in any direction—a desire is awakened.

Training of Desire.—The impulses must be trained in their relation to desire as well as in their relations to an idea. Indeed, the complaint sometimes made that school training leaves children bright and quick intellectually, but without corresponding moral training, is largely due, so far as it is well-based, to lack of training of the desires, or of the *emotional side of the will.* We notice then

(1) *Desires are trained through a development of the emotional nature; whatever interests is desired.*—The development of *interests* is, therefore, as important for the development of will as of intellect. The connection of *love* and desire is so close that, in popular language the terms are identified ; and there is this warrant for the identification, that whatever one likes one also desires to possess. *Sympathy* is a powerful coadjutor

in training desire. The manifestation of desire by one tends to awaken it in another. As soon as a child wants something, his playmates generally "want it too," even though it was previously indifferent. Rivalry may sometimes be appealed to in order to awaken desire, but in most cases sympathy is more effective. A teacher of strong desires will gradually find his pupils reflecting his own wishes and aversions, while the lack of permanent and controlling desires on his part, generally shows itself in the school.

2. *Desires are trained by satisfying or failing to satisfy impulse*.—Impulses that are always thwarted die out to some extent. Having no expression there is no experience of satisfaction to recur in the form of desire. On the contrary, the constant arousing and satisfying of some impulse, originally feeble, will by the cumulation of images of satisfaction gathering about that impulse, strengthen desire. The practical problem with a boy called stupid often is to search out and systematically gratify some impulse which has never been allowed to express itself. This done, definite desire is produced, and the boy is quickened into the exertion of his own powers to gain satisfaction in the future; having tasted the fruits of gratification, he never falls back into passivity. There is a moral as well as an intellectual application of this same principle. A selfish child should be made to feel the gratification of satisfying what generous impulses he does possess; an untruthful child, the satisfaction of stating things as they are, etc. While moral action is not constituted by action for the sake of gratification, it is often none the less true that it is by experiencing gratification from moral conduct that the child is led to desire moral conduct for its own sake.

3. *Desire is trained by awakening discontent with present attainments and interest in untried activities.*—There is desire for anything only when the idea of that thing seems more satisfactory than the actual state. To lessen satisfaction with the

actual state has, therefore, the same result in awakening desire as to increase the satisfaction of the ideal end. Though a child cannot be made to feel the satisfaction of generous conduct, he may perhaps be led to realize the unsatisfactory nature of selfishness. Pupils should be trained to the thought of their *possibilities* not yet made actual. Once make a pupil feel that he *can* do something, even if, as yet, he has not done it, and desire to do it will be awakened. Hardly anything is more important in the personal relation of teacher and pupil than inducing the pupil to believe in his own capacities and possibilities. A person to whom a new possibility is open, has a new world before him. It may be questioned if the transforming influence which religion often exercises, is not largely due to the effective belief it gives in new and hitherto untried personal possibilities. Real belief in the possibility of an achievement is the most efficient kind of desire for it.

4. *Desire is trained through the cultivation of the imagination.* —Imagination both *widens* and *strengthens* desire. It widens it, because it does not leave desire dependent upon the precise forms of old satisfaction, but, under the influence of love, hate, etc., creates new conceptions—desires for honor, fame or wealth, etc. Imagination strengthens desire, for, to allow the mind to dwell upon any image is to endear it to the mind. When we imagine anything we think of it as real, and wish, in some degree to make it real. If imagination habitually dwells upon some idea, this idea is apt to become the controlling desire of the mind. An artist imagines beautiful forms and scenes so vividly that he is impelled to produce the realities that correspond. By the same principle a child whose mind is filled with impure images, is impelled to impure desires and actions ; and, fortunately, a child whose imagination is filled with graceful, harmonious and pure ideas is stirred to corresponding desire and activity. The teacher can offer no more practical prayer for his pupil than that of Socrates, that he

may have "*beauty* in the inward soul," for this insures almost of itself that the "outward and the inward man be at one."

II. The Realization of the Desired Idea.—We have studied the first step in volition : the formation of the idea of an end, and of its accompanying feeling of want. We have now to study the realization of the idea—the way in which it is changed from an idea into a presentation, into an actual fact. If there is but one desired end, the manner of realization may be illustrated as follows : The child forms the idea of handling a colored ball. This idea suggests, by contiguous association, that of reaching out the arm and grasping the ball ; and thus the end is reached. In other words, the idea of the end suggests, by association, the means necessary for reaching the end. In more complex ends, *attention* is active, rather than association, and first analyzes the end into the means or steps which lead up to it, and then combines them so as to reach the end. In either case, there is no factor involved which has not been previously studied.

Conflict of Ends and of Desires.—But generally the case is not so simple. There is not merely one idea in the mind which immediately proceeds to suggest the means of its own realization, but there are various ends desired, and these conflict with one another. The child who wishes to play with the ball may also wish to look at his picture book, or he may have been told not to play with it, and he desires to obey this command. One cannot have his cake and eat it too. In case of conflict it is out of the question that the desired end work itself directly out. Before this can occur the conflict must be decided, and some one end emerge as the real end of action. The various steps in the settlement of conflict may be stated as : *deliberation, effort* and *choice*, all together constituting *control.*

Deliberation.—The beginning of deliberation is checking, or, in technical language, *inhibiting* the carrying out of action. The child stops or pauses before doing what he wishes to do. During the pause, he considers and reflects in the degree in which his mental powers are developed, He weighs the value of the end proposed, compares it with other ends, and in general calls upon all the reasons that would lead to action in one direction rather than in another. The process in a child is, of course, largely unconscious; it is not meant that the child consciously sets himself to weigh reasons, pro and con, regarding an action. But the conflict between desires arrests attention, and, the mind dwelling upon the conflict, various considerations are suggested by association.

Effort.—In some cases the child *wants* to act in one way, but feels that he *ought* to act in another. He wishes to play but ought to study, for example. In this case what is *desired* and what is *desirable* do not coincide. If the child does not recognize anything that is desirable, different from what is desired, there is no conflict. He continues to do as he wishes to do. Or, if the act is not only desirable but desired (that is, if duty and evident satisfaction go together) there is no conflict; the child does what he ought to do. But in many cases the child recognizes that he ought to desire one action, while he actually desires another. Here *effort* is required. It requires effort to *arrest* action in the direction desired; it requires effort to *prefer* what should be preferred.

True effort consists *in reinforcing by additional ideas, desires and motives, the side felt to be the weaker.* It may be true that action follows the strongest desire, but it is also true that we have the power to call up considerations and feelings that strengthen and that weaken the force of a desire. The idea of obligation itself, if it has been frequently acted upon, becomes a very considerable force, and if ideas, images and emotions are clustered about the idea of that which ought to be done, it gradually becomes not only desirable, but desired, and action follows in that direction.

Choice.—The end of conflict, following deliberation and effort, is choice. Choice may be defined as *the selection of a certain end of action and the identification of self with it.* In choice, the self throws itself into one desire, and gives that all the strength of the self. While desire manifests a *possible* àct or state of self, choice affirms that this possibility shall be made *real*, and that other possibilities shall not be realized.

Character and Retention.—By character is meant the *self as possessed of definite powers or abilities, and of permanent predisposit.ons or desires corresponding to these abilities.* The make-up or character of a man is shown by what he *can* do, plus what he continually *tends* to do. Character is formed by retention. It is the organized residuum or result of all past actions. In the beginning there are inherited instincts and impulses. These are acted upon; some are encouraged; the end of some is consciously adopted as motive to action. Each activity leaves behind an effect which renders it easier to act in that way again. The accumulation of such effects creates a *tendency* to act in that way. In the same way something is retained from each desire, and this leads desire in the same paths in the future. Character is thus organized tendency and desire.

Choice and Apperception.—Choice corresponds to apperception. Indeed, it *is* apperception *practically* directed It is the selection and assimilation of some course of action. In knowledge, apperceiving is bringing the mind to bear through its organized centres of experience, upon presented sensations. In will, it is bringing to bear the organized centres of ability and desire upon the presented impulses. The result in both cases is that the presentation is connected with the acquired results of past experience. Since apperception and retention mutually depend upon each other, it follows that the relation of character and choice is a reciprocal one. Character is organized decisions or choices. Choice is the expression of character.

Choice builds up character and character is manifested in choice. Every choice enters into the building up of an organ of choice and thus decides future decisions.

Control.—Finally, we may say that *a desire or impulse is controlled when it is brought into connection with character.* Every one has certain organized groups or systems of desires and of tendencies to action. When an impulse or desire does not express *itself* merely, but expresses a relation to one of these groups, it is in so far controlled, and it is controlled in the highest degree when it is brought into relation with the totality of such groups—with character. A desire may come in contact only with a superficial and simple group of desires and tendencies; comparatively the conflict is brief, effort slight, and the resulting choice unimportant. Another desire may send roots into all the groups. Here the conflict is prolonged, for each of these groups must be allowed due consideration; effort is severe, for the conflicting claims of these groups must be reconciled, and choice is important, influencing the entire future of the self, for it affects each of the centres that together make the self what it is. But since there is *no such thing as character in general,* since *character is only the totality of all the groups of fixed tendencies, ideas and desires,* it must be remembered that however unimportant any *one* choice may be (since affecting only one centre), yet it is by the cumulation of such single acts that each centre is built up and character formed.

The Training of Character.—It may be said that self-control is obtained by the proper training of desire, and by the subordination of impulses to the law of their ends. But after our study of the realization of an end we can add some further points.

1. *Self-control is reached through habitual action.*—Character is built up through successive acts. From each act something is "retained," which thus becomes influential in controlling future activity. Character is the sum and result of all these

activities.   It is significant that our words " ethical " and " moral " both find their origin in words signifying customs or habits.   Character, good or bad, is in very considerable degree the outcome of acts which in themselves are neither good nor bad, but only *customary* or habitual.   A child in his earliest years has instincts and tendencies, but no character.   Day by day, as he is directed in actions which are right, and yet which he does not do simply because they are right, he forms the *habit* of right action, he grows in love of such actions as he constantly finds satisfaction in them, he forms a tendency, which is almost instinctive or natural, to repeat them.   Then as his reason develops and he sees the true nature of such acts, he is prepared consciously to choose them because they are right. The acts are now right, not only externally, but also internally ; that is, they have a right motive and purpose, as well as conform outwardly to the demands of morality.

2. *The formation of habits is largely under the control of others: thus self-control is trained through external control.—* It is in the facts just mentioned that the educator finds at once his opportunity and suggestions as to methods.   Character is largely the result of unconscious habit : and the teacher has it in his hands to aid in the formation of habits.   While the influence of education in training character has often been exaggerated, as when it is supposed that certain systems of education will turn out a certain kind of product with the fixity and certainty of machinery, the influence is so great that it stands in no need of exaggeration.   Nature contributes its share, but nurture has its part also.   " The virtues," says Aristotle, " come neither by nature nor against nature, but nature gives the capacity for acquiring them and training develops it."

3. *Self-control is trained by habits of self-reliance.—*While the young and immature, almost characterless child, is highly susceptible to external discipline in forming his habits, it should not be forgotten that the sole end of this external control is

self-control. The habit of decision can be formed only by repeated personal decisions. Choice, as we have seen, is identification of self with a desire. No one but the self, therefore, can choose. One can do much for another, but he cannot choose for him. The teacher may and should supply all the possible *conditions* of right choice; he must check hasty action, he must encourage deliberation, he must suggest all reinforcing motives, but *the act of choice* belongs to the child. If, therefore, no opportunity for decision is given, if the educator does everything for the child, as soon as this external prop is removed the fact that no habit of choice has been formed reveals itself in weak and in wrong action. The child of the streets has often a better training of will than the favoured child of culture, because the former has always to choose for himself, while the latter is surrounded with influences that do not allow decision.

4. *Self control is trained through recognition of idea of Law and strengthening regard for it.*—We have already seen that impulses work towards an end, and that this end once reached becomes the law to which they thereafter subject themselves. This gives a multiplicity of laws; as many laws as there are ends. But as the child grows in intelligence he frames the ideas of larger and more comprehensive ends, and thus of more inclusive laws. Finally he rises to the generalization of *law ;* of law in general, not merely a particular law for each particular impulse. There is set up a general permanent standard— conformity to law—by which all impulses and desires may be measured ; and if the sense of obligation is correspondingly developed, it is felt that they *must* be referred to this law as their standard. The conception of such a law gives self-control even in new circumstances, for it is felt that there is *some* law to be followed, and there is cultivated the habit of searching for this law. The habit of referring desires to law which is felt to be obligatory, constitutes *conscientiousness.*

5. *Self-control is trained through the conception of an ideal or perfect self.*—With the growth of the child in intelligence and in conscientiousness, the conception of character is enlarged. It includes not only the actual self, the result of past decisions and actions, but an ideal self. There is nothing mystical about the conception of the ideal self; it simply includes over and above actual attainments, the idea of capacities or possibilities not yet realized. Desires are measured not merely by their reference to the actual state of character as the organized result of past experiences, but by their reference to the development of *possibilities* of character in the future. Desires in line with the development of these possibilities, however much in contrast with past attainments, are stimulated and reinforced, others are arrested. A *perfect* character means also a *completed* character—a character with all capacities realized. When such an ideal is made the end of activity, desires are controlled in the highest degree ; they are controlled by relation to past attainments and by reference to future possible attainments. Such self-control is *freedom*.

Kinds of Control.—The foregoing considerations may be rendered more specific by a brief consideration of the various kinds of self-control. These may conveniently, though soemwhat arbitrarily, be classified as *physical, prudential* and *moral.* In the first place a child has to gain *control of his body.* This includes everything by which the child is enabled to use his body as an instrument in executing any volition, walking, articulate speech, writing, etc., etc. Then, a child has to be able to control his speech, his actions, and even his thoughts and feelings *with reference to his own welfare.* And finally, he must be able to control himself, *with regard to what is demanded of him by the obligations of morality*—first as they are embodied in the requirements of others, and afterwards as he recognizes his own obligations to his own and to others' personality

I. Physical Control.—This is of importance in the education of will, both for its own sake, and for the discipline of volition afforded by it. The necessity of a child's being able to control his senses and his muscles is so evident as not to need illustration. But it must also be remembered that in learning to control them he is exercising all the factors that enter into self-control of the highest kind. He is subordinating his impulses to law; he is forming and guiding desires; he is employing self-restraint, effort and choice.

Relation of physical to moral control.—It is thus obvious that the training of the impulses of physical activity is a very important factor in moral training, aside from all moral *uses* the training is put to. A child cannot learn to write, to sit still when necessary, to prepare and recite lessons at certain times (considered merely as physical processes) without exercising self-control; and so, in these actions he forms *habits* of self-control, which, when subordinated to right motives, constitute morality. There is therefore, a decided *moral* as well as intellectual side to the training of the eye, the ear, the tongue and the hand. " Kindergarten" and "manual" training are tributary to specifically ethical culture. It is said that in a certain reformatory, part of the prisoners were subject to definite physical training, gymnastic exercises, etc., and that they not only gained intellectually and in personal appearance, but in general moral character. And this is what one might expect.

Process of physical control.—No new principles are involved in physical control. Association and attention acting upon the impulses and instincts explain the results. In particular, the two functions of analysis and synthesis are employed in gaining control of the physical self. In the first place, all impulses are vague. Aside from one or two primary instincts, they are diffused through the entire muscular system. An infant has very early the impulse to walk, but the impulse instead

K

of being distinct and confined to the proper muscles, expends itself through all the muscles. So, a child when learning to write moves his whole arm, and even his body, face and tongue. Learning to perform some physical act consists, therefore, in the first place, in the *differentiation* and *localization* of the impulse. And in the second place, it consists in the *uniting*, the *interconnecting* of these differentiated impulses. To walk is to combine and co-ordinate a series or succession of distinct muscular impulses. In articulate speech, a series of motor impulses of vocal organs, tongue, lips, etc., must be connected, and then this series must be properly associated with a series of auditory sensations, and this with a series of ideas. That is, in order to speak, the child must control his vocal organs; to control them he must have as a standard the images of the sounds which he is to make; and if these sounds are to mean anything, they must be connected with ideas. Similar complex combinations are involved in writing, playing musical instruments, reading aloud, etc.

Results of Control.—1. *The idea of what can be done becomes more extended and more definite.*—Not only is the act more definite, but the *idea* is more definite, for, as we have previously noticed, it is only when an end has been reached that we know what the end is. A baby has no *definite* idea either of what a word sounds like or how to speak it, until he has succeeded in pronouncing it. And the *idea* becomes more *extensive* just in proportion as the act combines more impulses. An infant lives in the present because his *actions* do not extend their significance beyond the present. Compare with an infant a youth who is learning a trade. Here all actions have a unity in their reference to the end aimed at, and the youth's *ideas* gain a similar unity and comprehensiveness. His consciousness takes in a wide future range.

2. *Abilities and tendencies are created.*—We come again upon the fact of retention. Movements become organized into the

structure of the body, and through the effect that each act produces, the act is easier in the future; since easier, it tends to be repeated in preference to acts requiring more energy; being repeated, habit is formed. Isolated acts have become *power* to act. That which has been acquired by hard labor becomes spontaneous function, becomes play. These abilities become *tendencies*; that is, the person follows or acts according to them unconsciously or automatically, and unless he exercises effort, he falls into these habits so easily that they seem to to control him. He apparently becomes the creature of what he has created.

3. *The amount of stimulus and effort required is lessened.*—This follows from the two principles already stated. When, in writing, the impulse is diffused through the entire body, it is clear that the most of it is wasted. When it is confined to the fingers, there is less draft upon the energies required. In an infant, the original stimulus to activity is an excitement of the whole organism. There are chance and random movements, but actions directed to an end occur only when the whole organism is stirred by a demand for food. Then strong affections of a single sense—as a bright light, or a loud sound, rouse activity; then a perception of moderate force suffices the sight of a play-thing induces activity; the sound of a word, is stimulus to repeat the sound. Then a suggestion or injunction from another suffices; the child does what he is told to do. Then, at last, an *idea* originating in his own consciousness is sufficient stimulus to action. Thus there are gradations between affection of the whole physical organism at one extreme, and the mere idea at the other. And, of course, as habits are built up, the amount of necessary effort is lessened until, as just mentioned, it may require effort *not* to act rather than to act.

II. **Prudential Control.**—As soon as physical control is made a means to something beyond itself, the stage of pruden-

tial control is reached.   When a child speaks, not for the sake
of learning to speak, but for the sake of some end beyond, the
control is not only physical but prudential.   It thus begins at
a very early period in life.   Prudential action *involves all
action for the sake of any end felt to be satisfactory, excepting a
moral end.*

Results of Prudential Control.—We have already
studied desire, deliberation, choice, and the intellectual processes which enter into control.   There is nothing new involved in prudential control, excepting the *kind of end* for the
sake of which the control occurs—some recognized satisfaction.
Accordingly we turn at once to the results of prudential control
in the formation and development of character.

1. *Action is more deliberate.*—Since the action aims at some
recognized satisfaction, it is necessary to weigh and compare
means and ends.   The child cannot follow his impulses immediately, but must reflect upon them to see which will
reach the most useful end, and what steps he must take to
reach the end he decides upon.   In this way character becomes
thoughtful or *reflective.*

2. *Action takes in more remote and more comprehensive ends.*—
The satisfaction may be one which cannot be reached in a day
or even in a year.   If such a remote satisfaction is desired, it is
evident that all acts between the time of choice and the realization of the end, must be controlled with reference to the one
end.   For example, consider a person studying a profession
or learning a trade.   The end may become very inclusive it may
be health, or wealth, or political honor, or success as a teacher
or author.   Such ends are exceedingly complex, involving an
indefinite number of minor acts of restraint, effort and choice.
Thus character gains *unity* and *continuity.*

3. *Action is more determined and persevering.*—While only a
resolute or determined person is likely to be persevering, the

terms are not synonymous.   Resolution or determination has reference to the choice of ends.   A determined or firm person is one who chooses definitely and fixedly; he knows what he wants and is not to be induced to change his purpose.   Having settled upon his end, he is now persevering in attempting to reach it.   Persevering thus relates to use of means, as resolute does to choice of end.   A persevering person is one not turned aside from an end because it is not immediately reached, because obstacles present themselves, because other agreeable ends suggest themselves.   *Resolution and perseverance give character permanent stability.*

4. *Action becomes more intense or energetic.*—As prudential control is obtained, action becomes forceful, manifesting increased power.   This does not mean excitement.   It is not measured by the amount of effort *apparent*.   A person who appears very intense is often, like a puffing engine, not doing much. Physical energy is defined as power to do work, and so volitional energy or intensity, is measured by its result, by its capacity for doing, not by apparent activity.   A teacher should avoid the idea that there is any value in mere activity, in going through a set of motions or performances; the value is in what the activity accomplishes.   Energy renders character *effective*.   If we sum up what has been said, it follows that a thoroughly controlled will involves *deliberation* before choosing, *certainty and singleness* in making the choice, *tenacity* in clinging to the choice once made, and *energy* using all appropriate means for realising it.

III. Moral Control.—

There are no new processes involved in moral control   It differs from physical and prudential control only in the *end* to which the volitional processes are subject.   It aims at controlling the impulses and the desires by the *law of good character*, and not by the law of physical action or of personal welfare.

Relation to physical and prudential control.—It is of great importance to the teacher to realize that moral control considered simply upon the side of volitional factors that enter into it, namely, desire, effort, choice, etc., is the same as physical and prudential control, and that only the *end* or *motive* differs. This fact gives two principles for the teacher's guidance.

1. *Every act of will, whether directly moral or not, may be rendered tributary to formation of Moral Character.*—It was shown, when speaking of the intellectual faculties, that their training is largely *indirect*; that memory, for example, is trained in training perception; that thinking is trained by right perception and memory. The same law of indirect culture holds in moral training; and it is fortunate for both teacher and pupil that such is the case. Every act of attention on the part of the pupil, every concentration in study that excludes distracting stimuli, every physical restraint, as sitting quietly when necessary; every form of physical control, as guiding the pen in writing; every subordination of present pleasure to future satisfaction, requires the same activity of will that moral conduct requires, and results in a training of character through the formation of habits. If the teacher's methods and his own purpose are not mechanical but moral, if an ethical spirit animates him, this *ethical spirit will lay hold of all the details of school work*, and make them subservient to the development of character in the pupil.

2. *These processes, not directly moral in themselves, when subordinated to right motives, become moral.*—In other words, in order to develop morality, the teacher does not have to resort to some new processes, to some kind of activity and training distinct from all employed before, but has to awaken love of what is right and to stimulate the pupil to make this love the motive of his actions. Moral action, in a word, does not regard a distinct kind of action, but a distinct kind of *motive*. The teacher who

is making use of all possible methods to give the pupil proper control of his physical and of his mental activities, and who, at the same time, by example, by sympathy, by correction, by awakening admiration of good characters and good acts, and, if necessary, by direct precept, is inspiring in the pupil love of the right, is doing all that can be done to build up moral character.

Relation of motive to moral action.—A few examples will make clear the relations of motive to moral action. Both lying and truth-telling, considered as external acts, and considered internally with reference to psychological processes entering into them, are the same. They differ in the kind of motive which inspires each. The act of a surgeon in performing an operation that leads to the death of a patient, and the act of a murderer are, as acts, alike. The difference, again is in the motive that led to each act; the reason for which it was performed. It is then not the outcome, the result of an act that makes it moral, but the motive, the reason in which it originates.

Motive and Responsibility.—This is the reason why persons hold themselves, and are held by others, responsible or accountable for moral action, and not for prudential action. The *result* is often, perhaps generally, beyond one's control; the *motive* never. For example, a man wishes to become rich. His attaining wealth, while partly depending upon his own industry, foresight, etc., yet depends also upon forces of nature and society which he cannot govern. These forces may defeat his best plans, and thus, considered from the standpoint of result, his act is a failure. Yet he does not blame himself for the failure, so far as it depends solely upon outside agencies. But when one is untruthful, one recognizes that the failure lies not with outside forces, but in himself. His choice or motive was wrong, and for this choice, as his own act, he holds himself responsible

Motive and Character.—It is also evident that moral action forms character in a sense in which other action does not. In prudential and physical control, only the processes, not the result, make character. In moral character the result makes or is character. One touches what a man *has;* the other what he *is.* A man's wealth, health, knowledge, social standing deeply influence his being yet they do not make it. But a man's will is himself, not something which he has. When, therefore, a man *chooses* to be good, not merely wishes in a vague way that he were or might mysteriously become good, he *is* in so far good. The choice, the selection of the motive makes him what he is. The set or bent of a man's will constitutes his character, and this set or bent is constituted by the ruling motives of his life.

Character and the Sense of Obligation.—We have seen before that the relation of character and choice is reciprocal. This holds in moral action. A constant choice of the right *makes,* *is,* upright character ; and this, in turn leads to a strengthening of the sense of obligation, increasing the power of right motives to control choice. We cannot overestimate the evil of evil choice in leading to evil results ; but more disheartening yet is the fact that wrong choice and action weaken the sense of obligation, and thus lessen the force of good motives. Almost the worst thing that can be said of a pupil is, not that he does this or that bad thing, but that he seems to have no idea of obligation—of duty. The well-spring of moral action is dried-up, and good deeds come, if they come at all, only by impulse or by accident.

The Growth of Idea of Obligation.—To a child the sense of obligation can come only in connection with particular acts. This or that deed is right or wrong. And it comes at first negatively rather than positively. That is, it comes through restraint ; the child is forbidden to do this or that thing. The impulse is met by a restraining power, and in the conflict of natural impulse to *do* with the injunction to *forbear* doing, the child gets his first moral experiences. Then come positive injunctions to do certain things which his impulses, if left to themselves, would not do. Gradually the experience is generalized. There comes the idea of *law*, of something always obligatory standing over against impulse to control it both by arresting and by guiding it.

The Performance of Duties—While a large share of the moral education of a child consists in developing his sense of obligation, it is, of course, also important that he be trained to *act* upon recognized obligation. In general a child who really *feels* obligation is impelled to act accordingly; the obligation becomes a concrete motive or moving power. But there are other forces which act *along with* the force of obligation, and which re-act upon it to strengthen it. There is, first, the force of habit, as already mentioned. A right action often done tends to be repeated, independent of its rightness. Secondly, there are certain lower impulses and motives which may be called in by the educator: the desire for reward, to escape punishment, for future gratification, for the approval of others, etc., while not *moral* motives, may be judiciously employed by the teacher as forces co-operating in right doing. A manipulation of non-moral motives leading to moral acts constitutes, especially with younger children, a large part of the work of the educator.

And, thirdly, there are motives which, if not originally moral, become such with a very slight development. These are especially pity, sympathy and love. Such feelings tend to identify the child with those about him—first in the family, then in the school, then in the wider relations of society. This identification makes real the claims that others have upon him; these claims, the rights of others, are not mere abstract obligations, but are his own interests. He is interested in them as he is in his own wants and desires. This identification also extends the range of obligations that the child recognizes; whatever obligations the one whom he loves and admires recognizes, he also feels that he ought to recognize. And finally such an identification weakens the motive that tends most strongly to wrong conduct, *selfishness*, namely. It takes the child beyond his own personal gratification and widens his being, his character. Only that can satisfy him which satisfies others. This feeling, if properly trained, must finally cause the person to recognize, practically if not theoretically, his identity of interests and purpose with those of *all* other persons, and must change the bare feeling of obligation into a powerful social motive.

Results of Moral Control.—1. *Generic or Immanent Choice.*—This term implies two things; first, that the result of forming a moral habit, or mode of moral control, forms a *general* motive in that direction. It creates a *state* of choice. A child who has the organized habit of truth telling does not have to exercise specific choice in each case; but has a general governing intention or purpose which controls all cases. It implies, secondly, that this general decision *continues* in action even when there is no immediate cause for action. A temperate man's temperance does not cease to exist when he is not satisfying some appetite. The choice is immanent in him; that is, it remains *permanently* to direct the course of his actions.

2. *Automatic and Intuitive Decision.*—A person who has fixed habits of action does not have to hesitate a long time before acting. An immature character may have a long struggle before choosing, but a thoroughly good or a thoroughly bad character has no such struggle; such a person chooses automatically. Fixity of character shows itself also in intuitive *recognition* of what is right and wrong. An immature character has often to reflect long in order to decide what is good or bad, but a formed character makes its decision at once.

3. *Regulation of Desires.*—The formation of desires is, if we omit moral considerations, as natural as the origin of impulses; the desires are the direct result of the psychical constitution.

But when moral motives are recognized, it is seen that obligation extends to the desires. Desires, as well as acts, may be wrong, and need checking. A settled character decides what desires can be entertained as well as what acts shall be performed. Character thus finally decides the emotional bent of the person.

4. *Effective Execution.*—Character forms a *reservoir of power* back of the choice. An immature character may desire to do a certain act, may choose it, and yet be overcome by opposing temptations. There is not enough force back of the choice to guarantee its realization. But character is a multiplied volition which guarantees the execution of the chosen end. A person with fixed character, moreover, takes pleasure in certain desires and acts, and this pleasure, the abiding interest which he has, leads him to act.

CHAPTER VII.

MIND AND BODY.

The mind must be developed as completely as possible. The mind must also be able to use its developed powers in an effective way, so as to accomplish as much as possible with them. To reach these two ends, the body must be *healthy* and must be *well-trained.* The teacher should, therefore, know something of the mutual relations of mind and body that he may fully realize the importance of the *corpus sanum* for the *mens sana,* and that he may be able to infer something as to methods to be employed in bringing about the ideal relation between them.

Importance of Body for Soul.—The soul of a human being is not pure spirit, but embodied mind. This one fact makes it necessary that in his methods the educator should always have reference to physical and physiological conditions.

It is through the body that the soul is connected with nature ; with those vast and also minute forces which make up this whole universe. And the body connects the soul with material universe in two ways : on the one hand, it makes the soul a *recipient* of the influences coming from it ; on the other hand, it makes the soul an *agent*, a power capable of affecting or influencing nature. All that comes to the soul from without, comes through the body ; all that the soul can give to the world without, it gives through the body.

Relation of Sense-Organs, Muscular System and Brain, to the Soul.—In more detail, all sensations come through the *sense-organs ;* all activity of will is manifested through the *muscular-system ;* all processes of apperception, and retention, of memory and thinking are accompanied by activities in the *brain and nervous system.* The body is, therefore, not only an *instrument* of mind, but its processes enter, as an *integral factor*, into mental processes and results. If a sense-organ is defective or is diseased, the corresponding sensation is absent or abnormal ; if entirely wanting, one department of knowledge is evidently cut off ; if it is distorted, resulting knowledge is abnormal. Indeed, the distortion of the sensation often leads to a distortion of the mental process that interprets it. A person with abnormal auditory sensations often comes to interpret them as voices of demons, or as the voice of one commanding him to do some deed. This hallucination, in turn, becomes an "apperceiving organ," that is, other perceptions and ideas are assimilated to it ; it becomes a centre about which many ideas gather and are correspondingly distorted. On the other hand, if the sense-organ is well controlled, considered simply as a physical instru-ment, perception becomes definite and accurate, and this *tends*, at least, to produce correct and clear habits of thinking.

The same may be said of the relation of the *muscular system* to the will. The muscular system is not only a necessary means of carrying out the decisions of the soul, but its culture or non-

culture is directly reflected in the development of the will. Un-
steady, vacillating, or irritable physical habits, are apt to mean
similar habits of attention and choice. The dependence of soul
is not confined, of course, to its relations to the sense-organs
and muscular system ; the eye, the hand, are parts of the body,
consequently their condition depends upon the state of the and
entire organism. The circulation of the blood and nutrition of
the body will reflect themselves in sense-organ, in muscle, and
in the state of the brain. Hence, the culture of the whole
body is as necessary as that of any special organ. The health of
the body as a whole seems to be intimately connected with the
emotional condition. The organic or common sensations coming from every part of the body, form, it is probable, the
underlying emotional back-ground or disposition, and every
disturbance of the health of the organism is reflected in a
disturbance of the emotional attitude. Fresh air, exercise.
repose are, through their relation to the emotions, as much
demands of moral hygiene as of physical.

Mind and Brain.—Less is known, of course, of the direct
relations of mind and brain than of the direct relations of mind
and sense-organs, and muscular system. But there is good reason
to believe that every psychical process is accompanied with
change in the brain-centres, and leaves behind it an alteration
of their condition. Lesions of the brain are accompanied
with greater or less loss of mental function, and insanity is
always found to be accompanied with some cerebral change.
The character of the blood that goes to the brain, the nutrition
of the body and of the nerve-centres, manifest themselves
in the mental states. Mental over-work, lack of change, or
excessive stimulation, are as disastrous as their analogous physical disturbances. On the other hand, statistics show that
well-balanced and thorough mental activity is conducive to
good health and long life, through the correct habit that it
induces in the physical organism.

Structure of Nervous System in Man.--The details of this belong rather to anatomy and physiology, but it may be well to recall some leading facts. There are two kinds of nerve-tissue, the cellular, which is generally gathered into ganglionic masses or *nerve-centres*, and the fibrous aggregated into bundles, known as the *nerves*. In man these are arranged so as to form the cerebro-spinal system, including the brain, the spinal-cord and the nerves going from the brain and the spinal-cord to the various organs of the body. These nerves are generally classified as *motor* or *sensory*. The motor are *efferent*, that is, they carry impulses from the central organs to the muscles and thus induce movement ; the sensory are *afferent*, that is, they conduct stimuli from the sense-organs to the brain-centres and thus occasion sensation. For example, light is reflected upon the retina of the eye ; the resulting stimulus is transmitted by the optic nerve to the brain ; nervous changes take place there corresponding to the assimilation of the sensation, to its association with other sensations, and thus result in the formation of a percept, say the recognition of an orange; other cerebral changes occur corresponding to a determination to get the orange ; an impulse goes out along a motor nerve, the muscles of the hand are stimulated, and the orange is grasped. The cerebral changes corresponding to the higher psychical processes are generally thought to occur in the cortex of the brain, a comparatively thin rind of ganglionic matter surrounding the fibrous mass of the hemispheres of the brain.

Elementary Properties of Nerve Structures.-- Every nerve structure is *irritable* or *excitable ;* that is, capable of receiving stimuli and of responding to them by the exercise of energy. Every portion of the nerve tissue is also capable of *conducting* these stimuli, or is capable of transmitting its own excitation to some other point. The fibres are much better conductors than the ganglia or nerve centres, and hence are sometimes, but incorrectly, treated as the sole conductors.

Nerve tissue also has the power of *summation*, that is, it is capable of transforming, or summing-up, a number of separate, minute shocks into one continuous and more prolonged stimulus. It also has the powers of *inhibition*, and of *plasticity*. By *inhibition* is meant that the nervous system is capable of arresting or controlling stimuli. If a neural organ had only the property of excitability, it would use up all its energy in responding to every stimulus that affected it, but being capable of checking the amount of energy expended in answer to a stimulus, it is able to keep a reserve force constantly on hand. Indeed, it is probably this reserve force that acts in opposition to the stimulus affecting it, and by antagonizing it, arrests the outflow of energy.

By *plasticity* is meant that the nerve tissues are altered in structure by every process that they undergo. A nerve organ that has responded to a stimulus is not the same that it was before. This property of plasticity is also termed *facilitation*. A neural structure that has acted in one way once, acts that way more *easily* in future; indeed, it *tends* to act that way in future. This property is also termed *accommodation*. This term expresses the fact that a nerve structure that has received similar stimuli, or undergone similar processes a number of times, becomes specially accommodated or adjusted to that kind of stimulus or process. It is evident that plasticity and inhibition are closely connected. The more a nerve structure tends to act in one way, the greater resistance it will offer to all stimuli exciting to a different course of action.

Psychological Equivalents.—It is evident that sensation, interest, and impulse, answer in some way to the property of excitability. They all stir the soul to action, either intellectual or volitional, or both. And as the physiological stimulus is controlled and guided by the inhibition exercised by the central organs, so the psychological excitations are brought under the control of the less superficial "apperceptive organs."

That is to say, upon both the physiological and the psychological sides, we have, on one hand, stimulus to activity, and, on the other, organized capacities or tendencies (" faculties ") that respond to the stimulus, and that, by the manner of their response, control it. And it is only as the stimulus, whether physiological or psychological, is inhibited or regulated, that it becomes effective or of any value. The sensation is controlled by the intellectual capacities that connect and interpret it ; the impulse is controlled by the habits of desire and choice with which it is brought into relation.

Excitation and Inhibition.—A right balance of the two sides of excitation and inhibition is necessary for proper physical or psychical activity. Without excitation there is dullness, inertia, laziness, lack of incentive ; without inhibition, there is instability, excessive irritability and vacillation. There is no self-control, physical or mental. Every stimulus excites activity to a high degree, and thus exhausts power, nervous and psychical. It is a noteworthy fact that a fatigued nerve is relatively more excitable than a fresh one. So fatigue generally shows itself psychically by inability to control attention, and often by irritation of temper. The reserve force of the brain centres is exhausted, and the stimuli are comparatively stronger. Hence the evil effects, mental and physical, of over work and over pressure in school. Some psychologists think the different temperaments are due to the mutual relations of the stimulating and the inhibiting power. The psychological equivalent of *plasticity* is, of course, *habit* and *retention*. There is a change in the structure and function of the nerves, and especially of the nerve centres, at the basis of the change that the mind undergoes. And retention, in building up habit and character, builds up future self-control, just as plasticity and inhibition are connected.

Localization of Function.—One of the most important topics in physiological psychology, as well as one of the most important pedagogically, is that of *localization of function.* To what extent do definite portions of the brain correspond to definite mental functions and capacities ? The details of this question are much disputed, but there seems to be growing agreement of opinion upon the following points :

1. There is *original indifference* of function. That is, prior to experience, either of the individual or of the species, there is no localization. Every part of the nervous structure is equally prepared to exercise every function.

2. As the result of *use* certain functions become more or less confined to certain portions of the brain. This would be a necessary result of the properties of plasticity and accommodation. Use depends not so much on the structure of a part as upon its motor, sensory and cerebral *connections.*

3. The more *mechanical* the function, the more readily (and hence perfectly) it is localized. Thus the processes ordinarily called purely mechanical, like breathing, circulation, etc., have definite local centres. The spinal-cord and the lower parts of the brain, aside from their conducting functions, seem to be groups of centres for regulating mechanical functions. Walking and other physical habits seem to have definite centres. Articulate speech almost always has its nerve-basis in the third *frontal* convolution of the left hemisphere.

4. Mental *capacities,* whether intellectual or volitional, have *ill-defined* and *changeable* centres. That is to say, the capacities of assimilating and of recognizing various kinds of sense-impressions, and of co-ordinating and controlling various kinds of motor impulses, have centres in the brain. The centres have no definite outline, however, and probably overlap one another. By calling them changeable we mean that if a centre in one hemisphere is destroyed, the function may, through use, be assumed by a corresponding centre in the other hemisphere. If this is also destroyed, it is probable that other parts of the brain, having proper nerve connections, may be substituted.

L

5. Memory, thinking, choice, etc., have *no* definite localization.   There is no *general power* of memory, but only retention and recognition of various original experiences. Each idea has its own memory, as it were.   Hence the centre of memory is supposed to be the same as that of the original idea.   In other words, the same parts of the brain are active in remembering that were active in the original perception.   The agreement of this physiological fact with the precept laid down for training memory will be noticed.   Thinking is relating various memories, images and ideas. .It cannot have any one centre, therefore, but all parts of the brain involved in the original perceptions and in the images, must be active in thinking.   Physiologically as well as psychologically there is no abstract or formal faculty of memory or of thought, apart from *what* is remembered, *what* is thought about.

6. *Ideas* are not localized.   Some have written as if each idea had a separate cell in the brain, and were then connected with other cells, by fibres corresponding to the association of ideas.   This cannot be true, however, for an idea is the *result* of associations and relations.   It is not an entity in itself, but is a complex result of many factors and processes.   The idea of a ' dog,' for example, involves elements coming from all the senses ; involves motor elements used in speaking or writing the word dog; involves, in an educated person, words corresponding to the same idea in several languages ; and involves all the manifold knowledge a person has about the habits, varieties, etc., of dogs.   Almost every kind of idea may be thus involved in an idea, apparently as simple as that of dog.   All portions of the brain corresponding to these elements must, therefore, be active when we have the idea.

Educational Principles.—Aside from being convinced of the necessity of thorough culture and care of the body the teacher may, by the foregoing brief summary, be confirmed in certain educational principles already laid down.   *First*, he may see that the idea of organization of faculty, through retention of the result of every experience, which has been so much emphasized, has a physical basis and efficiency. *Secondly*, he may see that it is a physiological impossibility that there should be specific direct training of any one faculty. The faculty can be trained only through the material assimilated, and the assimilation of the material requires the activity of the fundamental mental processes and functions. Educate association and attention, educate analysis and synthesis, and to a large degree memory, thinking, etc., will take care of themselves. *Thirdly*, as no cell or fibre has originally any particular function in itself, but acquires functions only through its connections, so, mentally, *relations* established by association and by attention are more important than the isolated sensation itself.

CHAPTER VIII.

SUMMARY OF PRINCIPLES.

We shall now go over the psychological discussion, select the principles of most importance for the teacher, and rearrange them under appropriate heads, that we may, as far as possible, derive general maxims for the guidance of the teacher. After having done this we shall be in a position to criticise some of the current maxims, recognizing both their value and their limitations. The educational principles to be gathered from our present knowledge of psychology may be classified as follows :

I. Bases upon which instruction should rest.

II. Ends at which instruction should aim.

III. Methods which instruction should follow.

I. Bases of Instruction.

1. *Always base instruction upon some activity of the pupil.*

This is a principle which holds good from the beginning ; from the primary stage to the final, or university stage. Education is the development of the psychical activities, and must, therefore, begin with some spontaneous manifestation of the activity to be educated. This activity may appear in the form of an impulse, an interest, a habit, an exercise of effort, an associating or relating activity, according to the degree of development,—but personal or *self-activity there must be.*

2. *Always base instruction upon some interest of the pupil.*

This principle, again is co-extensive with the whole range of education. The interest may belong to the activity put forth, to the object upon which the activity is exercised, to some remoter end, which it is hoped the activity will reach ; it may not have originally belonged to the activity or to its object, but may have been transferred to it from something else interesting, or it may be induced by appealing to social motives (sympathy, love), or to rational motives (desire of knowledge, of progress, etc.)—but *personal interest there must be.*

3. *Always base instruction upon some idea already existing in the pupil's mind.*

In the current phrase, knowledge must proceed from the " known to the unknown." A fact or action absolutely new and unlike anything in the pupil's mind, cannot by any possibility be lodged in that mind. It can gain entrance only by being taken hold of by some idea already there. Instruction consists in supplying nutriment to some idea already in the mind so as to make it grow into a larger and more accurate idea, rather than in forcing or pouring something into the mind from without. There are two principles which we have repeatedly had occasion to notice which strengthen that just laid down : one is that we always learn with what we have already learned ; the other is that an idea (however vague) of what is to be done must precede any doing.

II. Ends of Instruction.

1. *Aim at making instruction significant. This includes : first, make each subject, as a whole significant, and second, make every statement within the subject significant.*

(*i*) There is no evil in education greater than teaching subjects so that their actual *bearing* is lost sight of : teaching them as if they were mere *studies* instead of real bodies of fact. The divorcing of knowledge obtained by study in school from that obtained spontaneously out of school, is one of the things the teacher must be most constantly on his guard against. Children may study geography and not find out that they are simply extending and classifying the knowledge about the world that they have been getting ever since they were born ; they may study history without realizing that they are but enlarging their knowledge of real men and real deeds ; they may study grammar without finding out that they are simply defining and analyzing what they have always had some *practical* knowledge of. All is remote, arbitrary and consequently meaningless and burdensome. None of the educational reforms of the last generation has been more important than that in primary methods which has connected *studies* with ordinary ways of gaining knowledge and with ordinary kinds of knowledge.

(*ii*) Every new statement of fact or law must be explained, illustrated and acted upon, so as to gain significance. It must be translated into old perceptions, and must be transformed into personal actions in order that its meaning may be fully apprehended.

2. *Aim at making instruction definite.*

Every lesson should have a point, and every question upon that lesson should have a point, precise, salient, unambiguous. Irrelevant matter should be excluded : the teacher must avoid the introduction of confusing examples or analogies. Objects presented must plainly illustrate j st the point desired ; if they do not in themselves, attention must be fixed upon the relevant points of the object. A great deal of scientific experiment and illustration by the teacher is practically wasted because the pupil observes only the sensational result, or because the experiment illustrates so many points beside the one in hand. Again, *every expression, every form of language used by the pupil must be definite* so far as the extent of knowledge and the idiosyncracies of the pupil permit. Finally the teacher should remember that knowledge is naturally anything but definite. Vague and cloudy ideas come first, and they will in many minds remain vague to the end unless the teacher is constantly alive to the necessity of arousing mental activities to work upon them.

3. *Aim at making instruction practical.*

Instruction is practical when, as has been explained, ideas lead to action and action is based upon ideas. In the period when everything that a child learns *counts*, and when he is learning more *rapidly* than at any other time in his life, namely his first five years, there is no divorce of knowing from doing. Every idea the child gets is acted upon, and every idea is got through action. We shall have an ideal method of education when this same connection between knowledge and action, (though the activities need not be physical) is continued through all school years, and is joined to a *regular* system of means and ends for securing it.

(i) Instruction is practical when it leads to the formation of right habits.

Instruction given *simply* for the sake of conveying information cannot be practical. The information must be given for the *sake of the habits formed,* the discipline of intelligence, emotion and will produced. A right understanding of this principle shows what is the true function of *drill* in educa tion. There must be drill, there must be a mechanical side to education, but it is all important that the mechanical be confined to its proper place —the training of habits, the organizing of capacities. Drill, for its own sake, apart from its influence in building up right habits is the most powerful of the forces at work in severing school work from the real world, and in making it artificial and unreal. Imagine a child out of school drilled and redrilled upon some facts he has gathered in conversation or in reading, as he too often is upon facts learned in school ; drilled as if the sole value of the facts consisted in the extent to which they lent themselves to purposes of drill : would not the result be that these facts would become unreal and distasteful ; that interest would die out ; that the sense of proportion, of the difference between the important and the unimportant, would be destroyed, and that, by dwelling on what is familiar to the degree of tediousness, habits of mind-wandering would be formed ? But when drill is used simply as *means* and as means to forming right habits in the subject studied, whatever it be, these evil results are avoided, and the *proper union of knowing and doing is systematically secured.*

(ii) Instruction is practical when it leads to the organization of new faculties and powers.

The subject of retention has been so often alluded to that there is no need of dwelling upon this principle here. It is evident that if instruction is carried on with a view to the *effect which ideas apprehended have upon the mind,* it will lead to the production of new capacities and powers ; that, instead of an accumulation of isolated and dead facts in the mind, there will be an assimilation and digestion of them, by which they will be worked over into centres of new activity and apprehension.

(iii) Instruction is practical when it develops the fundamental psychical powers, Association and Attention, Apperception and Retention.

It is not upon the *specific* knowledge acquired, nor upon the *specific* habits formed, nor yet upon the *specific* powers gained, that the pupil will have most to rely after he leaves school, and upon which his success in life will most depend. It is the cultivation of the *mind* in its fundamental capacities, its powers of forming proper connections, of apprehending readily and accurately, of retaining firmly and for long periods, of concentrating and directing attention, that decides whether or not the person is educated for life.

Fortunately the four ends mentioned are all met by the same methods. The *best* methods of acquiring knowledge in the subject of arithmetic are also the surest to develop right habits of dealing with arithmetical relations, and the most effective in organizing mental faculties. And the methods that form right habits and organize new powers are also the methods which are surest to discipline, cultivate and develop the fundamental powers of mind, and to give association and attention ability to deal with whatever questions present themselves.

III. Methods of Instruction.

1. *Teach one thing at a time.*

This does not mean simply that geography is to be taught at one time, history at another, and so on. It means that every subject is to be so presented that the mind's activities may be directed, all its energies *concentrated*, upon one point at a time. Operations that, to an adult, have become so habitual that their various factors are consolidated into one simple process are, to a beginner, highly complex, and it is necessary for the teacher to select these various factors, present them in logical order, and drill the pupils upon each one of them separately. When the question is as to the *special* methods to be adopted in teaching some subject, as reading, arithmetic, etc., the first step is to discover what mental operations the mind must go through in grasping that subject ; the next step is to arrange ways by which the child's attention may be confined successively to each one of these constituent operations, beginning, of course, with the simplest.

Example.—Reading aloud is to an educated adult a comparatively simple matter. The wrong methods, once in use, went upon the principle that it was a correspondingly simple matter to a child, and, therefore, endeavoured to make the child's mind work in three or four directions at once. The result, naturally, was that some of the aspects of reading were slighted, and that none of the processes involved in reading was efficiently and economically performed. For, consider how complex the operation really is. First, attention must be paid to the visual sensations in order to recognize the written word ; then there must be the mental operation of combining the letters and words ; then of paying attention to the ideas symbolized by the words ; then, in order to pronounce the words with expression, attention must be paid to the auditory sensations represented by the words ; then to their association with the motor impulses required to make the sounds ; and then to the proper inflection, pitch, emphasis, etc., that will **give** the full meaning of what is written. The analysis could be carried farther, but here we have six distinct operations, to each of which separate attention *must* be paid if the child is to learn to read well. How much better, therefore, the methods which select the various operations and train the child in them, one by one, than the methods that present all in a mass and compel the pupil to pick out the processes for himself.

Meaning of Analytic Methods in Education.—Every right method is a way of assisting some normal psychical process (page 4), and this method of " teaching one thing at a time " finds its justification in its relation to the mind's *analytic* function. The immature mind cannot perform the necessary analysis for itself; if it could it would need no instruction. But it is overwhelmed by the mass of facts confronting it. It is the function of the teacher so to *subdivide and analyze the material*, that the pupil's *mind shall work analytically.* A pupil who notices the sounds that his teacher is making, and then attempts to reproduce them, is performing mental analysis. There is one thing presented to him, and all his attention is concentrated upon that one thing. *An analytic method in education always consists in resolving a subject into its component members, and in presenting these members, one at a time, to the mind's activities to work upon.*

Advantages of Analytic Method.—Its main advantage is, of course, that it is based upon and aids a fundamental function of mind, one which must be used if knowledge is to be gained. But there are minor advantages which may be noticed.

(i) It economizes mental Energy.—When the mind is called upon to pay attention to something which contains a number of unfamiliar factors, it is really called upon to attend to that number of subjects at once. The result is that mental energy is diffused, scattered and largely wasted. There is *greater strain* upon the mind than if one point were presented at a time, but *less is accomplished*.

(ii) It defines mental Products.—A distinct mental product is one which has by attention been differentiated from others (page 59). Paying attention to one thing at a time, therefore, necessarily makes distinct what is attended to. On the other hand, when subjects are presented, *en masse,* as it were, everything is undefined, vague and blurred.

(iii) It excludes irrelevant Material.—The tendency of the mind to associate whatever is presented at the same time whether it should be connected or not, has been noticed (page 32). Unless pains are taken to select one thing and fix attention upon that, the mind is almost sure to include much that should not be included. When a pupil tells a teacher that "Columbus knew the earth was round because he balanced an egg on the table ;" it is easy to laugh at him ; but the probability is that these two statements had been presented to him in such juxtaposition amid a jumble of facts that his mind naturally associated them.

(iv) It prepares the way for Memory.—It has already been sufficiently repeated that memory is not a general power, but that there is a memory for everything learned, depending upon the vividness, distinctness and connections of the original apprehension. When one thing is attended to at a time, the requirements of correct apprehension are so well met that remembering follows *naturally.*

(v) It forms the analytic Habit.

When we say that a man has a trained mind, that he has his mental powers under good command, we almost always mean that he is able in any subject he takes up to seize upon its important points, to distinguish them clearly, and hold them firmly, no matter how complicated and confused the subject upon its surface. This means that he has acquired one of the best, if not the best, results of intellectual training—an *analytic habit of mind ;* a habit of grasping and defining leading facts and principles. If educators invariably follow the principle here laid down, the inducement to form this habit is strong. Paying attention to " one thing at a time," the mind is gradually led to *look* for the " one thing " which underlies a varied mass of facts ; it feels irritated and ill at ease until this unity is discovered, so that finally the pupil is *able to dispense with the teacher's preparatory analysis.*

2. *Teach in a connected Manner.*

This principle bears the same relation to the Synthetic Function of mind that the one just given does to the analytic function. The method based upon it may be termed, therefore, the *synthetic* method. This method demands that certain conditions be met both upon the side of the pupil and of the teacher.

It demands of the teacher:

(i) *Unity of aim, or an Educational Ideal.*

A teacher who does not have, in every detail of his school work, a purpose larger than that detail, must not only fall into a mechanical way of teaching, but must teach in a disconnected dispersive manner. There is no one end which runs through his class-work, his discipline, his intercourse with pupils, etc., welding them into a unity. But a teacher possessed of a practical ideal, that of forming *good habits of mind* in his students, will by this ideal connect all details, no matter how diverse they may be in themselves.

(ii) *That the teacher be systematic.*

The teacher must have a definite and comprehensive idea of what he is going to do in a given term. He must have his plans laid for an educational campaign. He must have a conception of what he is going to accomplish and by what means.

(iii) *That instruction be graded.*

There must be gradual advance from the easy to the difficult, from the simple to the complex, from the familiar to the novel. It was a saying of the schoolmen that nature never makes leaps. In this respect, instruction should "follow nature." It should have the continuity, the silent, imperceptible yet inevitable progress that marks natural growth.

So far as the pupil is concerned, the synthetic method requires:

(i) *That knowledge begin with presentation. This is for two reasons: because in training the perceptive powers all the powers of the mind are trained, and, because representative knowledge must be capable of translation into presentative.*

That knowledge should be connected is our general principle. It cannot be connected if there are representative or symbolic ideas incapable of translation into presentations. Such ideas would be isolated and meaningless. Nor can it be connected unless there is an orderly development or unfolding of the powers involved in getting knowledge. The necessity of translating images and concepts into percepts has already been dwelt upon, and so we shall occupy ourselves here with the other part of ₍the maxim. This is sometimes stated : Train the faculties in the order of their development, first, perception, then memory and imagination, then reasoning. But a more adequate statement would be : *Train perception always, and in such a way that the other powers shall grow from it.* For the first statement seems merely to imply that memory, imagination, etc., come *after* perception, losing sight of the important fact that they come after, only because they come *from* perception. In other words, all mental activities are exercised in perception, and exercised in such a way that they naturally and gradually pass into higher forms.

Activities involved in Perception.—If perception were the same as having sensations, this principle would not be true ; and any educational system which puts the *chief* emphasis upon the senses, inverts the true order. Sensations are necessary, as affording *stimuli* to call forth the mental powers, and as affording *material* upon which these powers shall act. Sensations must be attended to, must be associated, must be idealized and retained in order to become knowledge.

A right training of perception trains, therefore, all the mental activities involved in it, instead of merely heaping up sensations, or even training the sense organs alone. For example, take the intuitive method of teaching numbers. Here the child learns, say that ．．and ．．．are the same as ．∷ and as ˙｜∷ If the sensations the child gets were the only result of the process, the method would be useless. For the time must come when he will have to grasp the relations involved, and experiencing sensations any number of times, would not give any preparation for the *apprehension of relations*. But in reality, the child relates the sensations of ．．and of ．．．and only because he relates them does he *perceive* anything.

The child *makes* or *institutes* the relation, and thus necessarily prepares the way for *conception* or the *conscious grasping of the relation*. He performs, without recognizing its full significance, a *kind* of relating identical with that performed by the most advanced mathematician in the highest branches, and so far as the child grasps the *meaning* of elementary ideas in any subject, he is employing, however unconsciously, the relations whose conscious apprehension constitutes *thinking*.

The two Factors in Training of Perception.—In order to establish a connected growth from perception, there are, in its training, two points in particular, to be looked after. One is *identifying* the presentation with what has already been presented, *recognition ;* the other is the *discovery* of something implied in the perception, but not apparent on the surface, its *differentiation*. The recognition of the presentation implies, of course, that former knowledge, organized capacities, are brought to bear ; that what is now perceived is assimilated to what was formerly perceived. This ensures not only the recognition of the new presentation, but the strengthening of the acquired faculty by its exercise. This recognizing activity is evidently involved in the simplest perception, as *e. g.* that by which the child sees that c-a-t spells cat, and is also involved in that by which the older student *identifies* a botanical species, perceives the principle which covers a mathematical problem, or sees that the form of some given Greek word illustrates a law of euphonic change.

But there should be in all perception a *new* factor as well as an old. The child who sees that . . and . . . is the same as 'i: : sees it only by putting together the first two number-forms and *taking apart* the last. He perceives the identity by discovering it, by making it. So when a child puts the sounds of the letters c,a,t to make the word, he not only *recognizes*, but he *discovers*. In higher education we have clearly the factor of discovery in scientific experiment, in the demonstration of original propositions, in the analysis of unfamiliar plants, in the dissection of animals, etc. But it is a mistake to suppose that experiment and an element of original investigation are confined to advanced pursuits, or to natural and physical sciences. They are involved to some degree in every act of perception which gives new knowledge, and education should be so directed as to employ in all stages this acquisition of new knowledge by perception. New knowledge is obtained only through an *act of construction, or synthesis,* and this is, in reality, an *act of discovery*. It should be noticed that the new combination of these two factors of recognition and discovery renders knowledge *connected*. The old is made the basis of apprehending the new, while the new is made the means of extending or developing the old.

\ (ii) The synthetic method demands that facts be connected together by the laws of association and by the relations of unity and difference so that they form centres or groups of ideas.

An isolated fact is learned by the pupil only through sheer force of impressing it on his mind. Both brain and mind are plastic in childhood, and there is no doubt that the child can store away multitudes of comparatively unconnected facts. But this method does not train mental power; it gives no strength to old capacities, and no aid to the organization of new. Furthermore, this method draws wastefully upon mental energy ; the facts are learned by an expenditure of force, and are carried by expenditure of force ; in both ways, the mind is burdened. But facts learned by associations and relations, strengthen and form faculty in the very process of making the connections, or appropriating the material. Further, the mind gains instead of losing in carrying power by its assimilation of facts so learned. These connected ideas serve as centres about which allied ideas gather ; thus they carry others, instead of having to be carried by the energy of the mind.

Training of Connection of Ideas.—It is impossible here to lay down detailed rules for connecting ideas in various studies. There are, however, some facts bearing upon the subject which may be called to mind. First, this connecting activity is *normal* to the mind ; the mind strives to connect whenever it can, and the teacher can accomplish much by presenting material so that the child's mind is drawn on naturally from one point to another. Again, a unity of feeling, or of *interest*, will connect ideas or subjects otherwise diverse. Children at play thus unite all kinds of ideas. The story has recently been told of children who began by building houses in a sand pile, and went on gradually to the development of agricultural, manufacturing, railway and commercial establishments, comprehending in all a vast number of different activities. A unity of interest made the transitions. And so it will be in schools. Again, the subjects of reading, spelling, writing, composition, history and geography may undoubtedly be better interwoven with one another than they have hitherto been. Indeed, of all the branches of study in earlier years, arithmetic is the only one which does not lend itself easily, and almost inevitably, to union with other studies if the principle of interconnection is once grasped.

(iii) The synthetic method demands that the groups of ideas thus formed be used as organs for acquiring new knowledge.

This principle has two sides. A pupil who has learned, for example, the simple arithmetical operations must, on the one hand, constantly use them ; must add, subtract, etc.; and, on the other hand, must gain new arithmetical knowledge as an expansion or development of these operations. Old knowledge must be exercised in gaining new presentations, and these must be assimilated or appropriated by being brought into organic union with acquired knowledge. Old knowledge identifies or grasps the new presentation, the new presentation strengthens, expands and organizes old knowledge. There must be apperception on one side ; retention on the other.

Applications of Principle.—The principle requires, first, frequent *reviews* of former knowledge. Reviews have as their purpose not merely repeating former knowledge, and thus impressing it more deeply upon the mind, but also its grouping and classifying. It is important that the pupil should be led to form the habit of re-arranging what he has learned ; of bringing it under its proper heads, and of placing these heads in their proper relations to one another. In reviews, therefore, the *serial* order should often be changed for a *topical* order. A trained mind, after having amassed many facts, always endeavors to reduce them to as few principles as possible. This process not only assists the mind in grasping the real meaning of the facts, but it trains thought and memory. The reasoning powers are trained in the effort to discover the underlying principles, and to connect the facts with them. The memory is developed because only the principles have to be remembered ; the facts cluster about them as instances or illustrations.

The principle requires, secondly, that there be mental *preparation* for engaging in studying or in learning. That is, before a pupil enters upon the study of a new subject his mind must be prepared for it : before he takes up a new topic or principle, his mind must be prepared, and before he sets himself to learn any lessons there must be preparatory adjustment of mind. This preparation consists, partly, in stirring up ideas already in the mind, in re-awakening interest in them, and in calling them into activity ; and, partly, in forming transitions, in showing how these ideas lead naturally to something else.. Without this preparatory activity no *attention* can be given (pages 61 and 62), and hence what is studied is not connected with what has previously been learned, and there is no assimilation nor comprehension.

This principle requires, thirdly, that old knowledge be *exercised*. There are two injunctions of equal importance to the teacher. One is that new knowledge be not simply *impressed upon* the mind : the other is that old knowledge be not simply *stored* or passively retained *in* the mind. Constantly employing what has been learned guards against both these errors. To use grammatical principles in analyzing speech, in correcting errors, in constructing new sentences, etc., enlarges and organizes these principles, and at the same time causes what is learned to gather about them, and to gain meaning from them. Old knowledge and new facts are thus so connected together that both are made vital. Kept apart, both are dead. Just as the body must have nourishment in order to keep itself living, and just as food by becoming nourishment is itself transformed from dead to living material, so with the mind and its food-studies. Unless the mind constantly uses what it has gained to gain more, it loses what it has possessed ; and unless what is gained is connected with mental power already existing, it is a burden rather than a gain.

Analytic and Synthetic Methods.—We may sum up our discussion of methods by calling attention to three facts. 1. All special methods are only applications to particular branches of the analytic and synthetic methods. 2. These two methods do not exclude, but supplement, each other. 3. They are not to be confused with physical division and composition.

1. Since the fundamental powers or functions of mind are analysis and synthesis, since all that is ever learned is learned by being distinguished from and connected with other ideas, it follows that *all educational methods must rest upon these powers.* Any method in any subject that has value, must appeal, to some extent, to the discriminating and the unifying functions of intelligence, and the best method is that which appeals to them in the most systematic way, and which stimulates them to the fullest and most intense activity. In his knowledge of these powers every teacher has an instrument by which he may test for himself the value of any special method which is proposed.

2. Since mental analysis and synthesis are not separate, much less opposed, functions of mind, it follows that analytic and synthetic educational *methods* cannot be opposed. Indeed, we should rather speak of the analytic and synthetic aspects of an educational method, than of an analytic and a synthetic method. It follows that discussions as to whether geography, for example, should be taught by an analytic *or* a synthetic method, rest upon failure to understand the meaning of the terms used, and of the mental processes involved. Methods of teaching geography must possess both phases, or else some necessary mental operation is left unperformed. What is usually presented as the synthetic method, beginning, namely, with the locality familiar to the pupil and making divisions of land and water known from it, is, in reality, both synthetic and analytic. It is synthetic, because it connects what the pupil has to learn

with what he already knows ; it begins with presentations and translates representative ideas into them.   But it is also analytic, for, by such operations the vague outline-knowledge of the world which the child has is transformed into knowledge of the definite forms of land and water, etc., that make the world what it is. When a child learns that one geographical element is a lake ; that a lake has islands, bays, capes, peninsulas, etc., etc., the process must be an analytic one.   The fact that the child may make the analysis by noticing a pond in his own dooryard, does not change the process of mind from an analytic into a " synthetic " one.   And this illustration is typical.   While in some methods, one aspect may predominate over another, yet so far as the method is justifiable, it must be both analytic and synthetic.

3. The error of opposing mental analysis and synthesis generally arises from the prior error of confusing them as mental functions with physical operations having the same names. Physical analysis, or division of a whole occupying space into smaller parts *is* opposed to physical synthesis, or the composition of smaller parts into a larger spatial whole.   Thus, in geography, that method has been called synthetic, which begins with the small part of the earth known to the pupil, and then advances to the larger world ; while the analytic method is supposed to mean beginning with information about the earth as a whole, then taking up smaller subdivisions as continents, and gradually coming down to the smaller divisions of country, village, etc.   But this misapprehends the real meaning of *mental* analysis and synthesis.   The terms do not refer primarily to any difference in the size or extent of material objects.   Mental analysis does not divide spatial wholes, but renders *ideas definite*, that is clear, both as a whole, and in details ; mental synthesis does not join parts of objects or of space, but shows *how ideas are related* to one another, how they have a common meaning.   *Distinctness*, not separation, *unity*, not fusion are the

purposes of mental analysis and synthesis, and these not of material objects, but of *knowledge*.   (See pages 58 and 59.)

Illustration from Reading.—The same error is seen in many of the discussions regarding the synthetic method of teaching reading.   It is first taken for granted that some spatial unit must be found as the basis, and the question is discussed whether the unit is the letter, or the word, or the sentence. But in reality, what the pupil must begin with is the whole mass of sounds that he makes use of in pronouncing words. While these sounds in themselves are distinct, to *his* mind they have no such definiteness (see p. 80). Undoubtedly the various sounds *feel* different to the child, but this difference is not *known* or *recognized*. His first act must, therefore, be to notice some of these sounds, and through attention dwelling upon them make them distinct. *He performs an act of analysis.*   But at the same time, he must notice how these sounds go together to make words ; and his attention dwells upon the *relations* of the sounds.   Thus the pupil *performs an act of synthesis*, or combination.   By one act his knowledge of the primary sounds of speech becomes *definite ;* by the other, his knowledge becomes *connected*, By both acts, his fundamental mind functions are trained, and the habit of defining and unifying ideas is formed.

Relations of Knowledge, Feeling and Will.—While in the previous chapters knowledge, feeling and will have been discussed separately, nothing has been said about their relations to one another. This subject is, however, important to the teacher. Partly from the necessity of the case, partly from surrounding circumstances, and partly from the traditional school curriculum, *direct* instruction in our schools is confined mainly to knowledge. It is important to know in what degree this involves indirect training of feeling and will, and also in what degree it needs supplementing.

The Mind an Organic Unity.—The fact is that knowledge, feeling and will are so closely interconnected that it is impos-

M

sible to educate one without at once requiring and securing training of the other two. Aside from the fact that apperception and retention underlie all these, that the functions of analysis and synthesis enter into them all, and that the main principles of development (from the presentative and immediate to the representative and mediate, etc.) are alike in all, the mind is a unity, and primarily it is mind that is affected by education and not knowledge, feeling or will. There is but one mind, and knowledge, feeling and will are not three departments of mind, but three phases of its manifestation. Just as it would be impossible for the digestive organs to digest food without the aid of the circulatory, the respiratory and the nervous processes, and just as the digestion of food must re-act upon all these other operations, so the mind cannot know without the support of feeling and of will, and without the re-action of knowledge upon the emotional disposition and the volitional capacities. While in a material or spatial unity, the parts of the whole may exist side by side without influencing the structure of one another, as grains of sand in a sand-pile, in an organic unity, like the mind, each activity or member, is what it is by virtue of the other activities or members that influence it.

Dependence of Knowledge.—In all knowledge which is got by study or which requires voluntary attention, the will is evidently at work. Voluntary attention means attention directed by the will ; that is, attention which has an end before it, and which controls all the processes and ideas so as to lead up to this end. Study requires that there be control, physical and prudential, and generally, in many pupils, sometimes in all pupils, moral control. Without the aid and support of will, the obtaining of knowledge is a practical impossibility. Knowledge is also dependent upon feeling. *Interest* is a condition of attention, non-voluntary as well as voluntary. The mind may know, after a fashion, what does not arouse emotion, but it is a superficial and counterfeit knowledge. To *realize* the meaning of anything, to be *acquainted* with it, means to see it in its bearings upon the feelings. The *internal* appropriation and assimilation of presentations require not only that they be joined to older groups of ideas, but that they be transformed into interests and personal emotion: that they be known by the heart as well as by the head.

Dependence of Feeling.—When discussing feeling we called attention to two facts: one that feeling is *an accompaniment of activity*, the other that the various kinds of emotion, intellectual, aesthetic and personal, depend upon the kinds of objects or ideas about which feelings gather—that the distinction between them is *not so much in difference in them as feelings, as in that about which they cluster.* These two facts mean, in substance, that feeling is dependent upon will and upon knowledge, using will in a broad sense to include all psychical activity, and knowledge as the presentation of all sorts of objects and ideas. The education of perception and of thought, the training of attention and association must develop the intellectual emotions; the growth of imagination must bring about a development of the aesthetic feelings. Growth in personality, in recognition of other persons, in the recognition and practice of duty, carries along with it growth of the personal and moral feelings. The religious emotions are not susceptible of culture apart from their relation on the one hand to *ideas*, and on the other hand, to *conduct.* Indeed, it may be laid down as *a general principle that emotions may be cultivated and even permitted to exist only as motives to action and as the internal accompaniments of ideas.* Feeling of any kind that does not arise from *internal* acquaintance with ideas, from becoming at home with them, and which does not induce to action, results in unhealthy and morbid sentiment.

Dependence of Will.—Will involves, as its two essential components, *idea* and *desire*, one intellectual, the other emotional.

Without the desire, the side of feeling, action is slow and inert, having no stimulus. Without the idea, the side of knowledge, action is blind, unregulated, capricious. Every growth of feeling should result in strengthening some motive to action and in making action more energetic ; every growth of knowledge should widen action by giving it a broader end or ideal, and should make it more deliberate and reflective. The powers of will are trained both in the acts by which knowledge is acquired and by the resulting acquisition of knowledge. Learning must be based, if we go back to its ultimate foundation, upon some impulse ; and, as learning advances, this impulse is controlled by being brought into connection with ideas, and by being subjected to desire and choice. The process of learning is a volitional one from beginning to end, and as the facts of will are exercised, will must be trained. The knowledge acquired makes a basis for new activities of will ; it reveals new possibilities, and gives new laws by which to control conduct.

Education of Feeling and of Will.—It is evident from what has been said that the objection sometimes brought against present systems of education that they are *purely* intellectual, is aside the mark. Any system that really trains intelligence *must* train the emotions and the will. But unless the present system is perfect, it is evident that there must be a possibility of better training of feeling and volition than that we now have ; and, furthermore, that this training will give a better training of intellect than that now secured. But this will not involve any departure from the precepts already laid down. So far as present methods are what they should be, even as training the intellect, they rest upon the normal *interests* and *impulses* of childhood, and train these by subjecting them to association and attention, analysis and synthesis, thus necessitating emotional and volitional training as well as intellectual. Further reforms will discover more fully what the normal interests and impulses are, and will find better methods for calling out, ex-

ercising and developing the impulses, better methods for culturing and satisfying the interests. In a word, education is
primarily of the whole personality, and only secondarily of the
intellect, the feelings, or the will.*

Criticism of Maxims.—Having discovered the principles that lie at the basis of all educational maxims, we may
discuss briefly some of the current precepts.

1. *The Intellect is a Sum of Different Faculties, each of which
Requires its own Kind of Culture.*—This principle, while not
always, or even often, distinctly formulated, is assumed as
the basis of much pedagogical discussion. It violates the
true principle that intelligence has two fundamental functions
or powers, analysis and synthesis, both of which are forms of
relating activity. All faculties must, therefore, be stages in
the development of these functions, and hence, must be
trained to some degree by the same kinds of culture. (Pages
84 and 90.) Methods, for example, which attempt to train
language apart from thinking, or either language or thinking
apart from memory and perception, or which train perception
without reference to the relations of thought *implied* in the
perceptions, are inefficient, because opposed to psychological
facts.

2. *First Form Faculty, then Furnish It.*—This maxim is susceptible of an interpretation which makes it substantially correct,
but in any case it would be better stated thus : *Form faculty by
furnishing it.* The principle is correct in implying that the
organization and training of mental power is a more important end of education than the acquisition of a certain number
of facts. It is incorrect, so far as it seems to imply that
faculty can be formed apart from the activity of the mind
in acquiring knowledge, and apart from the reaction of
knowledge upon the mind. " For organizing mental faculty

---

* See Chap. vi., Training of Desires, Impulses, Character. See also
Part II, Chapter on Religious and Moral Culture.

there is no other means than organized knowledge." Mental power and knowledge are not to be opposed, or even separated, for they are correlative.   (See page 70).

3. *Learn to do by Doing.*—This precept has already been discussed. (See pages 45 and 129). The principle is true, in so far as it recognizes the fact that the self-activity of the pupil must be appealed to in all learning, and that it is through this activity that the subject gains meaning, and is apprehended. The principle becomes false when it loses sight of the ideal factor, the element of knowledge required for doing; and when it implies that the doing should be merely habitual or mechanical. It, therefore, requires a supplement : *Learn to do by knowing.* We might combine the maxims, and say: *Learn to know by doing, and to do by knowing.*

4. *Proceed from the Known to the Unknown.*—This maxim, as requiring the teacher to make what is familiar the basis of identifying or acquiring what is unfamiliar, is in line with correct psychology. Some educators have opposed the principle, by saying that since all learning involves a new element, and this new element transforms what was previously unfamiliar or vague into the familiar and definite, instruction really advances from the unknown to the known. But the words are not used in the same sense in the two maxims. The maxim, " proceed from the known to the unknown," means utilize old knowledge in acquiring new;" while the maxim, "from the unknown to the known," certainly does *not* mean " make the unknown the basis of *acquiring* the known." It means that it is through the presentation of the unknown that what was previously known is enlarged and strengthened, or that the presentation of the unfamiliar is necessary to the *development* of the familiar. From the known to the unknown corresponds to *apperception.* From the unknown to the known to *retention.* That is, one expresses the action of the mind

upon the presentation; the other, the effect which the presentation has upon the mind.

5. *Proceed from the Concrete to the Abstract.*—This precept also has been already referred to. (Page 80). Taken literally it is impossible, for there is no concrete knowledge with which to begin. Nor is it true as implying that definite knowledge is easier to get than general knowledge. It is just as difficult, requires as much preparation, as much mental energy, and as much maturity of mind, to make a clear distinction as to make broad generalization. Both processes, in fact, occur together as different aspects of comparison. To transform knowledge from hazy into definite, and from isolated into connected forms, are both ends of instruction, and the educator cannot safely assume that either process has been already accomplished before his work begins. Undoubtedly many who use the precept have a correct meaning back of it, but this meaning would be better expressed: *Develop representations from presentations.*

6. There are two maxims apparently wholly opposed to each other, often seen in educational works: "*Follow the order of nature, not the order of the subject, first synthesis and then analysis,*" and "*Proceed from the whole to the part.*" Regarding the first principle one author writes: "If in language, or in grammar we begin with grammar and pass to its divisions, learn of what each treats, take up parts of speech, and the properties of each, etc., we teach by analysis. If we begin with words, learn that they are of different kinds, as names, action-words, quality-words, etc., then learn their properties, and pass gradually up to the subject, grammar, we teach by synthesis. It is evident that the synthetic method is the method of nature, while the analytic is the logical order of the subject." But, what is really "evident" is that the method here termed synthetic is just as much analytic as synthetic. It is synthetic, because it begins with what is most familiar to the child, and advances to that more remote from his present at-

tainments ; it is analytic because it begins with the vague out-line-knowledge of words the child has, and fixes his attention upon differences of function and value, hitherto unnoticed, in words (by which some are nouns, others verbs, etc.) and thus *defines* his knowledge. Thus we get another illustration of the fact that the two methods cannot be separated. The other precept, " from the whole to the part," is correct, if it be clearly borne in mind that the ' whole ' does not refer to the objective whole, that is, the whole as it exists apart from the child's knowledge, but to the vague outline existing in his mind, the *subjective* whole. Instruction must begin with this and draw out and emphasize some one aspect, or relation of it, thus clearing up knowledge. The two principles, that of " whole to part," and " first synthesis then analysis," while opposed to each other if wrongly interpreted, supplement each other if each be understood as it should be.

7. *Teach Only What is Understood.*—The maxim, in its true meaning is identical with the precept already laid down. *Make instruction significant.* It must be remembered that a great many things are both interesting and significant to a child that are not so to an adult—for example, the forms of letters and of words, the sounds of speech simply as sounds, etc.

8. " *Teach Ideas before Words,*" or as some give it, " *Teach things not names.*" In its latter form the precept is, taken literally, meaningless. *Things* cannot be taught till they have been transformed into meaning and ideas. And language is one of the chief means of transformation. In the other form the maxim is valuable as a protest against a *merely* verbal instruction, which makes children glib reciters of rules, definitions and textual statements, and even expert performers of arithmetical operations, or of grammatical analysis, and yet leaves them with no recognition of the *meaning* of the subjects. But the maxim, so far as it seems to underrate the

value of language in aiding knowledge of objects, is, as already noticed (page 108), wholly erroneous. We may notice a few reasons. First, consciousness which is wholly presentative, that is, which does not contain a symbolic or representative factor, is meaningless. (See page 74). Language is the simplest, easiest and most efficient way, upon the whole, of introducing this representative factor into the mind. What it means can be seen by comparing the knowledge of deaf mutes with that of speaking people ; and by calling to mind that the first step in educating deaf-mutes is to give them some form of language.

Secondly, words make knowledge of objects both general and definite. They make it general by fixing attention upon the *class-qualities*, upon the *generic* properties of the object. They make it definite by seizing upon some quality of the object and making that a handle, as it were, by which the object may always be grasped. The mind is always restless till it knows the name of an object; if there is no recognized name, one is given as soon as possible. This is not only for the convenience of communication, but for the purpose of defining the object to one's self. It fixes the object, singles it out of the mass of surrounding and similar objects, and gives it an individuality of its own. The development of language in the race and in the child, shows clearly that names, at first, simply express the most salient or prominent quality of the object. Indeed, to a baby, the name *is* the most definite quality the object possesses; he repeats the name every time he sees the object, not to call the attention of others to it, but to *re*-call the object to his own mind; in other words, to define it. That animals do not have language is as much because their knowledge is vague as because it is not generalized.

Thirdly, names are condensations, concentrations of past knowledge. They introduce the immature mind at once into a fullness and richness of knowledge which it would take the child years to learn for himself; which indeed he would never learn. It is a common-place to say that a school-child of to-day may have more astronomical knowledge than Sir Isaac Newton had. The reason is found in language. Words sum up and condense into themselves the science and civilization of the race. A right use of language in teaching, therefore, is necessary to lift the child from his individual isolation and put him, as regards knowledge of things, upon the plane of his race. Much could be said of the necessity of language as an instrument of general culture, but the three reasons given are confined to the one point of the relation of names to the knowledge of objects.

9. "*Let Education follow Nature.*"—This precept is so vague that it might be dismissed at once. But in spite of its vagueness it is sometimes employed so as to do much harm. Its only true meaning is that educational methods should rest upon psychical processes normal to the child's mind, and should stimulate and train them. It is sometimes perverted to mean that there is some force called Nature which will carry on education of itself, and which should not be interfered with by educators; or, that Nature lays down laws so clearly that the educator need not have special knowledge or art of his own; or that Nature provides models so distinct that no one can err in following them, and so perfect that the teacher cannot improve upon them. All this is either mythology robing itself in the garb of science, or it is a vague way of covering up ignorance with the pretence of knowledge. The teacher must, indeed *know* the *nature* of his *pupil*. He must, like the Great Teacher, know what is in man in order that he may educate him for manhood, but, unlike the Great Teacher, he has need of definite study to find out what man is—what he is in actuality and in possibility.

CHAPTER IX.

THE METHOD OF INTERROGATION : ART OF QUESTIONING.

General Method.—We have seen (page 167, *et seq*) that special methods of instruction rest upon Analysis and Synthesis, and that the Analytic and Synthetic Methods in education are not independent but *complementary*, being in fact but different aspects of the one psychological method which must be followed in all normal instruction. Without perplexing the student, therefore, with a minute classification of methods, it is only necessary to state that we may appeal to the Analytic and Synthetic functions of mind chiefly in two ways, viz. : by *direct, continuous Exposition* (the Expository Method) ; or *by Interrogation* (the Socratic Method) ; *i. e.*, we may by **Questioning**, with occasional expositions or suggestions, direct the learner in the processes of *Recognition and Discovery* (page 172). The method of Questioning is of most value in primary and intermediate education, and that method we shall now study.

Of all the qualifications that go to make the successful teacher, ability to question well is probably the most important. The prime object of teaching is to get the learner to think for himself. This means that his mind is in the proper attitude and that the material for thought is properly presented. These conditions secure a vital, organic relation between the prepared mind and the presented material, that is, the material really enters into the structure of knowledge, and its acquisition enlarges the structure of mind.

Importance of the Art.—To secure these conditions and to test the value of the results, judicious questioning is the surest means. It may be said, indeed, that the Art of Questioning is the Art of Teaching. Whoever can question well can teach well; whoever fails in this point fails in all. Natural endowments, accurate scholarship, professional knowledge and experience, are required for excellence in this method of instruction. Valuable as the method is, no great prominence has hitherto been given to its study in institutions for the training of teachers. It seems to have been taken for granted that if a teacher knows a subject well he can question upon it well; an outgrowth, or perhaps a modified form, of the long prevalent error that knowledge of a subject is identical with ability to teach it. The fallacy of this assumption is now generally recognised. Learning, energy, enthusiasm, knowledge of the theory and practice of teaching, will prove comparatively ineffective without this Socratic qualification, ability to question well, the rarest of attainments, the *Master Art* of the teacher's calling.

Principles and Practice.—Skill in the art of questioning is to be acquired as skill in any other art is acquired, by long and patient practice; one learns to do by doing; one learns to question by questioning. But, in accordance with what has been established in our psychology, here, as everywhere, the co-ordinate maxim has its place: *By knowing, learn to do.* Mere practice does not make experience in the true sense of the word; it must be intelligent practice. Rules of art are derived from principles of science, and unless the " doer " has a clear knowledge of rules and of their underlying principles, he is not likely to acquire artistic skill in their practical application. It is a common mistake to assume that mere lapse of time. as it were, results in experience. On the contrary, there is many a " practical " man—so far as time spent in " doing " is concerned—that is thoroughly unpractical, and many an " experienced " one quite without experience. An experience which is not the result of sound principles and their wise application, gives special powers and tendencies to work in the wrong direction, a fatal facility for leaving undone the things that ought to be done, and doing the things that ought not to be done.

It is not an uncommon thing to hear a teacher boasting of his long experience, and even claiming special privileges on account of it, who in his actual school work violates almost every principle of scientific method, and who, in consequence of his " experience," is beyond hope of improvement. It may be well, then, to indicate the principles on which the art of questioning rests, and since method in teaching is little more than method in questioning, to discuss as fully as may be, such practical applications as may help the young teacher to begin right, to continue right, and so, with the least possible waste of time and power, to attain that true experience which comes from *right doing* guided by *right knowing*

Division of the Subject.—It has already been suggested that teaching and learning are based on the two fundamental processes, Apperception—the process of taking anything into the mind ; and Retention—the *effect* which the material when apprehended, has upon the mind itself. These two processes are, as we have seen, mutually dependent ; there can be no retention without clear apprehension ; and, on the other hand, every new apprehension modifies mind, and so has its effect in interpreting new experiences. The teacher should, therefore, bear in mind that the two conditions of learning are, on the one hand, *proper presentation of material*, and on the other hand, *proper preparation of mind.* In the light of this principle, we may consider (I) The Objects of Questioning, or what may be accomplished by it ; (II) The Qualifications of the Questioner; (III) The Form and Matter of Questions; (IV) The Form and Matter of Answers. If the first topic is fully discussed, it is evident that the *principles* of the other three may be easily deduced. Since the two processes, apperception and retention, are reciprocal, the one necessarily implying the other, it is not easy to classify the objects of questioning as belonging definitely to one process rather than to the other. But it will be convenient to classify them roughly under these heads, *i.e.*, we shall consider the Objects, or Purposes, of Questioning as *(a)* concerned with *the Presentation of Material, or with the Testing of Retention ; (b)* as concerned with *the Preparation of Mind, or the Training of Apperception.*

I. Objects, or Purposes of Questioning.

Testing Retention.—Under *(a)* we may consider the following important purposes : 1. To Discuss Actual Knowledge ; 2. To Fix Actual Knowledge ; 3. To Extend, or Enlarge Actual Knowledge—the vague made definite, the imperfect made accurate, new knowledge imparted ; and 4. To Cultivate Power of Expression, and thus aid both these fundamental Processes ; this of course, belongs equally to subdivision, *(b)*.

Training Apperception.—Under *(b)* may be considered the following purposes : 1. To Excite Interest ; 2. To Arouse Attention : 3. To Direct Attention ; 4. To Cultivate Habit of Self-Direction of Attention, *i.e.*, Habit of Self-Questioning.

(a) Testing Retention : Presentation of Material.

1. *To Discover the Pupil's Knowledge.*—This is one of the first requisites in preparing to give a new lesson. For the new lesson must have some logical connection with what was previously taught ; it can be interpreted only by what has been retained from former lessons, and so it is impossible effectively to aid the learner to assimilate the new with the old, unless we know what the old is and how it stands in the learner's mind. If this is not known we may waste time in two ways.

Presenting too Easy Stimulus.—(See page 111.)—In the first place : We may dwell upon what is already perfectly known to the learner, and thus, by monotonous repetition of what has lost all charm of novelty, quench rather than excite interest. The tendency of certain modern methods is strongly in this direction. Ingenious minds have long been in travail to discover a royal road to learning ; they have at last discovered it by the simple expedient of removing difficulties instead of developing strength to conquer .them. It appears to be thought that the teacher can take the place of the learner by properly preparing the material, that is by atomizing knowledge, the mental aliment, and administering it in homœopathic doses to the recipient mind. Or, if it is admitted that the child must himself climb the arduous ladder that leads to the high plane of capacity and skill, the ladder, it is thought, can be freed from all its arduousness by indefinitely diminishing the distance between the rounds. If anyone thinks this is too strongly' put, let him open almost any educational journal or recent educational work, and he will find abundant proof of the prevalence of the theory : "develop strength by making things easy." Witness the infinitesimal doses prescribed in "model" number lessons, language lessons, etc. Witness the "mob" of questions that the young teacher is recommended to ask on three or four lines of a common reading lesson, a mere scrap which can never enter into organized knowledge nor have any effect in organizing faculty. Witness the trivial "development" questions recommended for the evolution of ideas which are already in the child's mind, if he has a minimum of brain-power, as clearly as they can be there, in his presumed stage of mental growth.

Questions should Stimulate.—Is it necessary, is it good method, to give forty or fifty pages of questions on the numbers from one to five? Are from 100 to 300 questions required for reasonable practice on the number two? as *e.g.*, How many thumbs on the right hand ? How many on the left ? How many on both hands ? John had one apple and his sister gave him another, how many had he then ? Two birds are sitting on a tree, if one bird flies away how many will be left ? How many eyes has Willie ? If he shuts one how many will remain open ? And so on, if not *ad infinitum*, certainly *ad* *nauseam*, in the case of every child with a modicum of brains. Such questioning at last loses all power to *stimulate*, and the answers become simply an exercise in " dead vocables." Merely verbal repetition cannot strengthen intelligence, and so *drill*— the mighty instrument of little men—may be carried to a point where it is not only useless, but positively pernicious.

In primary schools, perhaps in all schools, incalculable time is wasted in a wearisome monotony of drills, tending to form merely sensuous associations, and continued long after such associations have been actually formed. Let the teacher be on his guard against the atomic method in questioning—a cut-feed method which may be, presumably, suited to the capacity of the " missing link," but is a positive hindrance to an intelligent child.

It is safe to assume that where there is a healthy brain there is mind ; where there is mind there is capacity for attention, for self-active direction of normal power, and that this self-activity of mind works with effect, *because* it works with interest when operating upon material that challenges effort. There is little doubt that many a child loses interest in the inane things presented as mental pabulum, and is pronounced " dull " when he is only disgusted and " inattentive " when he is but attentive to his own more interesting trains of ideas. The conclusion of the matter is : do not waste time and mental force in asking too many questions of the past—questions which are below the child's actual capacity and attainments, which begin, continue, and end in the " concrete," which destroy interest, and hence disqualify the mind rather than prepare it, for the reception and elaboration of new material.

Teaching too Difficult Matter.—In the second place : The teacher must discover the child's knowledge in order to avoid the other extreme—the presentation of material, which is beyond the child's power to assimilate. This error, is in

Canadian Schools, more common than that described in the fore-going paragraph, and is perhaps equally harmful.   Learning is a process of interpretation, that is, the knowledge acquired yes-terday must be used to interpret what is presented to-day. There is learning, therefore, only when there is bringing to bear past experiences upon the new material.   If this material is "above the learner's head," how is it possible that there can be assimilation ? If A, B, C are related ideas in a certain topic, and the learner is in possession of A but not of B, it is worse than useless to present C to him ; his mind cannot be brought into relation with C.   There may be clear arrangement, fluent ex-position, and apposite illustration, and yet on the part of the learner there is neither knowledge-growth nor mind-growth ; and the teacher is left to wonder how so " excellent **a lesson** " should be to the pupil words and nothing more.   Even good teachers are prone to this error of asking questions of the future.   A teacher of zeal and energy is anxious for the pro-gress of his pupils ; he is tempted to forget that there is no possibility of forcing progress—which is a thing of growth re-sulting only from the self-activity of the mental organism—he gives a long but lucid lesson ; he has not time to test fully on retention, but finding that part of the lesson seems to have been fairly taken in, he hastily concludes that all has been appropriated, and so, when he proceeds to give a new lesson logically depending on the last, he finds, after much waste of energy and much discouragement to the learner, that he has been vainly appealing to groups of ideas and to a power of comprehension that as yet do not exist.

True Assimilation—It must never be forgotten that the apprehension—the interpretation—of the new matter must occur through what the mind has already within itself ; that is to say, the interpretation, the true assimilation, occurs not merely through certain ideas or groups of ideas held in the mind, but through an increased mental power—capacity in a

N

given direction, developed in acquiring such ideas. If, for example, a young pupil has mastered the number five, he is not only in possession of certain ideas concerning the number (such as 4 and 1 are 5, 5 less 1 is 4, etc.), but in getting these ideas his mind has acquired increased capacity for grasping number-relations in general. Thus, also, if a teacher attempts to teach the number 7 before the pupil has a clear apprehension of the number 6, he is not only appealing to ideas not yet in the child's mind—for 6 is a thought in 7—but he is assuming a higher power of grasping relations than the child has yet acquired.

What Is Known and How.—It is clear, therefore, that before beginning a new lesson the teacher must find out exactly what the child knows, and *how* he knows it, *i.e.*, how he has acquired it; whether by mere sensuous association (verbal memory)—in which case the ideas are held mechanically in the mind and *have no interpreting power*—or by true assimilation, in which case not only are the ideas there, but also the capacity to use them, Yet, it is to be feared, that with the majority of teachers, the object of questioning is to test *what* the child knows, rather than *how* he knows it; that is, the questions are a test of what is held mechanically in the mind, but not a test of power developed. The thoughtful teacher proposes to act on the maxim: "From the Known to the related Unknown." What course does he pursue? He endeavors to see clearly the logical connection of the new lesson with what is already in the learner's mind; he carefully analyzes it and notes the relations of the several parts so as to present the new material properly arranged; he tests the "known" in the learner's mind, and the power developed in acquiring it; he stimulates this power, and brightens up and brings to the front the ideas involved in the known; he leads the pupil to create for himself the relations between the new and the old. Thus there is real assimilation; there are both apperception and retention ; there is growth in organized power and in organized knowledge. In such instruction there is pleasure to the teacher from the conscious success in waking up mind, and pleasure to the learner from the conscious increase in apperceiving power.

2. *To Fix Knowledge : Retention by Repetition.*—The law of Retention is fundamental in all education ; it operates in the acquiring of any kind of manual dexterity, in forming labour-saving mental and physical habits, as well as in the higher forms of psychical development. It is the foundation of the Law of Repetition which is so important in the primary stage of education, and so useful in all stages. For example : A child, in imitation of his teacher, tentatively produces a certain articulate sound ; the approximately correct utterance makes clearer the idea of the sound; frequent repetition gives the power to make the sound *at will ;* on still further repetition there results ability to produce the sound without *effort, i.e.,* without the conscious intervention of the will. This illustration is typical of what takes place in all forms of physical and mental growth ; it shows how "doing" helps *knowing,* how "knowing" helps *doing,* and how both aid Retention, the process by which the material of instruction is wrought over into powers and capacities, tendencies and tastes.

Mental Activity to be Repeated.—The teacher should note that it is *mental activity in the act of apprehension* that is to be repeated, rather than the impression *on* the mind, which may be due to merely sensuous association, or rote learning. Even in what we have termed the mechanical stage, discipline is to be the aim, that is, there is to be suitable appeal to the opening intelligence. The law is, in brief, not impression and repetition of impression, but rather **Self-activity and Repetition of Self-activity.** Self-activity is to be awakened and guided chiefly by the method of Interrogation. The teacher makes a preparatory analysis of the subject ; he presents the results of this analysis point by point; by skilful questioning he guides the mind of the pupil in *discriminating* i.e., in working *analytically ;* he guides it in *identifying, i.e.,* in working *synthetically ;* he continues this method of education until an *analytic* (and synthetic) *habit* of mind is formed, and the pupil no longer needs the preparatory analysis and synthesis which it is the business of the teacher to supply.

In *perception*, the stage of intellectual development nearest to sensation, the child is to be guided in the formation of clear and adequate percepts of the objects presented ; the presentation and, therefore, the *re-*presentation, becomes clearer with each repetition, and the dim and vague mental outline with which the child started, grows into clear and definite idea.   So, if a pupil has been led to *apprehend the relation* of certain facts, and to think this relation again and again, the process fixes the thought in the mind, and gives increased power to deal with all similar relations.   Similarly with all forms of *reasoning,* or discourse.   A pupil has difficulty with an abstract argument, say the solution of a problem ; he is aided by judicious questioning to comprehend the logical connection of the several steps in the solution ; he repeats the reasoning for himself, re-thinks the relations—and at last, not only is the reasoned truth permanently retained, but there is also the beginning of a *habit* of logical reasoning.

Illustration.—By means of objects, a child forms a first intuition of the number *five ;* one presentation will not suffice, even if the objects are so arranged as to facilitate the mental act.   Herein, it may be observed, lies the source of many a sad mistake.   A teacher knows that there must be " objective teaching " in giving first lessons in numbers, but falls into the common error of assuming that because there are *concrete things* before the child there is *concrete knowledge* in the child's mind ; he forgets that the first idea is vague, indefinite ; that the mind must *act* on the material, and frequently repeat the act ; that the child must be made to *think* from the vague to the well-defined—the ' concrete ;' and, that the mental processes ought to be aided by proper presentation of objects.   For example, in teaching the number five, we do not begin with five dissimilar and unarranged objects ; this would be to commit two blunders.   We begin with *similar* objects, symmetrically arranged, as thus :

But even with this symmetrical number-form, one presentation is not enough.   On the basis of the several familiar forms, which the child has already learned, he must be questioned *through clear perceptions* into clear *conceptions*.   Every presentation becomes clearer until there results a definite idea of the number five, through a conscious recognition of its relations to the lower numbers.   Thus, in the foregoing number-form, the relations $5 = 4 + 1$, $5 - 1 = 4$,—*i.e.*, by questioning, $5 = 4 + ?$, $5 - 1 = ?$—can be presented in five different (though *related*) ways.   It seems plain that if the child, is led by clear intuitions to think the relations as presented in these number-forms, the " mental experiences " will blend into a lasting conception of the number.   Similarly, from the same number-form can be presented various intuitions of the relations $5 = 3 + 2$, $5 - 3 = 2$, *i.e.*, by questioning, $5 = 3 + ?$, $5 - 3 = ?$; $5 = 2 + 3$, $5 = 2 + ?$, etc., etc.   (See chap. on teaching arithmetic).

Again :   A boy will not at first clearly apprehend so simple a proposition as " Things which are equal to the same thing are equal to one another," much less will he draw the right conclusion from its application in a given case ; as *e.g.*, the line AB is equal to the line CD, the line EF is also equal to CD, therefore, *the lines are all equal to one another:* which is *not* the immediate inference.   From the conditions of a given arithmetical problem a pupil may discover the relations :

The selling price $= \frac{11}{10}$ of cost price.

The selling price $= \frac{9}{10}$ of cost price + \$20

And yet fail to see that the application of this axiom will at once give the answer. The pupil must be plied with many concrete examples, and he will have to be questioned and cross-questioned upon the principle and its applications, until he has acquired a clear apprehension of it, a *working* conception, which he can readily bring to bear in all cases in which it applies.

Once more ; when a child has fairly learned the number six, he will not, at first, solve off hand such a question as : If 2 apples cost 4 cents what will 3 apples cost ? Much less will he be able to comprehend its solution by the " Rule of Three," since the general idea of ratio and the complex idea of the equality of ratios, are quite beyond his grasp. But he *can be led* to solve the problem by taking its two steps, one at a time. By clear intuitions, he can be led first to *perceive*, and then to *conceive* that if 2 apples cost 4 cents, *one* apple will cost 2 cents ; and then by similar means, to see that if *one* apple cost 2 cents, 3 apples will cost 6 cents : As, *e.g.*

<pre>
Apple   • | • •   cents
Apple   • | • •   cents
</pre>

therefore *one* apple costs 2 cents ; etc. Thus forming clear perceptions from a few examples, he will quickly rise to a conception of such relations, and soon be able to solve similar problems without the aid of visible objects.

Relating Facts.—Not only is questioning the sure test of how the child's mind is dealing with the material, it is, as has been suggested, the best way to guide him in *relating the facts*. Though it is chiefly the mechanical aspect of association that comes into play in the primary stage of instruction, the main object, even here, is mental discipline, and, therefore a *rational* spirit must pervade the teaching. There can be, of course, no severe demand made upon rational comprehension, because this is only in the beginning of its development ; bnt facts can be presented in their proper relations — things can be associated by

the law of similiarity. It is by the *teacher's* preparatory analysis of the subject and by his judicious questioning, that the
child is brought to think *implicitly*, facts in *their relations*. He
does not grasp explicitly the underlying unity of the facts ; but
to some extent, related facts explain themselves (p. 83) ; and if
this *rationality of facts* has been carefully kept in mind by the
teacher during his Socratic lesson, there will be retention of the
facts in their relations, unconscious appropriation of their
rationality, which in good time will grow into conscious recognition of their logical connection.

Illustration.—If, for example, the facts of *six* have been
presented in clear intuitions **: : :** there will be a gradual, but
sure growth of clear *perceptions* into a conscious *thinking*
of the *relations* between 1 and 6, 2 and 6, etc.; 6 is 6 times 1, 1
is one-sixth of 6 ; 6 is three times 2 ; 2 is one-third of 6, etc.
Having learned thus much, he passes, easily (first by intuition,
of course) to the new facts : $6 + 2 = 8 = 4$ times 2, 2 is *one-
fourth* of 8, and so on, to 5 times 2, 6 times 2, etc. So, too, 6
$= two$ times 3 ; $9 = 6 + 3 = three$ times 3, 3 = one-third of 9,
and so on. That is, from the right presentation of objects,
the child forms clear perceptions which almost unconsciously
grow into a firm grasp of the relations of numbers in the Multiplication Table ; and thus, learning how to construct the table
for himself, he is not left to memorize it by *merely mechanical* associations. There must be repetition, of course ; the
table must be so thoroughly memorized that any pair of factors
instantly suggests the right product. But, if there are a few
repetitions of the *acts of apprehension* by which the several products are formed, the task of mastering the table will be im-
mensely lighter than if left to the symbol-memory alone.

Use and Abuse of Drill.—It is clear from the foregoing
considerations that *Repetition, Drill*, is necessary, for there is and
must be a mechanical side to education. Drill is necessary for

the formation of right habits, for the acquisition of skill in certain work in the primary stage of instruction, for the accumulation of the right experiences and the consequent development of mental and moral power in all stages ; but there is a point at which drill—repetition, ceases to be of any value for the growth of knowledge, or skill, or capacity, and becomes positively harmful. Unintelligent repetition cannot strengthen intelligence, ceaseless questioning on unimportant details, monotonous re-callings of mere sensuous associations, " thorough grinds " on what is already well known—destroy interest, which, as we have seen, is essential to *attention*, and so induce a habit of mind-wandering, the greatest foe that the educator has to confront. In primary schools, perhaps in all grades of schools, incalculable time is wasted in a repulsive monotony of drills. Dealing with the concrete as if the concrete were all in all—as if " from the concrete to the abstract " means to begin, continue and end with the concrete, is to ignore the fact that abstract thinking is the only true thinking, that the concrete is only means to end, and that so far as it delays the power to grasp the abstract, it defeats its end, hinders rather than helps psychical development.

The re-action against an imperfect method of instruction has led to the other extreme which is equally imperfect. Formerly children were rarely allowed to begin with the concrete. Now, the tendency is to keep them from rising higher than the concrete. It is, possibly, owing to this reign of the visible and tangible that so many teachers are deficient in power of abstraction and analysis. The trained mind of a trainer of minds surely ought to be able to see the fallacy in the inference, *some A's are not B's, therefore, some B's are not A's*, without the necessity of resorting to a concrete case, as, *e.g.*, some living things are not men, therefore, some men are not living things.

More than once we have found the majority of a large class hesitate to answer the question, *What is the A of the B whose A is C?* Before answering, most of them had to think of a particular case, as, *e.g.*, what is the length of a pole whose length is ten feet? *The power of abstract thinking may be taken as the measure of intellectual development.*

It ought perhaps to be mentioned that there is not unfrequently, excessive drill through a teacher's ability "to interest his class." But the thing is, not simply are the pupils interested, but are they interested in the main thought of the lesson? When pupils have been drilled on a lesson to the fatigue-point, or to the monotony-point, the teacher arouses the flagging attention by introducing an interesting "story," or illustration, in which the thought of the lesson is supposed to be repeated, and thus "more drill" secured. But the real interest is in the illustration and not in the thought it is supposed to illustrate. Children have been "drilled," say on the number *two*, ringing changes on one and one? nothing and two? two less one? two less two? till under the monotonous repetition interest and attention die out; but the teacher is for more drill, and so interesting stories, of which the heroes are *two* mice, or *two* cats, or *two* dogs, or *two* elephants, or *two* deinotheria. Undoubtedly there is *interest*, but it is not in the **two** ; it is in the mice, or the cats, or the elephants, or the deinotheria, and so there is no attention to the thought of the lesson, but amusement or excitement in the story. That sort of spurious attention is often seen even in advanced classes. College students sometimes miss the chief points of a lesson in chemistry through the brilliancy and variety of the experiments. It is possible to talk interestingly to a class without either conveying much information or developing much power—just as " A. Ward, the American humorist," interested many an intelligent audience by his lecture on The Babes in the Wood, while giving but little information about the " Babes."

Sense of Proportion.—In the right use of drill, therefore, the teacher should arrange his questions so as to have and to give due *Sense of Proportion, i.e.,* so as to repeat the great principles, leading thoughts, rather than subordinate details.　By the majority of teachers this important point is lost sight of.　In questioning, they make no distinction between the important and the unimportant, between the trivial points and prominent facts and their relations.　Lessons in reading, geography, history, are treated as if their value depended on the number of questions that can be asked upon them.　The child is questioned and re-questioned and cross-questioned, drilled and re-drilled to the very extreme of tediousness, sometimes on a lesson that is of little value as a whole, and sometimes on the equally unimportant details of a lesson in itself of value.　Take the following interesting lesson : " 'The rat sat on a mat, the cat ran to the mat, the rat ran into the box."　What are we to think of the model lesson that gives twenty-five or thirty questions on such stuff?　Or, of the mental condition of the " six years darling of a pygmy size " that is ruthlessly subjected to such an ordeal ?　What are we to think of a model lesson that gives three and a half pages of questions on seven and a half lines of an ordinary reading lesson ?　Suppose a child were to be subjected to such a " drill " on every fairy tale he reads, or every interesting story or biography, how long before fairy tale and story would become an utter abomination to him ?　Consider how a history lesson is ordinarily given ; note the infinitude of questions asked upon it, in utter disregard of the due proportion between the essential and the non-essential.　The inevitable result is that interest dies out, attention flags, and instead of assimilated knowledge and strengthened faculty, there is left a medley of vague notions and disconnected facts, whose only end is to be speedily forgotten, or to be reproduced in preposterous answers to (perhaps) equally preposterous examination questions.　By such excessive drill, the teacher makes himself a mere machine, and turns out mechanisms after his own likeness.

3. *To Extend, or Enlarge Knowledge.*—By questioning, vague ideas may be made definite, misapprehensions removed, and new knowledge imparted. It is a common maxim that nothing is to be told the learner that he is able to make out for himself. What he acquires by the exercise of his own powers will remain with him in more enlarged or more accurate knowledge, or at least in increased power of apperception. Of course, *Telling*, *Explanation*, and clear *Exposition*, are often needed. For, while it may be true that it is not so much what goes into a boy as what comes out of him that educates, it is equally true that nothing can be got out of him unless something is first put into him. It is almost a common-place that " Telling is not teaching." The truth of this depends on the mental attitude of the taught, and this again, depends chiefly on the kind of telling and the spirit and ability of the teller.

Telling ; Questioning.—Telling the right thing at the right time and in the right way, *is* teaching. Very often time is worse than wasted in a futile attempt to question out of a pupil what has never been questioned into him, and what he cannot by any possibility evolve from his " inner consciousness." It is one of the best characteristics of a good teacher that he knows exactly when and what to *tell*, as well as when and what to impart or to elicit by *questioning*. The " telling not teaching" maxim is thoroughly sound as a protest against the method of continuous lecturing. It is easy to lecture ; it is difficult to teach ; thus, many instructors are good lecturers but not good teachers. With clearness of thought and fluency of speech, they seem to expect that lucid exposition on the part of the teacher will prove an effective substitute for attention and self-activity on the part of the pupil. The lecturing method, the pouring in process, may have its place in the college lecture-room—though even there a little Socratic questioning now and then seems desirable—but the method is nearly worthless in the primary and the secondary school. The object lesson, the exposition, the demonstration, can be interpreted and assimilated only by what is already within the mind. This assimilating process—it cannot be too often repeated—is solely the learner's act and can never be dispensed with by even the most logical arrangement and lucid exposition on the part of teacher or text-book. But, as we have seen, the teacher may aid the learner's effort by presenting the new matter in its proper relations, and may lead him by questioning to see the old knowledge in clearer light, and to make for himself the mental connection between the new and the old.

Vague made Definite.—It has been said that the first ideas got by a child—no matter by what process of instruction—are necessarily hazy; his mental growth is from the vague to the definite by analysis and synthesis, either conscious or unconscious. And as these mental functions are undeveloped in the young learner, it is the business of the teacher to *guide* the learner's mind into analytic and synthetic working. Thus the vague is made definite, misapprehensions are corrected, and old knowledge is both clarified and enlarged by new growths of material with which it is rationally connected. If a pupil, by an erroneous answer, shows that he has not clearly grasped a thought, we do not forthwith tell him the correct answer. Guided by a few thoughtful questions he is made to discover the error and to think out the correct answer for himself.

Socratic Questioning.—The truth of his wrong answer assumed, he is led by Socratic questioning to a *reductio ad absurdum;* he then re-examines the argument; he discovers where the fallacy lies, whether in the premises, or in the conclusion; he makes the needed corrections; and thus, as an active co-worker in the process, he is sure to retain somewhat of real value, both in knowledge and mental discipline. The teacher must guard against the mistake of thinking that because he is using objects in teaching, the child's ideas cannot be hazy, and that clear talking will suffice. No matter how well a lesson may be given, no matter how skilfully the maxim "from concrete to abstract" may be applied, the careful teacher well knows that there are some points which are not clear to the learner; that, though there is a concrete *object* before the mind there is not concrete *knowledge* in the mind, and he will endeavour, by well prepared and connected questions, to make the knowledge broader and more definite.

Illustrations.—A pupil may have learned the definition of a straight line, for example, and repeated it again and again, and yet have a very inadequate idea of it. He has been told that a line has not breadth but "position only," yet he will retain a lurking suspicion that a thing which he has drawn from A to B, which he sees before his eyes, which he can blot out and replace, etc., must have *some* breadth. Besides, is he not distinctly told in Euclid I, ix, to describe an equilateral triangle on the side of DE (a line) "*remote* from A?" If he thinks at all, he is somewhat perplexed by this "remote" side.

An examiner testing a class on this proposition and suspecting that some of the class had but crude ideas of "straight line," "remote side," etc., put a few questions: Has DE, then, *two* sides? *It has.* On which side is the equilateral triangle to be described? *It is to be described on the side remote from A.* If one side of DE is *remote* from A, what may you say about the other side? *It is near or next to A.* Then, how much further from A is the *remote* side than the *near* side? *It depends on the width of the line!* This was the answer of an eager but perfectly sincere member of the class, and two or three others were quite ready to agree with him. It is not improbable that scores of pupils who have crossed the "Pons" in triumph, have very misty notions concerning the meaning and reason of construction in this proposition.

It is not, then, the mark of a cautious teacher to assume that even axioms and definitions are on their first presentation, clear to the minds of beginners. By examination and cross-examination they are to be guided in thinking till their vague outlines become clear and adequate conceptions. Many a beginner in geometry has very vague notions of the definitions and axioms that fall so glibly from his lips. Some have been known to affirm that when three lines AD, BD, CD meet in D, only two angles are formed; others have stoutly maintained that if the angle A D B be taken away, only the *line* CD will remain. Not a few imagine for a long time that the *base* of a triangle is necessarily the *horizontal* side,—the side parallel to the bot·tom of the page—, and are not a little perplexed on finding that another side (any side) may be the base, as in *e. g.* the figure of Euclid I, vi. A little thoughtful questioning would give pupils clearer ideas of *triangle, base, vertical angle,* "the other two sides," etc. The teacher cannot be too often reminded that the object before the mind does not ensure *concrete* knowledge; that first ideas are necessarily vague, that objects are used to aid teacher and pupil in *making* knowledge concrete.

Further Illustrations.—It may, therefore, be laid down as a safe rule that all imperfect mental products should be corrected by the pupil himself with a minimum of help from the teacher. Ideas obscure at first, remain obscure unless there is a growth into clearness by exercise of the mental functions by which they were apprehended, and by which they may be at once extended and defined. A pupil may have been taught the parts of speech, and the doctrine of grammatical equivalency; he will have to apply his knowledge many times before he apprehends it in its fullness. He must himself correct his imperfect thinkings on a given topic till he reaches perfect thought. Take the sentence " The charge is too trifling to be confuted, and deserves to be mentioned only that it may be despised : "

A pupil may have had a good deal of drilling on the parts of speech, and yet fail to see the force of " only " in this sentence. He will probably parse it as an " adverb " modifying *mentioned,* because that is the nearest verb. He should be led by questioning to correct his thinking till he reaches the truth :

What is only? *It is an adverb modifying mentioned.* What does *only* mean? *It means this one thing and nothing more.* But does the speaker mean that the charge deserves to be *only* mentioned, *i.e.,* that the bare mention of it would lead to its being despised? *No, that is not the meaning.* If that were the meaning where should *only* be placed? *It should be placed before the verb mentioned.* Well, what is only? *It is an adverb modifying despised.* Is the meaning, then, that the charge should be despised and nothing more? *That is not the meaning.* Omitting *only,* what have we? The *charge deserves to be mentioned that it may be despised.* Does the charge deserve to be mentioned? *It does.* For what reason, or purpose? *That it may be despised.* Is there any other reason? *There is no other reason.* How do you learn that? *From the word "only."* Then what is the part of *only* in the sentence? It affects the meaning *of the clause, " That it may be despised."*

Again, a pupil is asked to parse *but* in the line : "The paths of glory lead but to the grave." Reflecting for a moment, he concludes that *but* here is equivalant to *only,* and is probably an adverb, that adverbs modify verbs, and *but,* therefore, modifies the verb *lead.* Now, the careless teacher will pronounce the answer wrong, give the correction, and pass on without further concern, and his " teaching," for any lasting effect it can have on the minds of the learners, might as well be addressed to the idle winds. But a few questions will enable the pupil to correct his own errors, and not only does he firmly hold what he has thought out for himself, he has also increased mental power in the act of thinking.

For example : " But means only, and is an adverb modifying *lead.*" Well, what does *only* mean? It *means this one thing, and no other.* Does the poet mean, then, that the *paths lead* and *only,* that is, do nothing more than *lead* to the grave? *That* is *not his meaning.* Well, leave out *but,* and what results. The *paths* .... lead *whither? The paths of glory lead to the grave.* Consider whether there is any other termination? *There is no other destination.* How do you gather this from the line? *We gather it from the word " but,"* Then, what word or words does *but* affect? *It affects the meaning of the words, " to the grave."* And, grammatically, what is the phrase to the grave? *It is an adverbial phrase modifying leads ;* etc.

An Example from Arithmetic.—Owing to imperfect teaching many pupils who have "gone over" square measure have but misty notions of what is really done in finding the area of a rectangle. Propose to a class *e. g.*, to find the area of a rectangle 5 ft. long by 3 ft. wide, and ask a few questions on the work and its result :

What answer have you got? *Fifteen feet.* Does that answer need any correction? *Yes, it should be fifteen square feet.* How has the answer been obtained? *By multiplying 5 feet, the length, by 3, the breadth.* What quantity does 5 represent? *It represents 5 linear feet.* Many of the class will give this answer, for the word *length* is prominent in the "rule," and by repetition of the rule, their minds have become possessed by the idea of *length.* Now, the thoughtless teacher, on getting such an answer, will simply give the correct answer and pass on to something else, and so the pupils who gave the wrong answer have done *no thinking* in this correction of errors — have *apperceived* nothing—and of course will *retain* nothing. The careful teacher, by a few Socratic questions, will lead the erring minds to make the corrections for themselves. He gets them to recall the ideas that multiplication is only a short way of doing addition where all the addends are equal, that the multiplier as representing simply *how many* addends there are, is an "abstract" number, etc. He draws a figure on the board representing the rectangle whose area is to be found, performs the usual operation using say 5 for multiplicand, and 3 for multiplier. Then :

What quantity does this 5 represent? *Five linear feet.* What has been done with this ? *It has been multiplied by three.* What is the result ? *Fifteen "linear" feet*, say some. *No, fifteen square feet*, say others who having the trusty eye on the 15 square feet are determined to stick to the right conclusion in spite of their false premises. The teacher shows these close observers that it is not permitted to play such fantastics tricks with quantities—that having started with *linear* feet in the operation, with *linear* feet they must end. What have we done? *Multiplied 5 linear feet by 3, thus,* 5 × 3 = 15. Can the result be got in another way? *Yes, by addition, taking 5 three times as an addend, thus 5ft. + 5ft. + 5ft. = 15ft.* Does this operation work any change on the quantity which 5 represents? *It makes no change.* Then what is the sum of 5cts + cts + 5cts? *Fifteen cents.* And of 5 linear ft. + 5 linear ft. + 5 linear ft. *Fifteen linear feet.* But what is the area? *Fifteen square feet.* And so, by a few similar questions, they are led to see that the 5 of the multiplicand represents not 5 linear units making up the line A B, say, but the five square feet making up the first of the three equal rectangles which form the given rectangle.

Imparting new Knowledge.—By questioning not only is the vague made definite and misconceptions corrected, but also new knowledge is acquired and assimilated with the old. By the principles of the synthetic method (p. 173) ideas are connected into groups, and these groups are used to interpret and assimilate new groups. Old knowledge is to be brought into vital connection with new facts; and this vital union at the same time gives meaning to the new and strengthens and enlarges the old. To this end the analytic-synthetic method is employed under the form of interrogation; in *all stages* of learning the pupil should be trained in self-activity, *i.e.*, in self-education. Even in primary reading, for example, he has to do something for himself. Given the sounds of a few letters to start with, the pupil can almost independently discover the sounds of many others.

Having been taught to give sounds of *a* and *t*, and to form the word *at*, he may discover the sounds of b, c, f, h, etc. For instance, the picture of *a cat* is before him and he pronounces the word *cat*; the word is then written on the board; the pupil recognizes the familiar part *at*, and recalls its sound; he discriminates the forms of *at* and *cat*, and their *sounds*, and thus, with a few repetitions, gains a *definite* idea of the sound of *c*, as well as power to produce it ; and so on, with other letters, *b*, *f*, *h*, *m*, etc., as illustrated in the chapter on phonic reading. When he has learned to pronounce the three-letter words, of which *at* forms a part, he will quickly learn to pronounce when written, and to write when pronounced, all the new words which can be formed with the letters now familiar to him ; as, *e.g.*, pronounce *cab*, *can*, etc., and he will write them, or point them out on chart, etc.; or write *sap*, *man*, etc., and he will pronounce them. In all this, questioning directs him in identifying and discovering.

Even in the simple matter of naming numbers, the pupil's self-activity may be engaged ; for example, he is taught that the number made up of 3 and 10 (3 + 10) is named *thirteen* (three-teen), and of 4 and ten, *fourteen*. Then, name the number composed of 5 and 10 ? 6 and 10 ? etc. What then, does *teen* mean ? And, similarly, a number composed of two tens is named twenty (twain-ty = two-ty), of three tens, thirty (= three-ty) : name, then, the number made up of 4 tens ? of 5 tens ? etc. What then does *ty* mean ? So, in notation, when a pupil has learned through *intuitive* teaching, the relation between the tens and the units, and also the significance of the symbols 0, 1, 2, 3, etc., it is only necessary to tell him that *one* ten and *no* units is represented by 10, to enable him to infer the notation of *(a)* *two* tens and *no* units, *three* tens and *no* units, etc.; *(b) one* ten and *one* unit, *one* ten and *two* units, etc.; *(c) two* tens and *one* unit, *two* tens and *two* units, etc. (See chapter on Teaching Arithmetic.)

Illustrations.—(1) We give a few examples from actual work in the school-room.

When taught primary arithmetic by the intuitive method— especially from the graphic number-forms—the child, very early in his course, gains the idea of *division of a number into equal*

parts, which is, of course, the fundamental idea of fractions.
And by first using whole numbers in applying this idea, he will
have no great difficulty in mastering the principles and rules of
the Arithmetic of Fractions   For example :

Divide 2, 4, 6, 8, etc., by 2 ?
"   3. 6, 9, 12, etc., by 3 ?
"   4, 8, 12, 16, etc., by 4 ?
etc., etc.

Now take the *half* of 2, 4, 6, etc. ?
"   "   *third* of 3, 6, 9, etc. ?
"   "   *fourth* of 4, 8, 12, etc. ?

Here, to enable him to pass from the old to the new, it will
be only necessary to tell him that *to divide a number by* 2, is to
take the *half* of it ; to divide a number by 3, is to take the
third of it, etc., *i.e.*, that there is a change of *language* but no
change of idea. It may not, indeed, be always necessary to
make even this explanation. For instance :

An inspector was giving a lesson introductory to fractions,
according to the foregoing plan. He found, at the beginning
of the lesson, that the children did not know how to take the
half, the third, etc., of a number. He put a series of questions
in division, which all were able to answer : Divide 6 by 3 ?
9 by 3 ? 12 by 3 ? etc. And then, *without any explanation*,
asked a bright little fellow: what is the third of 6? After a
moment's thought the child replied *two ;* and then answered
without the slightest hesitation, the questions : one-third of 9 ?
one-third of 12 ? etc., and one-fourth of 4? of 8 ? of 12 ? etc.
The other members of the class soon caught the clew, and answered similar questions with equal readiness. The inspector
then asked the leader in this process of discovery and identification : How did you find out what I meant by the question,
what is *one-third* of 6 ? He replied, " *There are three two's in
six, and I thought you meant one of them.*"

At the end of the lesson, the class were able to answer such
questions as these : How do you find the half of a number?

The third?   The fourth?......The *n*-th?   How many *halves* has a number?   How many thirds? How many fourths...... how many *n*-ths? What is one-third of 6? *two*-thirds? *three*-thirds?   What is *one*-fourth of 8? *two*-fourths? *three*-fourths? *four*-fourths?   *One*-third of a number is 4, what is the number? *One*-fourth of a number is 5, what is the number? etc., etc. And the brighter ones of the class answered such questions as the following : *Two*-thirds of a number is 6, what is the number? *Three*-fourths of a number is 9, what is the number? etc.

(2.) Solution of Problems.— An army loses 10 per cent. of its numbers in its first battle, and 10 per cent. of the remainder in the second battle, and then had 16,200 men left ; how many men composed the army at first ?

What part of a number is 10 per cent. of it ? *One-tenth.* One-tenth of the army is lost, what part remains ? *Nine-tenths of it.*   One-tenth of this remainder is lost what part of it remains? *Nine-tenths of it.*   What part of the whole army now remains ?

$$\tfrac{9}{10} \text{ of } \tfrac{9}{10} \text{ or } \tfrac{81}{100}.$$

If 81 hundredths of the army $= 16,200$ men, what is one-hundredth ? *200 men.*

Then what number in the entire army ?

100 times 200 men *i. e.*, 20,000 men.

I sold a horse so as to gain 10 per cent.; had the horse cost $36 more, there would have been, at the same selling price, a loss of 10 per cent. Find the actual cost of the horse.

How many cost prices are mentioned ?
Two, the actual cost price, and a supposed cost.
What is the difference between these ? *$36.*
How many selling prices ? *One selling price.*
What part of a number is 10 per cent. of it ? *One-tenth.*
What relation between the selling price and the actual cost ?
Selling price $= \tfrac{11}{10}$ *actual cost.*

And also between selling price and supposed cost?

Selling price $= \frac{9}{10}$ supposed cost.

What inference from these relations? *No answer.*

$$\left.\begin{array}{l}\text{Well if } A = B \\ \text{and} \quad\; A = C\end{array}\right\} \text{ What inference?}$$

Answer, $B = C$.

State the axiom by which this is inferred?

Things which are *equal to the same thing are equal to each other.*

Then, what inference from the relations between the two cost prices?

$$\tfrac{9}{10} \text{ of supposed cost} = \tfrac{11}{10} \text{ actual cost}$$

Therefore?

Supposed cost $= \frac{11}{10} \div \frac{9}{10} = \frac{11}{9} = 1\frac{2}{9}$ of actual cost.

From this, what is the difference between the two costs?

The *difference* is $\frac{2}{9}$ of actual cost.

Complete the solution?

The difference is given $= \$36$.

$\therefore \frac{2}{9}$ *actual cost* $= \$36$, $\frac{1}{9} = \$18$, and *entire cost* $\$162$.

(3.) **Algebraic Example, Socratic Questioning.**—In the expression $a^2b^2 + b^2c^2 + c^2a^2$. What letters are involved? a,b,c. How are they involved? They are involved *symmetrically.* Taking the square root of each term separately, what do you get? $ab+bc+ca$. Is this result the square root of the given expression? *It is not.* If for a,b,c, I substitute respectively d,e,f, or p,q,r, or x,y,z, etc., will it make any difference in your argument? *It will make no difference.* If for a,b,c, there be substituted $a+b$, $b+c$, $c+a$, or $p-q$, $r-s$, $t-u$, will your answer still be valid? *It will.* When any quantities are substituted for a,b,c, does your argument still hold? *It does.* Is the expression :

$$(x-y)^2 (y-z)^2 + (y-z)^2 (z-x)^2 + (z-x)^2 (x-y)^2,$$

similar to the given expression? *It is ; for a,b,c have been substituted respectively $x-y$, $y-z$, $z-x$.* Now, taking the square root of each term separately, what do you get?

$$(x-y)(y-z) + (y-z)(z-x) + (z-x)(x-y).$$

Compare the result with $ab+bc+ca$. *They are, of course, similarly formed.* Is $ab+bc+ca$ the square root of $a^2b^2 +$ etc.? *It is not.* Then is $(x-y)(y-z)+$ etc. the square root of $(x-y)^2 (y-z)^2 +$ etc.? *It is not.*

But, said the teacher, **It is the square root of it.**

At this declaration the class were greatly astonished. What was wrong in the reasoning? Their curiosity was thoroughly aroused. They examined the reasoning again and again ; there was a general marshalling of all the ideas bearing on the matter, there was in a word, some close thinking done, before the fallacy was discovered. It would have been hard to convince that class, that Mathematical reasoning "condemns to a minimum of thought ; " that it is impossible to err in mathematical reasoning "because mathematical principles are self-evident, and the successive steps of the reasoning are equally self-evident."

(4.) Socratic Questioning, Positive—The following is an example of the positive extension of knowledge by questioning.   A class had been led to discover the two rational factors of

$$a^3 + b^3 + c^3 - 3\,abc,$$

and were now to apply the result to the resolution of certain similar forms, The teacher *told nothing*.

What about the symmetry of this question? *It is symmetrical in* $+a$, $+b$. $+c$. What is its linear factor? $a+b+c$. Its quadratic factor ?

$$a^2 + b^2 + c^2 - ab - bc - ca,$$

which can be put into the form $\frac{1}{2}[(a-b)^2 + (b-c)^2 + (c-a)^2]$.   Now let us consider the expression :

$$a^3 + b^3 - c^3 + 3abc\dots\dots\dots\dots\dots\dots\dots\dots(\text{I}).$$

With respect to what quantities is *this* symmetrical ? *No correct answer*. How may this be *derived* from the expression already factored ? *No correct answer*.   The teacher then proceeded to give a few questions leading up to the unanswered question.

How may $a+c$ be got from $a+b$?

A *few* answer correctly, others incorrectly.

What shall we do with $a+b$ in order to get a?

Take away $+b$.

What shall we do with a to get $a+c$?

Add $+c$.

Then how is $a+b$ changed into $a+c$?

By taking away $+b$ *and adding* $+c$, that is by *substituting* $+c$ *for* $+b$.

How shall $a+b$ be changed into $a-b$?

By substituting $-b$ for $+b$.

How shall $a^3 + b^3$ be changed into $a^3 - b^3$?

By substituting $-b$ for $+b$.

Now what is the relation of form (I) to the *primitive* form ?

It is derived from the primitive by substituting $-c$ *for* $+c$.

State, then, how form (I) differs from the primitive?

It differs only in having $-c$ *for* $+c$.

Well, we proved certain facts in the primitive form, what can you infer as to the corresponding facts in form (1)?

They can be got from the facts of the primitive by substituting —c for +c.

Then what is the linear factor in form (1)?

$a + b - c$.

The quadratic factor?

$a^2 + b^2 + c^2 - ab + bc + ca$, etc.

How may *other* forms similar to form (1) be derived from the primitive?

By substituting —b for +b we get a second form, and by substituting —a for +a we get a third form.

Give the factors of these two forms?

For the first case we have:

$a - b + c$ and $a^2 + b^2 + c^2 + ab + bc - ca$.

And for the second case:

$-a + b + c$ and $a^2 + b^2 + c^2 + ab - bc + ca$.

Can you suggest how *other* forms may be derived from the primitive?

For +b and +c, substitute —b and —c respectively.

What is the result?

$a^3 - b^3 - c^3 - 3abc$. The factors? $a - b - c$ and $a + b^2 + c^2 + ab - bc + ca$.

May other forms like this be derived from the primitive?

Yes, by substituting for +c +a, and again for +a +b.

And so at the conclusion of the lesson—which lasted about 20 minutes—the class were able, without a moment's hesitation, to write down the six derived forms and their pairs of factors.

4. *To Cultivate Power of Expression; Effect on Apperception and Retention.*—As intimated, this purpose of questioning pertains equally to the Testing of Retention and the Training of Apperception. In fact, it is on account of the powerful effect which the cultivation of expression has upon the fundamental processes of mind, that it is given a separate place among our Purposes of Questioning. The thought is: because words and the right use of words are *necessary* to both Apperception and Retention, therefore, the training of the language-power ought to be a prominent aim in all instruction.

Belittling Words.—In the re-action against mere rote-learning, there is a strong tendency to belittle words. " Words, words, empty words, teach things not words," is the cry. Doubtless the old plan was wrong, the plan of filling the memory with words and making little or no appeal to the intelligence.   The plan is very old, as old as education itself; for it is an easy plan, easy for the pupil, easy for the teacher.   The mind of childhood as we have seen, is exceedingly open to sensuous associations ; it can memorize words by connecting their successive sounds, with but little attention to their meaning.   But it is the work of the teacher to check, or to rather properly direct this tendency. He must see, indeed, that the child does not *simply* form a series of auditory sensations ; but equally it is his duty to see that this ready receptivity of the senses shall be employed in form- ing connections of ideas.   How is this to be done ?   Not by teaching words alone, nor things alone, but by teaching words and things, by making ideas of things clear and definite and this by fixing and defining them in words.   While, therefore, the teacher must be on his guard against teaching empty words, he must be equally on his guard against imparting empty ideas ; for if the word without the idea is empty, the idea without the word is little better than an airy nothing without a local habi- tation and a name.

Relation of Words and Ideas to Knowledge.— " The learner's knowledge," says an English writer, " consists in *ideas* gained from objects and facts by his own powers, and consciously possessed—not in words.   The words without the ideas are not knowledge to him."   This is but a partial truth. The learner's knowledge, if it is worthy of the name, if it is part of an organized structure, if its up-building has had any effect in organizing faculty, does *not* consist only in such ideas.   It con- sists in such ideas *made clearer, made more definite, made more comprehensive,* and *finally made incarnate in words.*   It is quite true that if a child were to memorize a series of words by merely connecting their sound-sensations, making the connec- tions absolutely without reference to meaning, the words would not be knowledge to him.   But it is equally certain that with- out words, or symbols of some sort, he would not be able to weld his sense-impressions into definite and permanent forms, and that such wordless mental experiences would not be knowledge in any true sense of the word. The truth appears to be that neither ideas alone (if there are such things that are of any worth) nor words alone, constitute knowledge, but ideas embodied in words ; and that this act of embodiment is a factor in the finished thought, and is an essential part of the process of organizing mental faculty by organizing knowledge. Let the teacher remember that, even in the primary stage, " to learn the name of a thing, and to learn how to use this name, involves much more mental action than is required in forming sense-peceptions about it."

Words and Clear Thinking.—Words, then, are not only the instruments for the expression of thought, they are also the instruments of the thinking process itself, Human speech is the complement of human reason, the gift without which reason would not be, and could not be what it is. Words are at once the test and the condition of the cultivation of reason, that is, there can be no thinking—deserving of the name— without words, and no explicit proof.that the thinking process is going on, unless its products are objectified in words. For the teacher, at least, the only proof of thinking on the part of the pupil, is expression, oral and written; and of clear thinking, is clear expression, oral and written. Definite thought means definite expression. Vague expression means equally vague thought. **No act of thinking is complete till its products have been set forth in words.** And the manner in which this is done marks the character of the thinking and the effectiveness of the teaching.

Thought Lessons are Language Lessons.—It follows that *every lesson should be a lesson in language.* It should be a lesson in language because it is a lesson in thought, and only so far as it is a language lesson is it an effective thought lesson. Every lesson, in all stages of learning, is given to awaken the self-activity of the child, to cause thinking. It is only by questioning that we can determine the matter and manner of his thinking; it is only by questioning that we can determine whether the final step in the thinking process has been taken, since this step is the act of expression itself. If we are giving a simple object-lesson for the exercise of perception, we know that the child has got the idea, and completed his act of thinking, when he has the right word for the idea, and can use it properly and promptly. If we give a lesson which demands the thinking of relations we know that the act of thought has been performed when it is expressed in definite propositions. So, in all the stages of intellectual development, the character of the mental product is shown in the character of the expression which we are able to elicit by the Socratic art.

We have already seen that clear Apprehension is necessary to Retention, and that clear expression is necessary to clear apprehension. The teacher must insist on ready and accurate utterance of the thoughts the lesson is intended to convey. If a pupil is unable to express the results of his thinking in any lesson, the teacher may be sure that they have not taken definite shape in his mind. The teacher must not be deceived by the earnest plea, "I know, but I cannot tell." This means nothing except, perhaps, that the mind is vaguely conscious of working towards more clearly defined thoughts. The thought-elements, mental nebulæ, are there, but the unifying and discriminating laws of Intelligence are to act still further, before distinct and finished forms appear. *Let the thing be clearly seen*, says Horace, *and the willing words will follow.*

Interaction between Thought and Expression.— From the relation between thought and language it may be laid down as a sound principle that direct and clear expression is preceded by clear thinking, and that the effort to speak with directness and precision reacts on the thinking process and contributes to clearness of thought. A maxim akin to that concerning Doing and Knowing finds place here. As knowing aids doing (page 182) and doing re-acts on knowing, so thinking aids speaking, and speaking re-acts on thinking. A man— much less a child hardly knows what his thought really is, till he has given form to it, *i.e.*, till he has clothed it in spoken or in written words. Everyone knows how thought grows in clearness with each attempt to clothe it in words.

The trained master of thought and speech clothes his thoughts at once in perfect language ; the word-embodied thought is a pure mental product, and it comes forth, whether in oral or in written speech, a thing of strength and beauty. But the immature mind of the learner is far below such power of thought and speech. A thought, as it first appears in his mind, is vague, and, in its expressed form, it bears the marks of this vagueness. But it is now before him in audible and in visible form ; this objectified thought is something that he can, as it were, study as an object. Guided by the judicious questioning of his teacher, and aided by the visible (or audible) form before him, he turns the thought over and over in his mind, each successive mental act being aided by the verbal expression of the preceding one—till at last the thought, as well as the expression of it, is as perfect as he can make it. The undoubted educational procedure, therefore, is : **First the Thought, then the Oral Expression of the thought, then the Written Expression of it.** Thus the interaction between thought and expression will finally result in the best expression of the best thought possible to the mind in its presumed stage of growth.

Questioning Best for Language.—From what has been said, the value of Interrogation as compared with continuous Explanation is manifest. A prevailing fault in primary and secondary schools is that the teacher talks too much and the pupil too little.   It is easier for the teacher to think and talk than to get his pupils to think and talk.   And it is a common error to suppose that clear thinking and expression on the part of the teacher, ensure clear thought and *ability* to express the thought, on the part of the pupil.   But only the pupil's self-activity educates, and speech, oral and written, is a necessary condition of self-activity.   The value of any lesson may be determined, therefore, by the amount of correct expression that it has called forth, and by this alone.   A lesson in which the teacher has done all the talking is nearly worthless.   A lesson during which the class have been questioned into clear and direct expression, and which ends with reducing to written forms the best that has been thought and said, is of permanent value, because it enlarges knowledge and strengthens and develops faculty.

Course to be followed.—What course, then, does the wise teacher follow?   As far as possible, in all stages of learning, he makes every lesson a lesson in correct expression.   By clear and correct language in his explanations and suggestions, and by clearly and definitely expressed questions, he stimulates the pupil to a similar clearness and distinctness of thought and speech.   At the beginning of the lesson he has the pupils correctly express the groups of ideas bearing upon the subject-matter of the new lesson.   In every imperfect sentence he sees the outward form of imperfect thought, and with an apt suggestion or a brief but lucid explanation, he questions the class into clear and well-defined thought clothed in chosen words.   He detects at once where mere verbal memory is at work in rule or formula, or reproduced expression, and questions and cross-questions the reciter till his empty words are filled with solid and connected thoughts.   Point by point he presents his matter logically arranged to suit the pupil's stage of development, and questions into a clear comprehension and a clear expression of the several parts. Concluding the lesson, he insists on a connected summary, and what was grasped and expressed in isolated sentences, is now reproduced in connected form; the ease and accuracy with which this is done being the test and measure of the thoroughness of the instruction and of its value in discipline. Finally, since it is impossible with large classes to give the necessary time to each member for the training of expression, he finds occasion as soon as possible after the lesson, for the written reproduction in improved form of all that had been thought and said.

If such a course as this is followed—and it can be followed in all stages, from the primary class that studies a lesson in a mere picture, to the advanced class that studies an important point in the philosophy of history, there will not be much need of desultory language lessons, and there will be undoubted growth of organized capacities and of organized knowledge.

Illustrations.—The rule to be followed is: in *all* classes, from the lowest primary to thehighest class, no thought without expression. If a child has had a lesson in which an idea has been developed, as that of an angle, or of the color violet, or of weight, the idea has not been clearly grasped, the lesson is incomplete, unless the word and the idea are so closely associated that the one instantly recalls the other. If an easy thought has been acquired, as that a cube has six faces, the prompt oral and written expression of the thought is the proof of the value of the lesson. If by the use of objects and practical examples, the facts about the number *four* have been taught and learned, there must be facility in expressing the facts, and ability to use them in making and rightly expressing applied examples; as *e. g.* three and one are four, four less one is three, etc.; Charlie has four cents, if he gives Susie one, and spends one for a pencil, how many has he left? Suppose a lesson on the text,

> *Politeness is to do and say*
> *The kindest thing in the kindest way:*

The children are led to a fair appreciation of this by an appeal
to experiences, perhaps incidents of the school-room or of the
play-ground; the kind thing done in the kind way, the kind
thing said in the kind way, are illustrated in the *concrete*—the
value of the lesson depends on the exact oral or written expression of what has been developed. A class has been led to
discover certain facts about water; water is a fluid, presses
equally in all directions, expands under certain circumstanees,
etc.; the lesson is not complete till the fragmentary thoughts
and expressions have been woven into connected oral and
written form.

From a primary lesson given on an angle, to a lesson on an
ode of Horace or a chorus of Aeschylus—wherever any instruction is given to strengthen the intellect or touch the heart,
the end is truly reached only when all that *can* be expressed is
reproduced in strong and beautiful speech.

More than half the value of classical study in the schools is
lost through inattention to this imperative law: *Train power
and skill through proper expression.* Too often teachers are
satisfied with the crude fragments of speech *disjecta membra*—
which are the product of the baldest construing. We have
known students to express surprise that Demosthenes is considered the greatest of orators; they had done much construing,
had done much of the author's work into a kind of English; his
thoughts but dimly seen, were hustled into the first clumsy garb
that offered from their meagre vocabulary; they had never
rendered a solitary paragraph from the majestic Greek into
the equally majestic English. What is the worth of such training either for enlarging knowledge or developing power?

Thus, too, many a student has read Horace, if we may be
pardoned the perversion of language, without ever having
caught a note of his lyric music. To such unfortunates, even if

the intellect fairly grasped the meaning of what they had read.
the words of Byron may well be applied :

> It is a curse
> To understand, not feel, his lyric flow,
> To comprehend, yet never love, his verse.

Of course there must be grammatical construing ; by fragments
of thought and language, students must be questioned till the
meaning is fairly apprehended; but we need not begin, continue
and end in vague thoughts, and scrappy sentences. Take the
lines of Horace

> Nequicquam deus abscidit
> Prudens Oceano dissociabili
> Terras, etc.

The thought is clear, the grammar is simple ; there could not well
be an easier piece of construing. Where then is the value of the
lesson ? It consists in *rendering the thought into the best English possible by the combined efforts of teacher and learner.* If,
patching together the fragments with which he began, the student ends with " the prudent god has cut off lands in vain by
the unsociable sea," the lesson is all but worthless. But the
work may be made of lasting value, if he be questioned and
cross-questioned on the poetic adequacy of different words, till
by the united effort of master and scholar, something approach-
ing Conington's fine lines is reached :

> Heaven's high providence in vain
> Has severed countries with the estranging main.

CHAPTER X.

METHOD OF INTERROGATION.—*Continued.*

Having studied the purposes of Questioning as concerned with the Testing of Retention, we shall now consider such purposes as more immediately relate to the Training of Apperception.

(b) Training of Apperception: Preparation of Mind.

Since the two processes are correlative, much of what has been said, under the first division of the subject, applies with equal force to the training of apperception, which we shall, therefore, study more briefly. The purposes to be studied under this head are: (1) To Excite Interest; (2) To Arouse Attention; (3) To Direct Attention; (4) To Cultivate the Habit of Self-Questioning.

1. *To Excite Interest.*—We have seen (page 164) that instruction must be based on the interest of the pupil. This principle is co-extensive with the whole of education. What the mind is interested in it will attend to, *i.e.*, it will exercise its activity upon it; what the mind is not interested in, has for it practically no existence. There may be interest in the mental activity itself, in the object upon which it works, in the end which it is desired to reach, and interest may be excited through personal or rational motives. All instruction is an appeal to some activity, and if this activity is free and unimpeded, it is naturally pleasureable. In the child, mental movement is as spontaneous as physical movement, and under right conditions, both ought to be equally a source of delight. It is the function of the teacher to appeal to these spontaneous activities so as to increase rather than diminish the pleasure

naturally arising from them. We may briefly consider how this free activity may be properly controlled and stimulated.

Clear Presentation, *and Interest.—In the first place:* by well-arranged and connected questions the matter may be presented to the pupil's mind in a way best suited to his capacities and attainments. In the course of questioning, the teacher is in continuous contact with the child's mind, and, therefore, he is less likely to present either too difficult or too easy stimulus. Questioned on properly arranged matter, the learner is led to make acquisitions for himself. His progress is one of invention and discovery ; his curiosity is kept on the alert ; he unexpectedly perceives the old in the new, he *identifies ;*—what was dim and obscure to him he gradually works into a luminous thought, he *discriminates ;* he pursues, in short, a method of investigation differing only in degree from that of the greatest thinkers and discoverers in philosophy and science, and feels the tonic thrill of healthful mental life. Thus, there is produced the *self-activity* which disposes to more strenuous effort, **and de-**velops self-reliance and a spirit of investigation.

The Clear Teacher.—On the importance of clear teaching we may quote from Arthur Sedgwick's admirable lecture on " Stimulus : "

For making boys think as opposed to merely cramming them, though there may be higher qualities, there are few more important than clearness. It may seem at first sight as if it was easy to be clear in teaching ; in fact there are few things that want more constant attention, and even preparation. To make his own words precise and clear-cut ; to put complicated things in lucid order and simple language : to search out for the point and emphasize that duly : to avoid formulæ as much as may be, and constantly to formulate afresh when the boys begin to use words by rote ; when there are difficulties, to shew exactly where the difficulties are : to lead on confused answers till the confusion, and the exact point of the confusion, become apparent : to cross-question neatly and succintly half knowledge, so as at once to expose its incompleteness and supply the deficiency ; to define exactly in a muddled head what is the particular tangle that has caused the

P

muddle : these are some of the marks of the really clear teacher, aud such clearness is **excessively** stimulating.

Sense of Power, *and Interest.—In the second place :* The clear presentation of material properly arranged for the learner's stage of intellectual growth, helps to develop this *sense of power*, of ability to grapple with difficulties which is one of the most potent allies of the teacher (p. 116). In this consists one of the best results of the Socratic art. Where there is much lecturing by the teacher, there is little real thinking by the pupil. He comes to feel that he is a mere spectator in a work in which the lecturer is the all-important factor. But, attacking difficulties as presented in thoughtful questions, he masters them one by one, and each successful effort brings a glow of satisfaction and a sense of growing power. Inspire a boy with confidence in his ability to do a thing, and the thing is already half done ; all his energies will be aroused to action ; all his ideas bearing on the subject will be brought to the front, and used by the quickened mind in assimilating the new material. To know when to tell, and when not to tell, to evoke the maximum of energy with the minimum of telling, is the mark of a teacher as compared with a mere expositor. There is, in general, too much talking by the teacher, and too little talking and thinking by the learner. This is, no doubt, partly due to defective teaching ; many teachers have neither the literary nor professional training to enable them to make the best of very imperfect conditions. But, it is also partly due to popular ignorance of the nature of education, which demands of the teacher more than he can possibly accomplish, and almost forces him to follow the expository method in the vain hope that what is clearly explained will be learned with the best educative results.

Time a Factor in Culture.—It is forgotten that time is a necessary factor in education which is an organic growth, the growing organism being a living soul in union with a growing body. And so, from a spirit of false economy, a double burden is imposed on the teacher. In proof of this, consider the number of pupils a single teacher is expected to " educate ;" the number of branches, disciplinary and practical, he is supposed to handle as educating instruments ; the high ideal he is expected to keep before him, and the short time allotted him to achieve his great work. Consider the swarms of little children that are usually found in " Primary Divisions," where, if our psychology is correct, is required to be done the most important part of the great work of education, the part that will tell with greatest effect on the welfare of the community. It is no wonder that even the earnest and able teacher, in presence of such a task and such conditions, is almost driven to substitute his own self-activity for that of the pupil, to do the thinking and talking that ought to be done by the pupil himself in the process of self-education. It is, perhaps, vain to hope that the multitudinous writers and speakers who are so ready with their nostrums for the " improvement of the teachers and the schools," may devote a portion of their energies to the removing of certain disabilities which make impossible the task now assigned to the teacher. And the watch-word of the first campaign in behalf of needed reforms, might well be : for the primary divisions, *double the time and half the numbers.* For the higher grades, *double the time or half the subjects,*—or better still, *double the time* AND *half the subjects.*

Law of Self-Education.—The teacher, then, is to use only needed explanation, and to have the pupil do as much as possible for himself. He is not to be too ready with his aid ; he is to develop the sense of power which contributes so much to awaken interest. Happily this source of interest can be drawn upon in all stages of instruction. Every teacher has seen the flush of pleasure on the face of the little child who has succeeded in doing what had threatened to baffle him. It may be the articulation of a single sound, or the making of a letter, or the drawing of a straight line ; it may be the combination of known letters into a new word, or the production of the written form of a spoken word, or the discovery that nine is three times three ; in every case there is a challenge to effort, and in every success, the thrill of conscious power. With but little telling, and much wise questioning, a class can be led to a fair mastery of the fundamental rules of arithmetic, and, then with less telling, and less questioning, they will master for themselves, fractions and all the so-called rules of that much-abused science.   And this is true of all the rational subjects of the school curricula.   A teacher who explains much, who anticipates every difficulty, and trusts nothing to the learner's independent investigation, is shorn of more than half his power. This is the tendency of things to-day.   There is too much coddling demanded by indulgent parents ; the teacher is expected to do everything for the pupil, who is to do little or nothing for himself.   Against this tendency, the able and faithful teacher must be on his guard ; he must arouse and deepen interest by developing conscious power.   *The boy must educate himself.*

Sympathy, *and Interest.—In the third place :* It has been seen again and again that sympathy (pp. 113, 120) and interest are great mental forces in the work of educating.   Where there is sympathy there is interest, with all that flows from it. Sympathy is the most potent force in the moral world.   Sympathy is in the world of mind what gravitation is in the world of matter ; by the one is maintained unity among the systems of worlds, by the other is secured the spiritual unity of humanity. In the school-room it is the greatest of forces.   To teach well, the teacher must get very near to the child ; the strong must put itself into vital contact with the weak ; " to become a teacher of children you must become a child."   This relation between teacher and taught, can be created by sympathy, and by sympathy alone.   For, it is impossible to get near a child, to win his affection and his confidence, without *know-ing* him, without a clear insight into the workings of his mind and heart.   And *this is the gift of sympathy.*   The seventh beatitude of the Divine Teacher is as sound in philosphy as it is deep in spiritual significance : " Blessed are the pure in Heart for they shall see God ; " that is, *Blessed are the loving,* the *sympathetic* in heart, for they shall *see things unseen by other* eyes

A man that has but little sympathy can never be a teacher in the best sense of the word ; lacking the gift of insight, he is but a blind guide ; he may be a hearer of recitations, an expositor of subjects, a martinet of discipline, an enforcer of spurious attention, a prince of rule and routine, but he has no power to touch the heart, and through the heart, to fashion mind into a form of blended strength and beauty. On the other hand, there is not a more beautiful sight than strong brain and kindly heart working on the plastic mind of childhood. It is hard to get implicit trust from children, but it is won through sympathy. In the general management of the school its presence is felt; but especially in lesson-giving, by the interrogative method, does the master's sympathy reveal itself and win the interest of his pupils. He feels *with* them, he knows that such feelings are *theirs*; for he projects his mind into theirs ; he is interested in the subject of instruction for their sakes; and they become interested in it for his sake ; he questions their minds into a communion with his, till the strong "sympathy of love unites their thoughts."

Mind to Mind.—The true teacher always knows when his mind is out of contact with the minds of his children ; he has at first, perhaps, pitched his questions too high or too low ; he has failed to excite interest because he has failed to create the necessary relation between their old mental experience and the new. But he soon corrects his error ; the sympathetic mind is keen to perceive and fertile in resources : he quickly touches the responsive chord, and he feels, and the children feel, that teacher and taught are one in thought and aim. There is perhaps no greater blessedness than such an experience ; the teacher knows that the bond of sympathy has been formed through which alone true educating power can pass. Through it, he becomes a child in heart without losing—rather increasing—his manly strength of intellect. He moves down from his superior plane of learning and power ; step by step he comes, till he reaches the lowly plane where children stand, and with a portion of that divine enthusiasm for child-humanity which marked the Divine Man, he draws them into a vital union with his strong heart and intellect. It is not irreverence to say that in the presence of such a teacher, the little ones press forward to touch the hem of his garment, and that with every touch there goes forth a quickening and transforming virtue of which the effects are as lasting as the soul itself.

Now, while the entire atmosphere of the school is one of sympathy, and thus influences the general school life, it is in actual teaching, *especially by the Method of Interrogation*, that it works with personal power. There is a focussing, so to speak, of the forces of sympathy, just as there is a concentration of the inellectual activity in attention ; in fact, the latter depends, in no small degree, upon the former. Under this condition effective teaching is possible. The teacher has an insight into every mind ; he adapts his questioning to its needs, and arouses it to normal action ; and breathless interest and brightening eye, prove that his labour is not in vain.

Arousing the Dull.—The questioning by which the teacher reveals himself to his pupils, and by which he forms and maintains a strong bond of sympathy with them, has the effect of animating even the dull members of the class into some semblance of life. This interest begins through class sympathy— sympathy of numbers, and is deepened by the teacher's interest in *all*. (Page 120). The teacher possessed of genuine sympathy, feels a special interest in those who learn with difficulty ; it is the heavy-laden ones whom he likes to encourage and to strengthen for the burden. The measure of the teacher's power is his ability to arouse the dull. Clever pupils will learn, even if the matter is imperfectly presented, and the teacher shows but little enthusiasm, but those of average ability, and especially the "slow of heart," can be aroused only by the touch of a master hand to the highest mental activity of which they are capable. Now, by the animated and judicious questions of the teacher, the interest of the whole class is deepened. The bright pupils are full of enthusiasm, those of moderate ability are on the alert, and the slow cannot escape the quickening influence. Mind acts on mind, enthusiasm begets enthusiasm, interest is born of interest, until the weakest members of the class share in a certain newness of life.

Nor does the teacher in his questioning fail to put questions suitable to the dull boys ; there is something within *their* grasp, and he leads them to feel this, and under the vitalizing impulse, even the dullest put forth unwonted energy, and the teacher has the surest proof of his success in the progress of those whom he had perhaps deemed incapable of learning. It often happens, indeed, that a child that had been all but stupid in one branch of study, develops a remarkable aptitude in another ; as when a student who has not taste or ability for science, discloses special aptitude for language, and *vice versa ;* or, occasionally one who is non-mathematical, shows a talent for literature.

Personality, *and interest.—In the fourth place :* Sympathy, we have seen, reveals itself and calls forth the sympathy of pupils, through questioning. The *lecturer* stands afar off ; he may excite admiration, but he cannot create the strong bond of sympathy which is the work of admiration and gratitude, and which is essential in all true education. But the sympathetic questioner works his way into the hearts of children. He is able to descend from his superior heights. With the clearer insight that comes from human sympathy, he has constantly before him the intricate points with which the child is wrestling, and affectionately aids the struggling mind into clearer light. And so, the child feeling again and again, the thrill that comes from conquest of difficulty, turns with blended feelings of gratitude and reverence to his inspiring leader. In this way is created a vital relation between the learner and the teacher, and everything that the one shows a deep interest in, becomes a source of interest to the other.

Sympathy united with enthusiasm constitutes a powerful *personality*. More than anything else, it is this personality that makes the successful teacher. Learning and method will be of little worth unless there is interest, enthusiasm in the work, for this alone can arouse the interest and stimulate the powers of the child. The fundamental principle is that person- . ality communicates itself, that there is developed in the pupil the same state of intellectual and moral consciousness that marks the teacher. If a subject has no interest for a teacher, it can have no interest for the taught; but sympathy, strengthened by enthusiasm will make the irksome, or even the repellant, attractive. Such a teacher, pursuing his calling under favourable circumstances, posseses all but unlimited power in the great work of mental and moral development. He takes the boys captive at his will; he makes an attractive subject still more attractive; he invests the indifferent with newly discovered charms; he reveals an element of beauty even in what was dry and harsh; in a word, he makes the pupil love what he himself loves, and hate what he hates; for a part of his own brain-power and heart-power, goes out in every lesson. He organizes faculty, capacity, tendency, almost at his discretion The despiser of classics becomes an enthusiastic student of Homer and Virgil; the hater of mathematics takes to geometry and the calculus; and the unimaginative plodder becomes saturated with love for the beauty and strength of Milton and Shakespeare.

Method of Personality.—No mechanical methods can possibly be a substitute for this personality. It is the power that ensures clearness, force, and permanent effect to all les on-giving; and especially is it this that moulds the character of the pupil. More than knowledge, it imparts love of knowledge and ability to acquire it; more than mere information about right and wrong, it forms *character*, which shows itself in a spontaneous and unswerving loyalty to conscience (page 154).

In the interminable discussions about "methods," therefore, it should be remembered that the true method for the **Educator**, is not to be found among the scores of ways, plans, devices, methods, that are so often enumerated : it is the *Method of Personality*. Erudition, knowledge of mind and normal method, have their place, a high place. But the highest place must be given to *Personality*. It is almost impossible to over-rate the influence of a strong personality. The most permanent influences history has known, or perhaps will know, may be traced to its forming and transforming power. It operates in the schoolroom, with far-reaching influence, because the teacher loves and respects infinitely the nature of the child, and comprehends the laws of its development. Too much reliance on methods *as methods*, makes education mechanical—dull, deadening, benumbing, destructive of vitality in both teacher and pupil. This is due largely to an immense exaggeration of the *mechanical* power of the teacher and its substitution for *vital* power. Give the pupil's mind a chance — do not destroy or enfeeble it by putting in place of it a machine which you yourself have modelled. Personality, not method, is the only power to produce personality; method based on recognition *of personality*—both formally and in its contents,—gives the mesmeric energy of the true teacher. In this informing spirit, sympathy united with enthusiasm, is the greatest factor. *Great thoughts come from the heart*; and, says John Morley, this is the truth that shines out as we watch the voyagings of humanity from the " wide, grey, lampless depths " of time. Those have been greatest in thought who have been best endowed with faith, hope, sympathy, and the spirit of effort.

2. *To Arouse Attention.*—The value of questioning in securing attention—*i.e.*, the exercise of mind-power—has been already referred to (page 37). A question is a challenge to attention ; a series of logical questions secures continuity of attention and consequent unity of thought. If there is to be any true learn-

ing—any true relation—between the mind and the object-matter, there must be *attention*—not counterfeit attention, but the positive exercise of mental energy. Questioning is the only means by which we can know that such attention is maintained. For what is this effective activity of attention, or what does it imply? It implies (page 61) the existence in the mind of ideas and groups of ideas essentially related to the new presentations ; it implies that these groups—forming an apperceiving capacity in the learner's mind—shall be brought to the front, made fresh and active, full of vitality, in order that the new and related groups may be so grafted upon them that an *organic growth* takes place.

In the early stages of learning this can be secured by questioning and by questioning alone. If the teacher simply explains, he is in the dark as to how the mind of the pupil is dealing with the explanations. There is no real attention, no creating of relations between connected points, unless the mind collects its forces in order to move from point to point in discovering relations. The teacher, then, having first clearly thought out what previous knowledge is necessary to enable the child to understand the lesson, calls up that knowledge by judicious questioning, gives it unity, freshness, vividness ; in a word, puts the studeat's mind in a comprehending, attitude and then, by a similar course of judicious interrogation, assists it in forming the inner relations between the matter of the new lesson and the freshened knowledge of the old.

Illustration.—If, for example, a master is going to give a first lesson on compound addition, he asks himself what is the relation between the new rule and the rules the pupil has already learned ? What ideas must be clear and fresh in the child's mind that he may firmly grasp the connection, *i.e.*, recognize in the (apparently) new the familar features of the old ? What are the resemblances, what the differences? The only differen e of course, is in the mode of notation— a *fixed* ratio in the simple, a *varying* ratio in the compound rule. He calls up in the learner's mind the old ideas that are related to the new rule, *e.g.*, that : (1) ten units make *one* ten, ten tens make *one* hundred, etc.; (2) in adding a column of units the tens of the aggregate are carried to the tens' column, and the units are placed under the units' column ; (3) in doing this we in effect *divide the sum* of the units by *ten* in order to find the number of tens to be carried ; as, *e.g.*, when the aggregate of the units' column is 57, and we consider this as 5 *tens* and 7 *units*, we really divide 57 by 10 ; etc. Thus, by recalling vividly to the learner's mind all the facts which are common to the two rules, the points of difference are seen to involve no new principle and are easily apprehended—the new is recognized as simply a modified form of the old.

So, in beginning fractions, a child is led to group certain ideas about the idea of *division* of a *whole number into equal parts*, *e.g.*, that a number has two halves, three thirds, four fourths, etc. ; that one of its halves is equal to two of its fourths, equal to four of its eighths, etc.; that three of a number's fourths is equal to one-fourth of three times the number, etc.

This grouping of ideas of interpretation is a necessity in all learning; It is the application of the old maxim, Pass from the known to the unknown. There must be preparatory mental adjustment, the *known* must be revivified, must be made ready, *then* there follows the process of attention, of making right connections, till the goal of the *unknown* is reached and found to be the *known* made larger and clearer.

In an ordinary reading lesson, for example, the child usually first reads over the lesson to get a " general idea " of its meaning. This serves as a centre of gravitation, it may be said, around which gather other ideas that come from further study and teaching. In other words, though this *general* idea may be vague, it is his starting point, it is what he will use when he goes over the lesson again, in acquiring a clearer idea of the whole by getting clearer ideas of its parts. And thus the process goes on till the whole is thoroughly assimilated.

3. *To Direct Attention.*—Concentration of mind upon any subject implies not only preparatory adjustment of attention, but also a *movement* in discovering relations of identity and difference (pp. 63, *et seq.*) After the initial act of attention, the stretching out of the mind with its prepared groups of ideas towards new matter, what follows ? There begins the movement towards a definite end, a process of defining and enlarging, discriminating and unifying. In the exercise of these essential functions of mind, the learner must be directed by questioning. His untrained mind cannot make the right preparatory adjustment of ideas, much less can it seize upon resemblances, notice differences and discover the law of connection which comprehends variety in unity. He is overwhelmed by the mass of materials that confront him. No matter how well the topic may be presented by text-book or lecturer, his immature powers cannot make the needed analysis, exclude the irrelevant, seize upon the salient points, and form the right connections. Thus, the teacher must make the required analysis, logically arrange the material, and skilfully question the learner in the line of related ideas till he has clearly discerned the relations. This work goes on from day to day, gradually forming a habit of noticing identities and differences, of forming essential connections, and ultimately developing a power of analysis and synthesis which leaves the learner largely independent of the teacher.

Whatever may be the subject matter of a lesson, there is an orderly way of presenting it, which tends to form the habit of concentrated attention, of clear and consecutive thought.

Illustrations.—If a lesson is to be given in arithmetic, say on the Least Common Multiple, the teacher will keep clearly before him the central truths, that the Least Common Multiple of several numbers must contain all the *different* factors found in the several numbers, and each of these in the *highest power* in

which it occurs.   He will not at first, of course, state the facts
in this abstract form; but they will guide him in questioning
the class through concrete examples up to a clear conception of
the principle. For the Least Common Multiple of 6 and 8, *e.g.*,
he proceeds somewhat as follows :

The factors of 6 ? *2 and* 3.
What, then, must any muliple of 6 contain ?
All the factors of 6 viz. 2 and 3, *i.e.,* 3 · 2..........(1).
The factors of 8 ?
Three two's, i.e., 2 · 2 · 2.
What therefore must any multiple of 8 contain ?
All the factors of 8, *viz.,* 2 · 2 · 2................(2).
What then must a common multiple of 6 and 8 contain ?
It must contain the factors (1) *and* (2).
Will not taking the factors (2) suffice ?
No, because a product of two's cannot contain 3, *which is a factor in* (1).
Well, taking the factors (2) and the factor 3, what results ?
The result is 2 · 2 · 2 · 3......................(3).
Is it not necessary to take also the other factor of 6, viz. 2 ?
No, for 2 is contained in the factors already used.

A different series of questions may, of course, be asked ; the foregoing
simply illustrates the principle under consideration, viz., that attention must
be *directed* by a series of connected questions starting from some basic
principle.

Again : Take the famous fifth proposition of Euclid, I., (the
Pons) : if a boy of common ability fails to master this proposition, it is because of poor teaching. As every one knows, the
fourth proposition is really the essential part of the " Bridge,"
and if this is thoroughly mastered, whence should difficulty
arise ? Question the boy into a thorough understanding of the
fourth proposition, and the key of Euclid is in his hands. He
will hardly stumble, much less fail, when he attacks the fifth.

In teaching the *Pons*, then, there is first of all, preparatory *adjusting*
of attention: the boy is tested upon his knowledge of the fourth proposition ; his knowledge must be practical, *i.e.*, capable of ready application to easy cases ; a few easy exercises leading up to the *pons*, are given,
etc. Then there is a *directing* of attention : there is first of all attention to

the enunciation, general and particular ; next, to the construction ; then to the demonstration in three parts, viz. :—part *first*, in which the equality of the two "larger" triangles is proved ; then part *second*, in which the equality of the two triangles on the base is proved ; lastly, part *third*, in which the results of the first and second parts are used, and the conclusion formally inferred. That is, the whole argument is subdivided, analyzed, and clearly presented in its several stages. With such a direction of attention by means of the well arranged questions, the boy's mastery of this famous proposition is assured.

This *Directing Attention* is of universal application. In a common reading lesson, in a simple poem, in a gem of literature, in a chapter of history, etc., there must be some *unity*, a grouping of ideas upon some principle, movement towards some end. And this unity must be apprehended and presented in the true spririt of the Socratic Art.*

4. *To Cultivate Habits of Self-Questioning*—The goal of attention is ability to grasp large wholes in one act, and to give at the same time, distinctness to the *parts*. This goal is reached through systematic exercise of the related processes of identifying and discriminating, that is, by the exercise of the mind's analytic and synthetic functions, which are best trained through the Method of Interrogation. The questioning which constantly appeals to the mind's native tendency to notice differences and to detect resemblances, must cultivate the habit of self-questioning, which may be considered the test of the development of attention. It is plain that every series of such questions as have been described, goes to form or strengthen this habit. This thing that I perceive, what is it ? What are the points which connect it with anything I have hitherto perceived ? Wherein is it like, yet different from, other things that I have known ? These facts that are before me—what relation have they ? These relations—are they comprehended in a wider law ? In this problem—what are the facts or conditions given ? What is the thing sought ? Are any of these conditions irrele-

---

* For examples in Literature etc., see Vol. on Detailed Methods of Teaching.

vant? What relations are explicitly given, what implictly? Such a spirit of enquiry calls into exercise all the activities of attention, its adjusting, selecting, and relating powers—and ultimately brings the highest degree of intellectual energy which the student can attain.

Clearly, this intellectual habit can be formed by logical questioning and by this alone. The pouring out processes whether by text-books, that copiously explain the easy and are silent on the difficult, or by teachers who with a fatal flow of words explain everything, works against independent investigation and the growth of power. The wordy teacher has been referred to; the wordy annotator deserves a passing notice. He is more to be dreaded than the wordy teacher. The young learner will sometimes venture to question the scientific or literary accuracy of the oral instructor; but he receives with unquestioning reverence the printed statements of the annotator.

In the course of a long experience, we have rarely found a young student bold enough to question a statement made by an editor of an English or a Classical author. In the lines:

> " Yet e'en these bones from insult to protect,
>   Some frail memorial still erected nigh,
>   With uncouth rhymes and shapeless sculpture decked
>   Implores, the passing tribute of a sigh."

Scores of students have been known to declare that "*yet* is an adverb modifying implores," because some of the editors had so disposed of it, and both teachers and learners had accepted this "note" on the meaning of yet. Evidently, the famous Elegy had not been considered in its unity, nor had there been any " directing of attention " to its related parts.

Take the well known lines of Horace:

> . . . .
> " Hunc, si, mobilium turba Quiritium,[*]
>   Certat tergeminis tollere honoribus ;"

It is safe to say that during the long reign of Anthon, thousands of students regarded *honoribus* as " a dative, a Græcism

---

[*] " *This* joys, if rabbles fickle as the wind
    Through triple grade of honours bid him rise."

for *ad honores*." They had never once ventured to ask whether *honoribus* might be *the other* case, and the Graecism, a fiction. We remember the amazement of a certain class and the indignant protest of their master, at the bare suggestion that there might be no "Graecism" after all. The habit of self-questioning, of independent thought, is not likely to be formed either by garrulous teachers, or verbose commentators. *Study the author, shelve the annotator.*

II. Qualifications of the Questioner.

We may roughly classify these under two heads, (*a*) Acquired Qualifications, and *(b)* Natural Endowments. Under *(a)* we shall consider a few of the qualifications that are indispensable in all good teaching :

(1) *Thorough Knowledge.*—Clear teaching is necessary and to this, thorough knowledge of the subject of instruction is essential. What a teacher does not know he cannot teach ; what he does not know well, he cannot teach well. To know a subject well, it must be known in its relations to kindred subjects. A single, isolated fact, or principle, as we have seen, is not knowledge ; to become knowledge, to have any effect on intelligence, it must be grasped in its *relations*. It follows, then, that an instructor must know of a subject far more then he intends to teach. If, in mathematics, for example, he is ignorant of Algebra, he cannot teach Arithmetic so well as if he were a skilled Algebraist. If he knows only the four fundamental rules of Arithmetic, his teaching of these will not deserve the name of teaching. Indeed, since all knowledge is one, it may be truly said that the broader and more thorough a teacher's scholarship is, the better he will teach even the elements of knowledge. He will know his topic better, for he will see it in its relations ; he will know its several parts better ; he will be more fertile in illustration and all skilled divices of the teacher's art ; he will impart some *educative* value even to the simplest

lessons.   They are clearly wrong, therefore, who take the ground that the primary teacher need " know " only what he is going to teach.   The primary teacher, it is sometimes argued, is to give the elements of reading, writing and numbers ; if he can read, write and cipher, he is qualified as an educator ; the *minimum* of knowledge to be imparted fixes the *maximum* of knowledge for the teacher.   If this view were acted upon, primary instruction would be of the most mechanical kind. The teacher is himself without interest in the subject which he feebly comprehends ; his own powers having never been called into vigorous action, how can he awaken interest and incite to vigorous effort ?   The truth of the matter is, that just because the primary subjects have in themselves but little culture-value, it is the more necessary that the teacher should have a liberal culture, as well as the power of insight into human nature. For, in this stage of development, above all others, it is the *method* rather than the matter, that is of greatest value.

The beginnings of knowledge which we have studied in our psychology, are the beginnings of moral and intellectual life. "The child is to be trained towards the perfection of manhood his nature brought into fullest activity on all sides, and his powers developed in harmonius completeness, so far as time and circumstances permit."   This view of primary work is not an ideal one which we may imagine but never hope to realize. The standard aimed at is easily within the reach of the earnest cultivated teacher ; it is far beyond the crude empiric whose fitness for the teacher's high vocation is an imperfect knowledge of the mechanical *trivium*, reading, writing and arithmetic.

In the more advanced work, it is a truism that good knowledge is necessary to good teaching.   The teacher must command the confidence of his class ; they must have respect for his character and admiration for his attainments.   Thoroughly master of his subject, he moves along with conscious, yet unpretentious power, and his boys look up to him as soldiers to

Q

an able leader.   Briefly, in all grades of teaching from the Kindergarten to the University, wherever there is to be true
teaching, wherever power is to be developed and character
formed, there ought to be broad and accurate knowledge and
a good degree of general culture. *Faculty is to be organized by
clear presentation of organized knowledge*, and, therefore, the imperative condition is : **To organize faculty, the teacher
must have organized knowledge.**

(2) *Preparation of Lessons.*—It follows that every lesson
should be thoroughly prepared.   However conversant a teacher
may be with the subject-matter of a lesson, he will know it
better for teaching purposes, if he makes special preparation.
He may have gone over the thing again and again, but if he
is about to teach it to a new class, it will have a fresh interest
for him.   *A strong mind never moves twice in exactly the same
groove ;* and, therefore, the trite subjects as they are reviewed,
will be broadened and freshened by increasing knowledge,
while interest is still further deepened by the power of sympathy.   Every teacher has felt the thrill that comes in teaching
even a familiar topic, when he realizes that the humble elements he is presenting have been seized by the mind of the child
to the awakening of new life and strength.   The teacher is
before his pupils as the dispenser of wonderful revelations, and
what to him is but the A, B, C, of knowledge, brings to them
the joy of discovery and the sense of growing power.   On the
other hand, most teachers have had the disagreeable feeling
that comes from half knowledge of a subject, or imperfect
preparation of a lesson.   A master imparts with lasting effect
what he has thoroughly prepared ; what, from want of preparation is only half knowledge, leads to feeble teaching.   Instead
of moving in conscious strength, he sees dimly, his step is
feebly wavering, and keen eyes are quick to see that he is in a
maze without a clue.   To be ready in resource, to have freshness of mind, to possess and to inspire confidence, to arouse

and develop mind, the golden rule to be followed in all teaching, from a lesson on the cube to one on Differential Equations, is : **Make Thorough Preparation of the Lesson.**

(3) *Analytic Power.*—The questioner must have a trained intellect; he should possess analytic power. " Present one thing at a time," is one of the soundest of maxims. This implies that the object matter has been analyzed, the connection of the several parts observed, and that the *one* thing is presented at the right time, and at the right place in the series. If the teacher is not guided by the unity of the topic, if his questions have no thread of connection, how can his pupils apprehend even the " one thing at a time ? " Once more, the *one* thing, in order to have any meaning, must have a logical connection with something else. Disconnected questions are the product of a muddled brain. And if that is the state of things with the teacher, it is with the pupil confusion worse confounded. Teach one thing at a time, but teach it in its right connection, so that the pupil re-thinking the related things, in the end reconstructs the *whole* with which analysis began. Thus he will be gradually trained to the exercise of the highest functions of the intellect. The analytic habit of mind is, perhaps, three-fourths of the intellectual qualifications of the successful questioner. A fruitful source of failure is the lack of logical method in teaching. Speaking generally, the untrained mind cannot be logical ; and the illogical mind cannot teach. The mechanical observance of mechanical methods cannot make him a teacher. His habits of confused explanation and jumbled questioning are incurable. **Therefore, cultivate the Analytic and Synthetic habit of Mind.**

(4) *Knowledge of Mind.*—All our previous study goes to show that a knowledge of psychology is indispensable to the true educator. It is with the workings of a *mind* that the teacher has constantly to do. His method is good, his skill is

great, only so far as they intelligently appeal to these mental processes and contribute to their highest results.   He may have been crammed with pedagogical formulæ, rules and devices, and methods and maxims, about "how to teach and how not to teach," but if he knows little or nothing of the laws, principles, and results of mental activity, his methods and his devices are likely to be only crude experiments, knowing no law, or unity, or definite aim.   The teacher, then, should know the laws of mind, and make all his expositions, all his questioning, tributary to its spontaneous activities ; he should ever realize that he is questioning a *mind*.   The *empiric* is saturated with the idea that his great aim is to question *about a subject ;* for him, the mind exists for the "subject," not the subject for the mind.   But the *Artist*, knowing the material he has to work upon, and familiar with the marvellous processes by which it grows and develops into the noblest thing on earth, subordinates method and all its instruments, to *mind* and its development.   Let the teacher remember that in the exercise of his highest function he is a **Questioner of Mind**.

(5) Practice in Questioning. — The reciprocal action between *knowing* and *doing* has been frequently pointed out.   Long and *intelligent* practice is necessary to skill in any art.   Let the young teacher aim *from the very beginning*, at excellence in the Art of Questioning.   In seeking the *way* to excellence let him remember : By *doing* alone, the way is endless : by *knowing* alone, the way is long ; **by Knowing and Doing the way is short and sure.**

(6) *Personal Endowments.*—Under this head but little need be added to what has already been advanced.   It has been seen that *personality* is the vital element in the qualifications of the teacher.   Energy, enthusiasm, decision of character, sympathy and the insight which comes from it, are the chief elements in a strong personality, and for this, no method, mechanical or

r.itional, can be a substitute. For, such a teacher, in no slight degree communicates himself. The mere tradesman, following with numb rigidity pedagogical rules whose meaning he has never grasped, drags his pupils through a dull and dreary routine of unprofitable facts, touching the intellectual and moral nature only to their lasting injury. But the strong-brained, and strong-hearted teacher, who also is impressed with the worth of the human spirit, will, while developing the intelligence of his pupils, plant in them moral feeling, and the sense of a universal love of man. Strong through patience, and hope, and faith, and sympathy, and the spirit of effort, he touches the intellect indeed, but touches also the moral and religious nature, inspires a reverence for the divine *spirit* of the Gospel, "which is operating with ever widening, humanizing, and enlightening influence on the destinies of mankind."

He who would attain the transforming power of the ideal teacher may well keep in mind the decree which Frederick the Great, with all his un-orthodoxy, thought it wise to issue to his Prussian teachers: "As far as the work of the school is concerned, school-masters are earnestly reminded above everything to prepare themselves for teaching by heartfelt prayer for themselves, and ask from the Giver of all good gifts, wisdom, and patience, that their exertions and labors may be blessed. In particular they are to pray that the Lord would grant them a heart paternaly inclined, and tempered with love and seriousness towards the children entrusted to them, that they may discharge the duties lying on them as teachers, willingly and without grudge, remembering that they can accomplish nothing, not even gain the hearts of the children, without the divine aid and Spirit of Jesus, the friend of children."

III. Matter and Form of Questions.

What is to be said under this head, also, follows necessarily from the purposes of questioning, and hence it will suffice to give a short summary of the characteristics of questioning as to *Matter, Form and Mode.*

(*a*) As to the matter of Questions.—(1) We may notice the following characteristics :

(1.) *Definiteness.*—Questions should be perfectly definite, *i.e.* unambiguous, precise, and corresponding to some assigned part of the subject.   Some teachers ask unanswerable questions, *i.e.*, questions which it is impossible to answer, or which could be answered in half a dozen ways.   (page 167.)   A definite question is given upon a definite portion of the subject matter, and in clear, terse and precise language.   Both of these rules are too frequently violated.   A few illustrations from "real life," may be given :

Illustration.—"What occurred in Palestine after the destruction of Jerusalem ? "   To answer that question would require on the part of the student an extraordinary gift of mind-reading.   "If you place *a over b* what does it mean ? "   The teacher had in mind a way of representing division ; but, a boy would have been quite right in respectfully asking for the meaning of "over," and "it."   "What influence do you draw from the fact that water, in freezing, contracts till a certain temperature is reached, and then begins to expand ? "   "What sort of quantity is $a^2 + ab + b^2$? " "In this poem, explain the devices of contrast and contiguity."   And so on.

A teacher in training was giving a twenty-minute trial lesson on "Partnership."   In starting to "develop" the idea of Partnership, he proceeded as follows :

" A man comes to the city to begin a certain business and finds that it will take $2,000 to start the business, but he has only $1,000, what will he do ? " No answer being given, the teacher said "surely some of you can answer," and repeated the question, stating the supposition and ending with "What will he do ? "   After another solemn pause, one boy said : " Please, sir, he would borrow a thousand dollars."   This was a very good answer, but not the required answer.   The teacher was plainly taken aback, but said : "No, the man was a stranger in the city, and could not borrow a thousand dollars, What would he do, think a moment?"   "After another pause, a thoughtful boy—who was perfectly sincere—said : Please, sir, if a man had a thousand dollars of his own, and had a good character, couldn't he *borrow* another thousand?" Which was a perfectly correct and business-like view of the case, showing considerable thought on the part of the answerer. The teacher was now driven to answer his own vague questions ; in other words, at the end of the lesson, the boys had learned that, in the opinion of the teacher, the man with "the one thousand dollars would try to find another man with a thousand, etc." That was the result of a twenty minute effort to "develop" the idea of partnership.

Vague questions have an exceedingly mischievous tendency. The thoughtful boy honestly endeavouring "to pay attention," is bewildered, and is likely to become inattentive to what he cannot understand. To the less conscientious boys, such questions are a premium on "guessing ;" they often hit upon the answers expected by the teacher, and so gain some credit through dishonesty.

(2) Logical Sequence.—In the *Second Place :* From what has been already said upon the necessity of presenting facts in their relations, it follows that questions should be *connected*, should proceed from one point, or topic, to another, with due regard to the unity of the subject. Even in elementary teaching, some order should be observed in questioning ; for, as already said, if facts are presented in their natural connection, there will be growth in the learner's mind into a *conscious* thinking of the relations. It may be stated once more that, in all grades of instruction, there can be clear thinking, and actual assimilation on the part of the learner, only when there are clear thinking (analysis and synthesis) and connected instruction on the part of the teacher. The most fruitful source of weak and ineffectual teaching to-day is, without doubt, the lack of logical power, and, therefore, of ability in clear instruction. Teachers are not, of course, responsible for all the preposterous answers which are given at examinations, and which are made to do duty in exposing the weakness of educational work. But there is no doubt that dispersive and discursive teaching and questioning are partly responsible. It seems impossible that

all the absurd answers are due to hasty preparation, or sheer stupidity. The candidates must, in some instances, have suffered from immethodical teaching and "discontinuous" questioning. Of such teaching, the candidate who gave the following answer was doubtless a victim : What are the characteristics of Goldsmith's poetical and prose works ? *He wrote both poetry and prose beautifully, his poetry being in general very lamentable and explanatory, and being five feet in length.*

Of course some license may be allowed in questioning on a familiar topic. In review-questions, a little "skipping round" may be permitted for practice in rapid grouping of ideas. In fact the serial order should give place to the topical (page 174) in all reviews for testing the thorough mastery of the work. When a teacher has presented a subject rationally, questioned the pupil into a perception of the meaning of the several parts, assisted them into thinking the proper relations, correct method demands that the pupil should now be able to analyze his mass of facts, properly group the elements, in a word, exercise independently the functions of analysis and synthesis. *To lead to the habit of connected thinking,* **Questions should have Continuity.** (Page 170.)

(3) Adapted to Capacity.—In order to stimulate, questions must be skillfully adapted to the capacity and attainments of the pupils, that is, they must not be too *easy* or too *difficult.* In either case, there can be no interest, and mind-wandering is sure to follow (page 192, *et seq.*) As a general rule, properly adapted and definite questions will not (*a*) include the answer, or (*b*) suggest the answer, or (*c*) be answerable by a single word, or (*d*) be unanswerable, or (*e*) be answerable by all. In the case of one-word answers there are many exceptions, especially in rapid review-lessons. But the safe, guiding principle is : *connected speech means connected thought* (see page 220, *et seq.*)

(4). *Due Proportion.*—Questions should repeat the mportant facts or principles of a subject rather than unimportant details. As the result of the analysis the central thought stands out prominently in the teacher's mind, the minor thoughts are arranged in proper relation according to their value, and all irrelevant matter is excluded. Questioning ought to result in a similar harmonious grouping of ideas in the minds of the learners. **Question upon the points of the lesson according to their importance.** (page 202.)

(*b*) **As to the Form of Questions.**—What has been said on the *matter* of questions will suggest the chief points as to their form. A few of these may be noticed.

(1) *Good Language.*—To secure definiteness, the language of questions must be concise, clear, and correct ; wordy, obscure, and incorrect questions imply vague ideas, and lead to the vagueness that it is the purpose of teaching to correct. Comparatively few teachers seem able to put questions in perfectly definite language. Even those who are fairly successful teachers would be astonished if their questions were reproduced *verbatim* in written form. They would indignantly challenge the accurracy of the " report." We have known questioners to change the form of a question three or four times before its final delivery, thus causing the class endless perplexity. **Muddled speech means muddled thought.**

(2) *Varied.*—Questions should be varied in form (1) to avoid monotony, and (2) to suit the subject matter of the lesson. Some teachers are the slaves of a changeless type of questions; they follow with fatal fidelity the same forms in fact-subjects, (Elementary Geography, *e. g.,*) in thought-subjects (Grammar, *e. g.*), and in action-subjects (Drawing, etc). *Monotony destroys Interest.*

(3) *Questioner's own Words.*—In general, questions should be given in the teacher's own words. This demands *thinking,*

and freshness of thought awakens interest. Do not be the servile repeater of the set questions of secular text-book, or Sunday-school Guide. It may be remarked that, in the case of words as well as of thought, the teacher is not to be a blind follower of the limited rule " teach only what the child understands." If the subject is within his reach, occasional " strange words " may be wisely used. *They are a stimulus.* They are explained by their connection with known words. We " explain words *before* using them ; " but, also, we *explain words* by *using them.*

(4) *Elliptical Questions.*—This is the worst of all possible forms, and should be rarely used.

(5) *Topical and Serial.*—It has already been pointed out (page 220) that the *serial* order of questions should be followed by the *topical* method.

Mode of Questioning.—A few words may be added on the *mode* of putting questions, (1) Effective class questioning is the result of a judicious use of the *individual* and the *class* methods, (2) In general, the questions should be addressed to the *class*, the answers given by the *individual.* (3) Unless the teacher is at fault, a question is not to be repeated; pupils must *attend* ; repetition of questions favours *inattention.* (4) As to *rapidity* : At the beginning of the lesson, questions for the grouping of ideas, for the adjusting of attention, may rapidly follow one another. During the course of the lesson, while the pupil is forming relations, *i. e., thinking* to the best of his ability, reasonable time should be allowed for the answer. Finally, in a review of the lesson, and in general reviews, question and answer should follow in quick succession. (5) Mutual questioning is an excellent test and stimulus. To put a good question upon a subject, one must know it well. A pupil, knowing he will be called on to put a question, is kept on the alert, he is *attentive;* and practice in questioning others helps to form the habit of self-questioning, the attitude of the thinking mind (page 238). (6) *Written Answers.* There should be frequent written examinations. From what has been said upon the relation of thought and language, it follows that written examinations are an essential factor in the process of mind training.

IV. Matter and Form of Answers.

Under this head there is little to be said that is not given almost expressly in our preceding studies upon questioning; a brief summary will suffice. (1) Good questioning secures good answering, or, in other words, good teaching secures good results. Thoughtful questions lead to definite thinking and expression. The general characteristic of good answering is, thererore, that it is the *pupil's best thinking expressed in the pupil's best words.* (2) Hence, *individual* answering is the rule, *class* (or sumultaneous) answering, the exception. Class-answering may sometimes be permitted in repetition, and in reviews of familiar subjects; it may, at times, be useful in encouraging the timid and animating the dull. But, for other purposes, the method is misleading, and if extensively used, exceedingly harmful. "It is astonishing," says Gladman, "with what readiness boys can take their cue from one another, so as to produce the appearance of unanimity, of a common knowledge. The wise teacher, however, knows that such apparently wide-spread skill is fallacious, and he will rarely employ a method in his teaching which admits of such misinterpretation." (3) If an answer is wholly wrong, it is proof of imperfect teaching, and the wise teacher will not hastily decide that an answer *is* wholly wrong. In some subjects there is but little room for difference of opinion, in others there is great room. Consider a question as to the force of a word in a given sentence, etc. The teacher who has his stereotyped answer, to which all other answers must conform, represses, rather than promotes, the pupil's self-activity. The pupil is fallible; the teacher is not infallible.   (4) If an answer is partly right, and partly wrong, it shows that the pupil is thinking, and the teacher, by kind encouragement, and perhaps a judicious question or two, is to guide the pupil into clearer light.   (5) Random answers should have no place.   If the teacher is master of his business, they will never find place.   Almost as rare will be the "Know— but cannot tell" answer.   The rule is: "**Cannot tell,**" **does not know.**   (6) Written answers are of the highest value.   Oral examination is not enough; for the best results there must be frequent written examinations, (page 220). They are an indispensable element in training.   Not that which goes into the eyes and ears of a student educates, but that which comes out of him in oral and especially in written form.   No student can be certain that he has mastered a subject till he has reproduced it.   This reproduction is the test of knowledge, and of the power which comes from the acquisition of knowledge.

Written examinations give a thorough mastery of the subject, demand activity rather than passivity of the mind, and train to the lucid expression of vigorous thought.   "They are," said Professor Jevons, "the most powerful means of training the intellect." **Examination is Education.**

CHAPTER XI.

KINDERGARTEN WORK AND SELF-INSTRUCTION IN PUBLIC SCHOOLS.

Grounds for Establishing Kindergarten Exercises.

When properly carried out, the Kindergarten receives the child at the age of three years, and applies the most efficient means known, to secure an all-sided development.   Wherever it is practicable, therefore, school authorities should establish Kindergartens in connection with the public schools. We have seen, in our psychology, that the soul is an organic unity—that there are not independent—much less antagonistic—" faculties," but that all the so-called faculties are only different stages of psychical development. It follows, therfore, that there is but one science of education. There is not one set of principles for the Kindergarten, another set for the Primary schools, etc. The principles of the Kindergarten are thoroughly sound; they are in the line of true psychology. But they are distinctive only in their *application, under specially favourable cireumstances,* to *a certain stage of human development.* In an ideal system of education, there would be a Kindergarten department in every school. It is likely, however, that the expense of establishing and keeping in operation fully equipped Kindergartens, will operate for a time against their introduction except in cities and towns. But cannot some of the Kindergarten exercises, or at least exercises embodying Kindergarten principles, be imported into the public schools as at present constituted? May not all the children of the country have a taste of what is calculated to make their early school days happy, as well as give them a better education and at least a touch of culture?

Can provision be made in Public Schools for the working of Kindergarten Principles and Methods?

In order to answer this question, we must ascertain upon what distinctive methods the Kindergarten mainly depends to secure the aims of education in its three great departments, Physical, Moral and Intellectual. We may then judge of the adaptability of such methods and principles to the altered conditions presented by the Public Schools.

1. Physical Education.—In the department of Physical Education, the Kindergarten, recognizing the law that the mind must be drawn away from the mere exercise as such, makes, elaborate provision under the disguise of plays of various kinds, for securing strength of body, beauty of form and gracefulness of bearing. In addition to this, the constant handling of material, and the various occupations of building, folding, weaving, etc., give delicacy of touch, quietness of movement, and deftness of hand.

The public schools, as at present constituted, have not the separate room required for this training, nor has the teacher the necessary time at his disposal. Excepting, then, the manual dexterity secured to the pupil by the exercises designed for intellectual development, it is doubtful whether much more can be done for physical training, than to ḷply the calisthenics at present common in the best Public Schools. In cities and ṭowns, however, by adopting the "Half-Time" system, time may be had for all the most valuable Kindergarten methods for physical education.

2. Moral Education.—In the department of Moral Education, it can scarcely be said that the Kindergarten furnishes any *method* different from that of the schools. It has, however, many marked advantages, as, *e. g.* : (*a*) Before evil habits have become fixed, the child comes under the influence of a society whose moral code is moulded and guided by a teacher familiar with all the ascertained laws of moral development. All psychology and all experience show how important is this early training. (p. 72). (*b*) Much more time can be spared for developing sympathy which not only goes out in kindly acts towards others, but is also the real basis of the moral feelings. (p. 121). (*c*) The *will power* is greatly strengthened by the constant employment of hand and brain in accomplishing the various kinds of work proposed for intellectual development. The importance of this hand training in educating the will, is very great. For, the child, in controlling hand-movements, in fact all bodily movements, is exercising the elements that enter into the highest kind of self-control. Train eye, ear, hand, tongue, and in the process the *doing* not only reacts on thinking—the development of intelligence—it also contributes, in no slight degree, to moral culture (p. 145). (*d*) The pupil is inspired by a spirit of order; patience is cultivated, habits of persistence are acquired; he learns to be " diligent in business," gentle in manner, and mindful of the rights of others. He is all the while gaining power to apprehend and appreciate the true, the beautiful and the good.

With the exception of this strengthening of the will-power and general development of the ethical nature by the employment of hand and brain—an advantage peculiar to the exercises for *intellectual* development, it will be seen that in the department of moral education, the superiority of the Kindergarten over the school is due rather to oportunity, than to any peculiarity of method. We should keep in mind, however, that the moral training resulting from Kindergarten exercises for intellectual development, will be so much gain to moral culture in the Public Schools. In fact, at this stage of development, intellectual, moral, and physical culture, may be almost considered as one.

3. Intellectual Education.—In the intellectual field, assuming development of power to be the chief work of the Kindergarten, what is really the principle, which working by means of the various exercises, draws forth and cultivates the mental powers? On reflection, it will be found **that it is the close attention which the child is obliged to give in order to perform the necessary movements in various pleasing constructive employments, that sets the mechanism of the senses in motion and thus secures the development of power.** The attempt **to do** under such circumstances that each forward step furnishes the necessary pleasurable stimulus for deeper attention and further effort, will be found to be the source of most of the good which characterizes the Kindergarten. The operation of the same principle, secures **skill**, itself one of the ends of education, since it is a product of intelligence. Once more, the pupil learns to know by doing, and to do by knowing.

Kindergarten, Rational.— From our psychology it seems plain that, in true Kindergarten work, the laws of early psychical development are closely followed. Instruction is based upon the impulses ; the hunger of the senses is gratified ; the correlative laws of knowing and doing are in continuous operation ; there is interest, natural and acquired, which secures non-voluntary attention ; the law of association works with effect, and good habits result ; the constant working for some end develops voluntary attention, the power of concentration ; from the very beginning, in the actions with things, there are partitions and constructions and designings and modellings, in a word, physical processes, which lead gradually to the conscious exercise and development of the essential functions of mind, analysis and synthesis ; in brief, since there is, under assumed favourable conditions, the best possible means for the training of Sensation, Interest, Impulse, and of the mental Processes, there is in that very fact, the best possible preparation for securing the highest results in the development of perception, memory, imagination and thought, as well as of the Emotions and the Will.

The Beginning of Wisdom.—*All the faculties, including reasoning, are the natural outgrowth of perception, or intuition,* (page 171).—Train the observing powers, it is urged, because perceived *objects* are simpler than *laws* and *abstract relations,* and prior to them. But also, and especially, train perception, because this training so touches all the mental powers, including remembering and thinking, that they will afterwards appear as naturally as blossom from plant and fruit from blossom. " Teach a child to understand ;" teach a child to *see,* and he will understand in due season. To the efficient, though perhaps unconscious, carrying out of this principle, is due the success of true Kindergarten instruction in developing the nature of the child. It follows, too, that the *efficiency of a system of education depends on the efficiency of its primary education.* A system which is weak in this, is weak in all. Clearly, then, if the principles and methods of the Kindergarten are based on true psychology, they should be *introduced as far as possible into every Public School.* Training perception is training all the mental powers; therefore, let ample provision be made for the best possible primary education, **this is the Beginning of Wisdom in every System of Education.** (Page 130.)

Happily, many of the Kindergarten exercises which are designed for the development of intellectual power and of skill, and which incidentally, yet powerfully, aid in moral culture, (page 145) readily lend themselves to the modifications necessary to their introduction into Public Schools.

The *expense* attending their introduction will be light—insignificant compared with the good that is sure to follow. The *time* taken for *direct* instruction need not exceed half an hour a day for first and second classes, and about three half-hour lessons a week for the other classes. There cannot be a doubt that the common branches will be learned with greater facility, and will have a far higher *educative* value. Lastly, if a *teacher* has had no special training for this work, he can easily qualify himself, with the help of a good Kindergarten guide.

The modified forms of Kindergarten work now to be described, have been found to work well. Under the altered circumstances, the teacher need not trouble himself much about the particular order of presenting the exercises. The important consideration is to keep up the interest, and for this purpose it is best to have variety (page 110). In dealing with those employments requiring considerable manual dexterity, such as *slat-work, paper-folding,* and *mat-weaving,* the teacher is at first apt to select too dfficult work. This will, however, be speedily corrected by experience.

1. Blocks and Building.

In dealing with the blocks, prepare for each pupil two boxes of thin material one 9⅛ × 4⅛ inches, the other 6¼ × 4⅛ inches,

R

inside measurement. Into the shorter box which we shall designate (*a*), put 24 bricks, 16 squares, and 8 pillars.

Into the longer box which we shall designate (*b*), put 24 cubes, 12 half cubes and 24 quarter cubes.*

It is found that the various kinds of blocks here mentioned can be furnished by an ordinary cabinet-maker at the rate of twenty-five cents per hundred, and the boxes at the rate of five cents each. Expense of material, therefore, is not, as generally supposed, a very important consideration.

Ordinary Object Lessons.—Although it is the close observation required to perform the synthetic, or constructive exercises, that furnishes the peculiar power of the Kindergarten, it is well to do *some* work of the ordinary "object-lesson" type. For example, having put into the hands of each pupil box (*b*), let the teacher select eight cubes from his own box, and form them into a large cube. At a signal from the teacher the pupils do the same. This is the *Third Gift* of the Kindergarten.

By *questioning* the pupils, lead them to *observe* the number of faces, the number of corners, the number of edges, in a cube. The terms right-angle, square, face, surface, parallel, etc., may, also, be learned in this connection.

Having examined the cube as a whole, divide it into two equal parts, the pupils doing the same. By questions, the pupils should be led to observe carefully the resulting regular solids. Divide each of these halves again, and proceed as before.

Make another division, and thus reduce the large cube to its elements.

The object-lessons with the cube may now be applied to give the pupils clear conceptions of the terms 'half,' 'quarter,'

---

* A brick is a block $2 \times 1 \times \frac{1}{2}$ inch.   The half cube is formed by dividing a cube
A square is a block $1 \times 1 \times \frac{1}{2}$ inch.   diagonally. The quarter-cube by dividing
A pillar is a block $2 \times \frac{1}{2} \times \frac{1}{2}$ inch.   the half-cube into two equal triangular
A cube is a block $1 \times 1 \times 1$.   pieces. ☞ Illustration, page 260.

'eighth,' and to make the pupils familiar with such useful facts as the following :

(*a*) The whole equals two halves.
(*b*) The whole equals four quarters.
(*c*) The whole equals eight eighths.
(*d*) A half equals two quarters.
(*e*) A half equals four eighths.
(*f*) A quarter equals two eighths, etc.

Illustration.

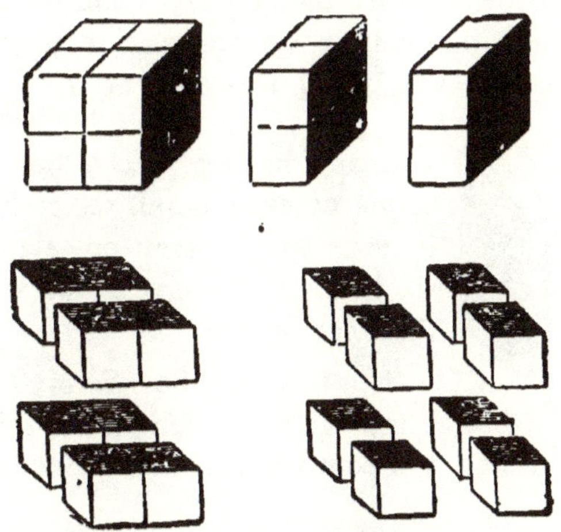

Again, having placed box '*a*' in the hands of the pupils, select from the one in your own possession eight bricks, and form a cube. This is the *Fourth Gift* of the Kindergarten·

By questions, lead the pupils to examine this closely, to compare it with the cube formerly dealt with (Third Gift). Lead them to compare the bricks of which it is composed, with the cubes of the Third Gift. How many faces has each brick ?

How many edges ?   Each face is an oblong.   Each face is a parallelogram, etc., etc.

Again, having placed box '*b*' in the hands of each pupil, let the teacher select from the one in his own hands, twenty-one whole cubes, six half-cubes, and nine quarter cubes. Now form these into a cube thus :

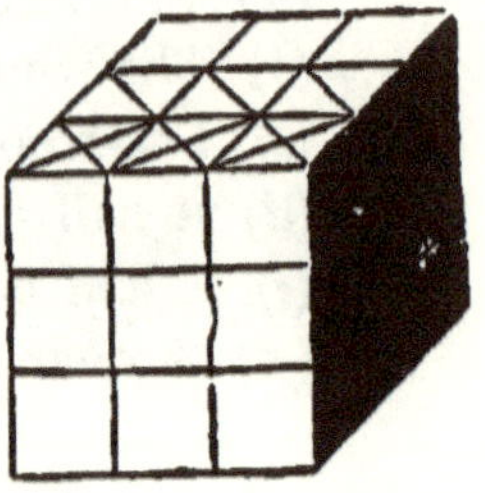

This is the *Fifth Gift* of the Kindergarten.   As in other cases, the pupils should be led by questioning, to make the same close observation upon this form, and upon the blocks of which it is composed.

Again, having placed box '*a*' in the hands of each pupil, select from the one in your own possession eighteen bricks, six pillars and twelve squares.   Now form these into a cube thus :

This forms the *Sixth Gift* of the Kindergarten.   Examine this form and the blocks of which it is composed in the manner already indicated.

Value of the Object Lesson Phase of Kindergarten Work.— These object-lessons on the material, are not very interesting. If the lessons be made long, or given very frequently, they may become irksome.   It would be a great mistake to give a long course of such lessons before entering upon the *constructive exercises.*   Short lessons, however, given occasionally will be uesful for the following reasons :

(*a*) They cultivate close observation.

(*b*) They make the pupils familiar with the material with which they are working.

(*c*) They lead to a practical acquaintance with a large number of geometrical forms and terms.

(*d*) They enlarge and enrich the pupil's vocabulary.

(*e*) They are a most valuable means of improving the language of the pupils.

Constructive Exercises with Blocks.—Without permitting the pupils to see how he does it, let the teacher build upon the table some such object as this, representing a bedstead: See figure page 265.

Keeping the form screened from view by a map or other means, arouse the curiosity of the little ones, to see the object behind the screen.   Their attention will be still further deepened by informing them that after looking at the object a very short time, they will have to **make** it (page 110.)   When the teacher has by some such means as this, excited a deep desire to see the object, and when he knows their fingers are itching to begin work, let the screen be suddenly removed. For a short time the object is contemplated in perfect silence. Knowing that they are about to be called upon to form the same object, their observation is keenly on the alert.   The mind swiftly compares the length with the breadth, notes the number and the kind of blocks used for the head and for the foot, marks the kind of divided blocks used, etc.   After the expiration of a short time, sharply give the command "Work," at the same time replacing the screen.

If the teacher has successfully conducted the work up to this point, it will be with a thrill of delight that the pupils proceed to carry out this command.   After a reasonable time has been spent in attempting to form the object, the teacher should give the signal to "Stop work.   While the pupils are "in position," the teacher should pass along and examine the work.   It will probably be found that a considerable number have failed.   These are thus taught by experience that their observations were, after all, too careless, and that closer attention must be given.

Those who have failed should have an opportunity to re-examine the object; but the time given for this purpose should be shorter than before. Having a keen sense of their former failure, the pupils, as soon as the screen is raised, will make the best possible use of their time. In a moment, *attention will be adjusted*, (page 53) the defects which caused their former failure, will be remedied. All will wait impatiently for the occasion to show that they are now able to do the proposed work. The teacher gives the command " Work," at the same time replacing the screen. This time they do not fail. It is obvious that exercises of this nature, repeated from day to day with various kinds of material, must cultivate some of the most important of the intellectual faculties.

In dealing with the *more difficult* forms, the teacher should direct (page 236) the observations of the pupils and take them over the work by successive stages, as follows :

Placing the object before the class, the teacher proceeds to question :

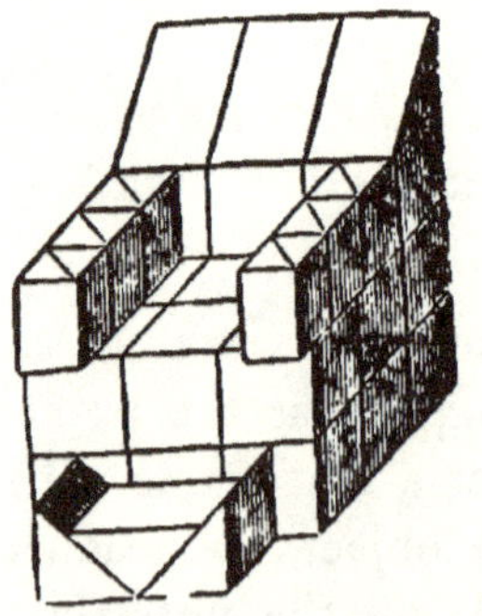

How many blocks form the width of the seat ?

How many the length of the seat ?

The seat is how many blocks high ?

The back is how many blocks high ?

What kind of blocks are used for the foot rests ?

What kind of blocks are used for the arms ?

After the object has been thoroughly examined as a whole, it should be reduced to its constituent blocks, and then rebuilt by the teacher and pupils, in successive stages thus :

The pupils being "in position," the teacher, in view of the whole class, places in proper form, the eighteen whole blocks for the seat. Then on the command, "Work," the pupils take the same step. The pupils resume position, and observe the teacher take the next step. This may consist in forming the back. On the command "Work," the pupils carry the work through the same stage. The pupils again come to position and observe the teacher take the next step, which may be placing the arms. At the command "Work," the pupils take the same step, etc. etc.

It is obvious, that the work of placing the material in position will be facilitated by marking off the tops of the pupils' desks, into inch squares. This is most readily done by means of a little toothed wheel fixed in a handle. It can be made by any blacksmith, and will cost but a few cents.

Language Training.—After the pupils can readily construct the given form, it should be employed as a means of still further cultivating the imagination, and of training in the use of language. For this purpose, the teacher should tell the pupils a story, in which the object just built, is made to play an important part. The imagined incidents should, of course, be made as interesting as possible. When all know the incidents, pupils should be successively called upon to relate the story. This effort on the part of the pupil at once lays bare the defects in his language. A very gentle criticism by the teacher should be followed by a renewed effort, and so on.

After the pupils can tell the *given* story fairly well, they should be encouraged to "make up" stories in connection with the object under consideration. Attempts of this nature have an educative value *distinct* from those just described. They appeal directly and powerfully to the creative imagination. Of course, the circumstance that the story is the product of the pupil's imagination, does not reduce its value as a means of training in language.

Desk Work, or Self-instruction for the Little Ones.—While the teacher is employed with other classes, the little children may be usefully employed as follows :—

(a) They may repeat the forms already taught.

(b) They may imitate forms placed upon the table in full view.

(c) They may build from a diagram placed upon the board, or printed on a large sheet.

(d) They may be left entirely to the dictates of their own fancy as to forms.

(e) They may write some of the stories which have been told in connection with the forms.

(f) They may invent stories.

It will be found, that the self-instruction here and elsewhere indicated in these pages, will simplify the difficulty of *keeping order*. The pupils become too deeply absorbed in these pleasant occupations, to give trouble; and thus, much of the school-room *worry* disappears.

The number of forms that may be thus treated is unlimited. Teachers should examine the illustrations given in " The Kindergarten Guide " No. 2 by Maria Kraus-Boelte and John Kraus. The forms on pages 265-6 are given by way of suggestion :

Forms of Beauty with Blocks.—After the pupils have been led to understand the simple underlying principle of the *balance of parts*, they may in a great measure be left to themselves in this part of the work.

They may be led to apprehend the balance of parts, thus :

What form is this? I shall now place a brick here (placing it at the top) :

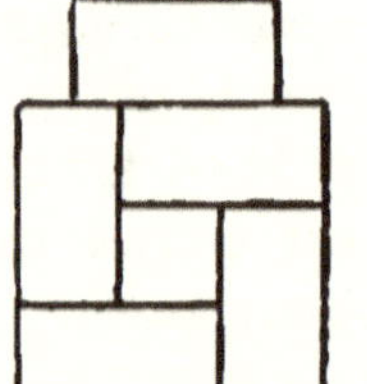

We now have this form :

Where should we place another brick to balance the form? The pupils will suggest that there must be one placed at the bottom.

The teacher may now say " I shall place a brick in the middle on the right side ; where should another go to balance the figure ? " etc. etc.

When the teacher has thus created, at the dictation of the pupils, a number of forms such as the following, it will be found

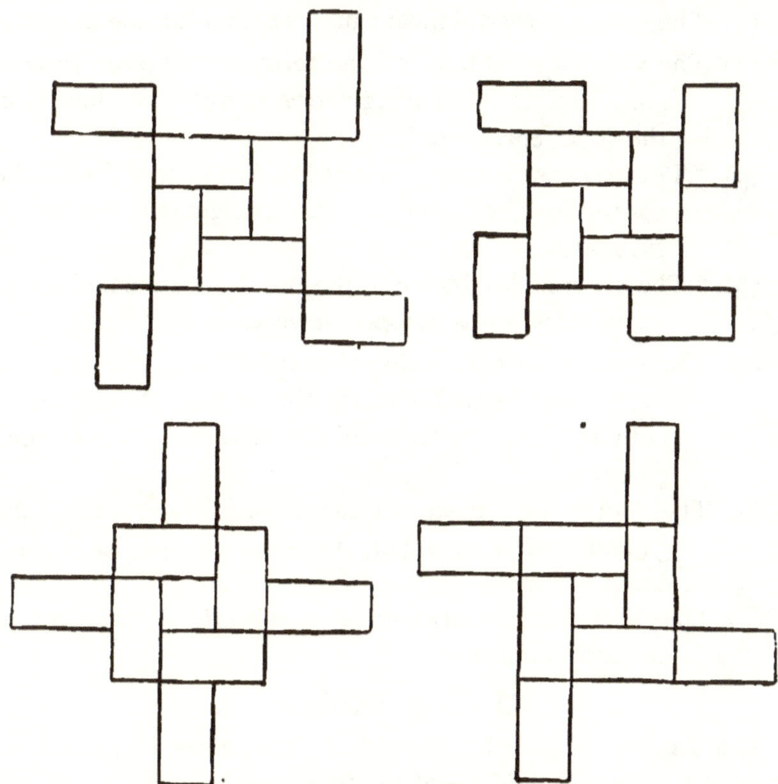

that the pupils will of their *own accord* apply the principle of balance of parts. They will now amuse themselves in making symmetrical figures with the blocks.

By way of suggestion, however, the teacher should occasionally place a new design before them for imitation. Thus, it will be found, that forms such as some of those on pages 272-3, (See also Kindergarten Guide) thrown in by the teacher, will prove very stimulating :

Value of Exercises.—(1) They greatly strengthen the power of *attention.*

(2) They are peculiarly fitted to impart energy and quickness to the powers of *observation.*

(3) They are a powerful means of strengthening the memory.

(4) The very imperfections of the forms develop *constructive imagination.* The imagination corrects all defects in the rude representation.

(5) * The constant attempt to express in material forms the conceptions of the mind, strengthens the **will-power.**

(6) * The attempt **to do** while the mind is stimulated on so many sides, imparts *skill* or *manual dexterity.*

(7) The practice of connecting the object built, with interesting stories, can be made the means of cultivating both the constructive and the creative phase of imagination.

(8) The telling of the stories mentioned in (7) under the guidance of the teacher, improves the pupils in oral composition.

(9) The Forn   of Beauty furnish a powerful instrument of aesthetic culture.

II. The Tablets.

The Tablets should be formed of thin pieces of wood well seasoned.   They should be of the following forms:

(1) The square, one inch to the side.

(2) The equilateral triangle, one inch to a side.

(3) The right angled isosceles triangle, each of the sides containing the right angle being one inch.

(4) The right angle scalene triangle, one of the sides containing the right angle being two inches and the other one inch long.

---

* The benefit claimed in Nos. 5 and 6 will be evident upon a slight examination of those kinds of work more especially designed for hand-training as **slat-work, mat-weaving, paper-folding,** etc.

(5) The obtuse angled isosceles triangle, the side opposite the obtuse angle being two inches long.

The following has been found to be a good arrangement of colours.

(1) The squares red on one side, and white on the other.

(2) The equilateral triangles, yellow on one side and purple on the other.

(3) The right angled issoceles triangle, red on one side and green on the other.

(4) The right angled scalene triangle, one side orange and the other blue.

(5) The obtuse angled isosceles triangle, one side black the other indigo.

REMARK.—It is found that all kinds of tablets can be supplied by a good cabinet-maker at the rate of sixteen cents per hundred. For Public School purposes, it is recommended that a sufficient number be procured to furnish each pupil with about 40 of each kind. A little paste-board box is all that is required to hold the tablets used by each pupil.

Object Lessons on the Tablets.—As in the case of the blocks, before the constructive exercises with any particular tablet are entered upon, the tablet should be made the basis of an object lesson.

Thus, by means of questions, the pupils should be led to count the sides and compare their lengths. The ideas represented by the words, parallel, perpendicular, oblique, etc., should be elicited. The different kinds of angles should be considered, etc.

Just as time permits, these object lessons should be extended beyond the particular tablet to the geometrical forms that can be made with it.

Thus, supposing the pupils to have mastered the equilateral triangle, the rhombus may be considered, and the pupils called upon to form this figure with two equilateral triangles.

The trapezoid may be considered and the pupils called upon to form this figure with three triangles. The rhomboid with four, etc., etc.

Again supposing the right angled scalene triangle to have been carefully considered, the pupils may be called upon to form an oblong with two of these triangles.

A large obtuse angled triangled with two.

A rhomboid with two.

A trapezum with two.

A rhomboid with four.

A trapezoid with four.

After the obtuse angled triangle has been discussed :

An equilateral triangle with three.

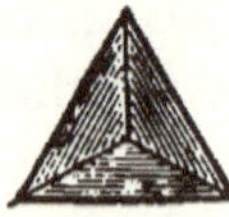

A trapezium with three.

A trapezoid with three.

A rhomboid with four.

A large obtuse-angled triangle with four.

A hexagon with six, etc. etc. :

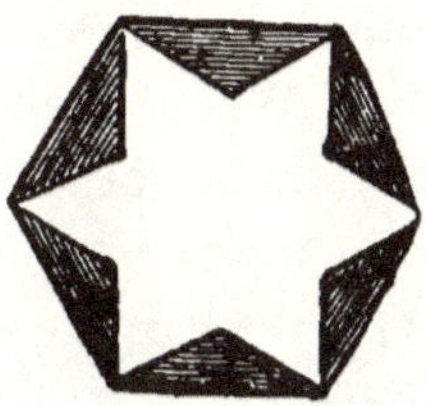

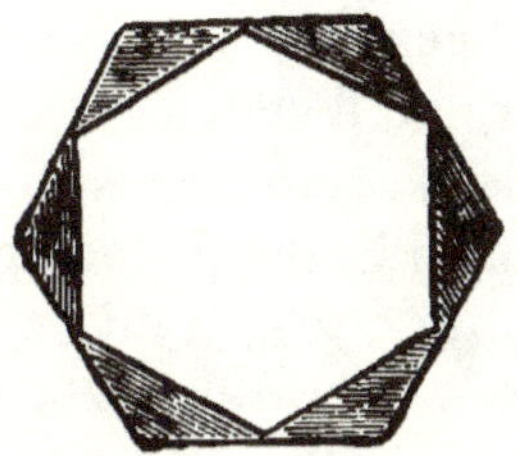

It is evident that work of this kind will make the pupils very familiar with the forms dealt with in elementary geometry. The teacher must not forget, however, that the *chief* value of Kindergarten work centres in the *constructive exercises.*

Constructive Exercises with Tablets.—The mode of dealing with the tablets will naturally follow the same general lines as that with the blocks.

As the forms made with the tablets represent the *pictures* of things rather than the *things themselves*, they can be exhibited to the pupils upon a vertical surface better than upon a horizontal one, such as a table. The following simple method is found to answer the purpose remarkably well :

(1) Hang against the wall a board 3½ ft. x 2½ ft., painted of a light drab color, and ruled or pricked into inch squares like the tops of the pupils' desks.

(2) Let the teacher set aside fifty or sixty of each kind of tablet for his own use, and have these furnished with little brads. The brads should project from the centre of each tablet about an eighth of an inch. In order to make provision for the different colors, **half of each kind of tablet should have the brad on one side, and half on the other.**

The teacher can now with the utmost ease present any desired form.

Self-Instruction with the Tablets.

(*a*) The children may repeat with the tablets any form already taught, and then *draw* the same upon their slates, or in their Kindergarten drawing books. This change of work, without the intervention of the teacher,—is found most valuable in securing long continued attention.

(*b*) They may produce new forms, either exhibited by the teacher, or dictated by their own fancy. When such forms have been completed with the tablets, they should be *drawn*, as mentioned in the foregoing paragraph.

REMARK.—Of course this kind of desk work, answers equally well for the work with the sticks, to be described hereafter.

The forms that may be thus treated, are inexhaustible. The teacher should examine " The Kindergarten Guide " No. 3, by Maria Kraus-Boelte, and John Kraus. Those given on page 273 are suggestive.

In dealing with the Forms of Beauty, those on page 274 are given by way of suggestion :

III. The Sticks.

Each child should be supplied with a number of square sticks such as are used in the Kindergarten. Some of these should be one inch long, some two inches, some three, some four, and some five. They will be much more interesting to the pupils, if colored. Such sticks are very inexpensive, and may be obtained from any dealer in Kindergarten material.

It has already been pointed out how the blocks and the tablets may be used, as the means of making the pupils familiar

S

with geometrical forms.   The sticks furnish peculiar facilities for repeating and extending such instruction.

Thus, the little ones may be called upon to form with sticks right angles, obtuse angles, acute angles, polygons, heptagons, hexagons, etc., etc.

The teacher must, however, as in the case of the blocks, or the tablets, exercise the same care to prevent such lessons becoming irksome.

The sticks also furnish excellent material for the study of numbers, each pupil performing the fundamental arithmetical operations for himself.   It cannot be claimed, however, that this method is peculiar to the Kindergarten, or that the sticks are superior to other counters.

Constructive Exercises with the Sticks.—In order to represent the forms to the class, the teacher should have a portion of the blackboard, ruled into two-inch squares, the lines being formed with white paint, and as thin as can be seen by all the pupils.   Upon these lines, the teacher may easily exhibit by means of the ordinary blackboard crayon, any form which he desires the pupils to produce by means of sticks upon the lines forming the checkered surface of their desks.

The following forms are suggestive : See page 276. Teachers should examine " The Kindergarten Guide," No. 4, by Maria Kraus-Boelte and John Kraus.

Kindergarten Drawing.

It is obvious that the sticks are merely embodied lines. The mode of dealing with part of the work, therefore, needs no explanation.   The following forms are suggestive : See page 277.

IV. Exercises for Hand Training.

For Public School purposes, perhaps the most valuable employments are Slat Interlacing, Paper Folding, and Mat Weaving.   These furnish an almost endless variety of choicest exer-

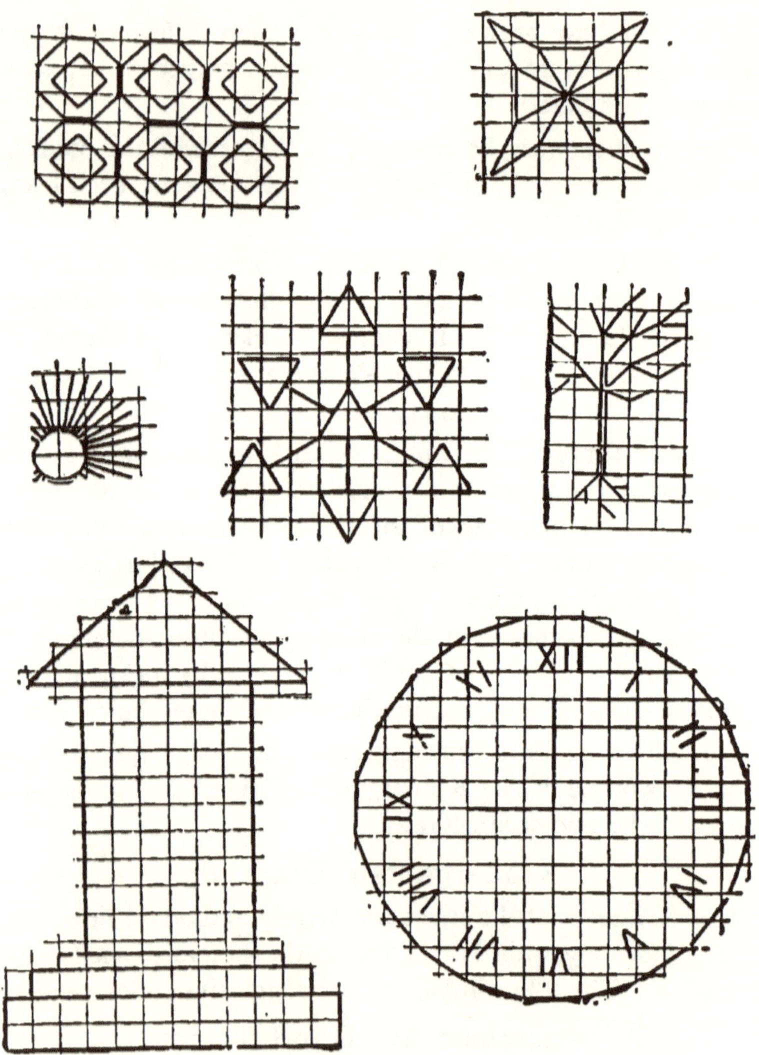

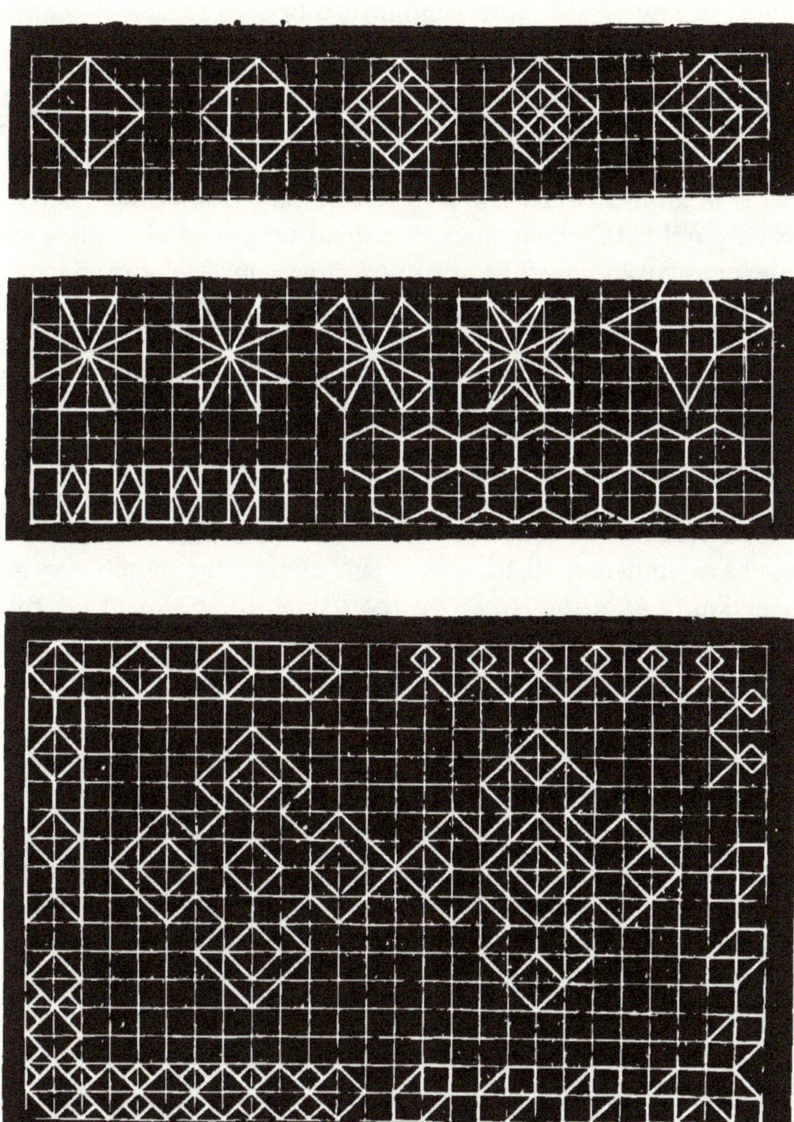

cises for training the hand. They are, at the same time, fully equal to any of the other employments as a means of mental training. Therefore, their value can scarcely be overestimated.

Slat Interlacing.—Slat interlacing consists in making forms by means of interlacing thin elastic wooden slats. For the purpose here contemplated, those ten inches long and two-fifths of an inch wide, are best. A number sufficient to supply each pupil with about sixteen, should be provided. They are inexpensive and may be obtained from any dealer in Kindergarten material. These slats are well adapted to give instruction in geometrical forms, but as these have received sufficient consideration in dealing with other material, it is best to proceed at once with the exercises for hand-training. In dealing with the simpler forms, the following method is found to work well :

The teacher, having made with the slats set apart for his own use, a number of patterns of the particular form he requires to have imitated, distributes them among the pupils for inspection. After the lapse of a short time, these should be collected, and the command given " to work." Those who fail should have another opportunity, but the time allowed for examination should be shortened, etc.

For the more difficult forms, the work should be divided into a number of stages, as in the case of dealing with blocks.

The teacher will be in a much better position to give instruction in this department of work, (in fact, in *all* departments) if he will take the trouble to read some of the little Kindergarten works on Slat Interlacing (Number 4 of the " Kindergarten Guide " by M. Kraus-Bolte and J. Kraus will give all that is required.)

The following forms are offered by **way of** suggestion.*
See page 279.

---

* Slat Interlacing furnishes one of the best forms of "desk work" for the pupils while the teacher is engaged with other classes. It should consist in imitating forms distributed by the teacher. Since in this case they are at liberty to look at the specimens as often as they please, the forms may be somewhat difficult.

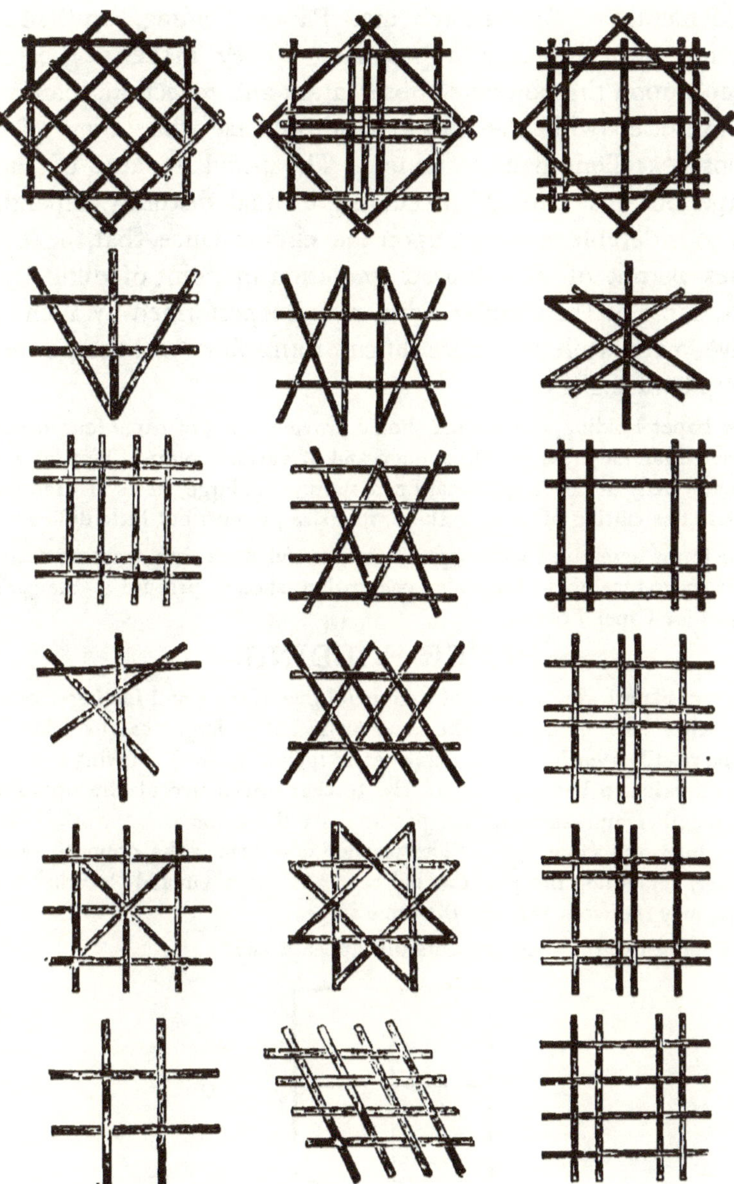

Paper Folding.—For the older First Book pupils, the employments of Slat Interlacing, Paper Folding, and Mat Weaving are peculiarly appropriate. They make a greater demand upon the powers of observation and reflection, than do the exercises with the blocks and tablets, while they give a most excellent hand-training.   The peculiar value of the occupations just named for securing manual dexterity depends in a considerable measure upon the circumstance, that the exercises permit of any desired gradation in point of difficulty. Thus, some of the simpler work, may be performed by a child of five years, while the more dificult forms fairly tax the powers of pupils of eight or ten.

For Paper Folding, the teacher should provide sheets of paper four inches square.   Manilla paper which is tough and of various colors is best for the purpose.   Any dealer in stationary can supply the large sheets of Manilla paper.   The cutting of these to the proper size presents but little difficulty.

The forms here given will suggest much useful work, but teachers desiring to introduce this admirable occupation should procure " Steiger's Designs for Paper Folding."

PAPER-FOLDING.

Having placed in the hands of each child one of the small folding-sheets, the teacher takes a sheet of the same form, but so large that its foldings may be readily seen by all the pupils (say 8 inches square.) Having secured close attention to her movements, the teacher brings two of the opposite sides together and smooths the paper.   At the command "work" the pupils take the same step.   The teacher now brings the opposite sides together, smoothing the paper as before.   At the command "work," the pupils carry the work through the same stage.

When opened, the sheet presents this appearance :

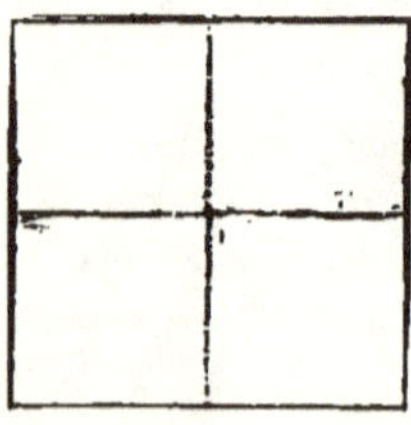

Fig. 1.

Now, bringing the opposite corners over each other and smoothing, the sheet presents this appearance:

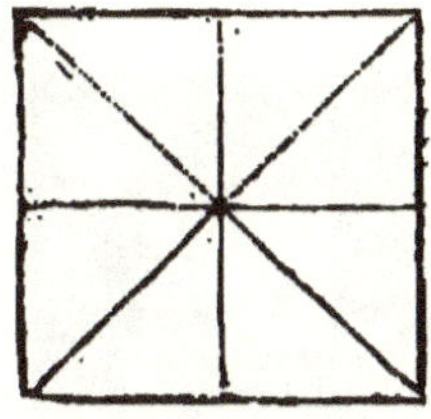

Fig. 2.

The pupils should not be permitted to advance to the construction exercises in Paper-Folding, till they can neatly and quickly secure the creases shown in Fig. 2.

First Basis.—The teacher having ascertained that all the pupils have creased their papers, she takes her large sheet creased in the same way, turns the corners upon the centre, and smooths the paper. At the command "work," the pupils do the same with their sheets. All, now, have in their hands, this form:

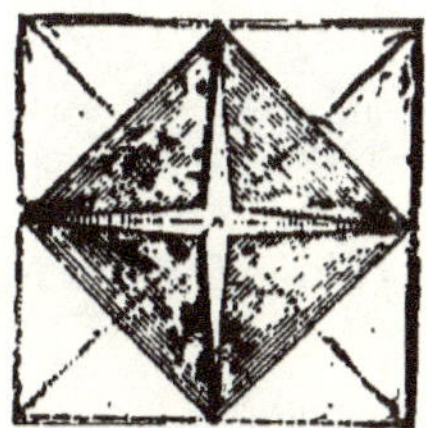

Fig. 3. (First Basis.)

From this form, other forms are made in endless variety. A form from which others are made is called a basis. Fig. 3, shows the First Basis in Paper-Folding.

Derived form, No. 1.—Let the teacher see that all the pupils have Basis No 1 in their hands. Now, taking the same form, (large) she turns the corners back on the middle of the four sides of square and smooths the paper.   At the command "work," the pupils do the same.   This gives us the following form •

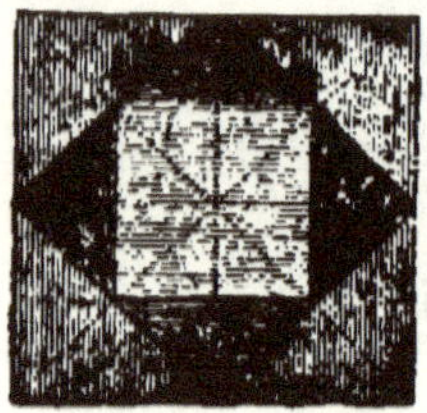

Fig. 4, (Derived Form, No. 1.)

Derived Form, No. 2.—Let the teacher see that all the pupils have "Derived Form No. 1" in their hands.   Now, taking the same form, (large) she simply bends in the corners.   At the command "work," the pupils do the same.   This gives us the following form :

Fig. 5, (Derived Form No. 2.)

Forms, Endless in Variety.—This system of producing new forms by slightly modifying old forms, may be carried on indefinitely.   As other bases may be assumed each as prolific as the one we have denominated First Basis, it is obvious that Paper-Folding is as rich in the matter of forms as any of the other Kindergarten occupations.

Forms Suggested.—The following forms produced from First Basis are given by way of suggestion :

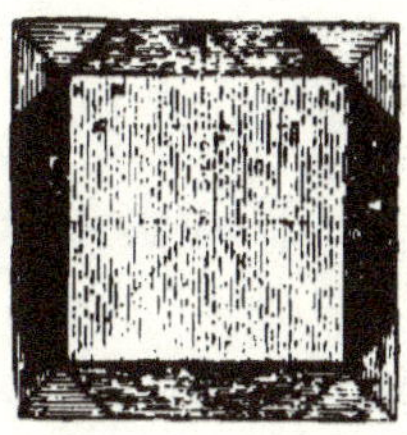 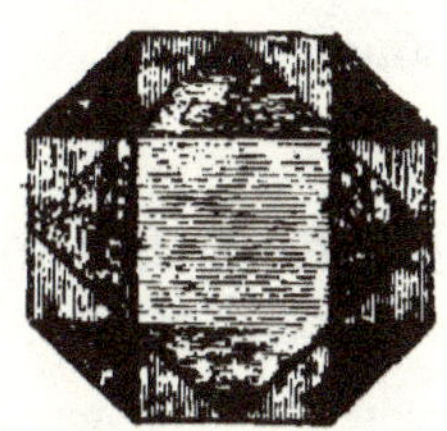 

Harmonious Blending of Colors.—After the pupils have had some practice in producing forms from a single sheet, they should be directed to take two or more sheets of different, but harmonious colors, and laying them over each other fold as if one sheet. This blending of colors adds, wonderfully, to the *beauty* of the forms and therefore to the *interest* in the exercises.

Paper-Folding as Desk-Work.—Paper-Folding opens up a magnificent field for Self-instruction.

(1) Pupils may be permitted to reproduce at pleasure forms already taught.

(2) They may be allowed to invent new forms.

(3) They may produce particular forms demanded by the teacher. For this purpose the teacher should make the required forms, with large sheets, and so place them that they may be readily seen by all the pupils.

Note.—Permissions to blend colors, should always be granted the pupils when engaged in Desk-work.

Mat-Weaving.—This occupation so interesting and useful to children, consists of weaving strips of colored paper into a leaf of paper differently colored. For this purpose the leaf, with the exception of a margin, is cut into strips, and the weaving is performed by means of needles of peculiar construction. A glance at the diagrams given below will clearly indicate the nature of the employment. The teacher's power of applying this admirable means of training will be greatly increased by examining " Steiger's Designs for Mat-Weaving.

Mat-Weaving furnishes an occupation for Seat Work unsurpassed in excellence, by any of the other departments of work.

The following diagrams are given by way of suggestion : See page 285.

The "Modified Forms" Under More Favorable Conditions.

For Public School purposes, it is believed that the exercises already outlined, are sufficiently varied. Without any change whatever in the present school arrangements at least *some* of them may be introduced. Where the teacher is much pressed for time, they will still be found of great utility as "Desk Work." It is found, however, that in large graded schools a much better plan is **to make room for them** by adopting the Half-Time System. By this system, the pupils in the First Book take only *part* of each half-day for the regular work laid down in the Public School programme, leaving the remaining part for other exercises. To illustrate how the arrangement affords the necessary *time* for Kindergarten work in large Schools, let us suppose that there are two separate departments doing First Book work, each department provided with a teacher employed *solely* upon the *regular* work of the programme. Now, for the pupils of these two departments, let us suppose a Kindergarten room with a teacher capable of doing Kindergarten work. Let us suppose the pupils of the two departments first mentioned divided into two sections, a junior and a senior section.

In the morning, the juniors of both rooms pass into the Kindergarten department, and the seniors into the rooms for ordinary work. After intermission, a change takes place, the seniors passing into the Kindergarten room, and the juniors into the room for ordinary work.

It is found that this arrangement gives time, not only for the employments described in the foregoing pages, but for those Kindergarten exercises designed for physical and moral training. The teacher of the Kindergarten department, not being held responsible for the pupils' ability to pass the promotion examination, turns kindly to those subjects on the Public School programme which are too often neglected. Thus the cultivation of the voice by simple songs, object lessons, and oral composition receive due attention.

Results Manifested.

In schools in which these modified forms of Kindergarten work have been adopted, the following results have been clearly manifest :

(*a*) The pupils have a much higher degree of general intelligence.

(*b*) They have a greater power of concentration.

(*c*) They have a much better command of language.

(*d*) They do better in arithmetic, getting the first ideas more readily, and also conceptions of fractions.

(*e*) They learn more easily the forms of letters and words, and hence reading comes easier.

(*f*) The exercises have completely displaced the inveterate idea that school is a pleasant place to go from.

(*g*) The little ones being delighted with the school, the interest of parents is awakened ; and the interest of the parents helps " the teacher to make the school."

Self-Instruction in Common Work.

Reproduction.—With the kindergarten exercises may be introduced much desk-work in connection with the ordinary lessons. The importance of " doing " in primary education has been often pointed out. **Reproduction is the test of self-activity.** And hence every lesson should be made, as far as possible, the occasion of self-instruction. It is of the utmost importance that during working hours, *all the classes should be always at definite work*. In a properly managed rural school, as goo l results can be produced as in any graded school ; because, from the force of circumstances, the law of self-education has a chance to operate ; pupils must help themselves, and self-reliance must, to some extent, be cultivated. In a graded school, where each teacher has but one class, there is, in general, too much teaching and too little independent work. The teacher is most of the time teaching and the pupils are most of the time trusting : with the ever-present help of the teacher they lose, or never fully acquire, the spirit of self-help. But in rural schools much time must either be given to self-instruction, or wasted in idleness. Let every teacher of a country school make provision for having all his pupils always at work, and, in real educational results, he may challenge comparison with the best graded schools.

Preparation of Lesson Provides for Self-Instruction.—The advanced classes can easily be kept employed. But for all classes, self-instruction work should be carefully considered and properly prescribed. Hap-hazard suggestions given on the spur of the moment, are all but useless. Definite work should be assigned for a definite purpose. Work given merely as "busy" work, from a vague idea that youthful hands ought to be doing "something," is the futile expedient of a feeble teacher. But work prescribed for a definite result in self-instruction is of the highest value. In educative results it is the most profitable work done in the school. Therefore, an important part of the honest teacher's preparation for every lesson will be *to determine the amount, the purpose, and the plan of the necessary self-instruction exercises.*

The teacher will have but little difficulty in assigning such work on the ordinary lessons of the day, and so interspersing them with the kindergarten exercises which have been described that they will not fail to be interesting, and, therefore, profitable.

1. *Writing and Drawing.*—Children should begin writing and drawing as soon as they enter school. Kindergarten drawing, the exercises accompanying the primary readers, and easy sketches of familiar things, will supply much desk-work. The sooner a child acquires some facility in writing the sooner he is ready to reap all the benefits of self-instruction.

2. *Reading.*—In learning to associate the sound and form of a letter, the child should make the letter, and should write the word when the letters of it have been learned. He learns the sounds, *e.g.,* of $\breve{a}$, *c*, *t*, and fixes their forms in his mind by writing them separately and together in the word *cat*. Even ability to rule his slate or paper neatly requires much attentive practice.

3. When a pupil has become familiar with some of the letters and their powers, he may be set to select the letters which form the names of objects presented in pictures. For example, from the picture of a pan, he may be asked to select the letters and write as neatly as he can the word, *pan*.

4. The child should write all the new words of a lesson, and, as soon as possible, should have practice in forming easy sentences from given words.

5. He should copy short sentences, especially proverbs, gems of poetry, etc., upon which interesting lessons have been given, and which it is wise to have committed to memory.

6. After a few exercises in telling stories from pictures—under the guidance of the teacher—it affords good practice to leave the pupil entirely to his own perception and imagination in interpreting suitable pictures.

7. Children are always interested in stories told by the teacher, and the reproduction of such stories is a valuable exercise.

Arithmetic.—From the beginning, arithmetic should supply useful examples for desk-work. For example :

1. There may be practice in making and varying the number-forms with blocks, or other counters, and on slates, *e.g.*, different forms for *five*, *six*, etc.

2. There may be practice in writing down the *sums* of pairs of numbers and the *differences* of pairs, first in words, then in figures ; *e.g.*, four *and* two are six.   Then $4+2=6$, $6-2=4$, etc.   Also in formal additions, of numbers, by means of figures, *e.g.*, $2+1+3=6$, the addends being arranged as in common addition.

3. After numerous problems have been solved by means of number-forms, there may be practice in making up easy problems, such as the teacher has given ; for example : Charlie has 6 cents and he pays 2 cents for a pencil for his sister, how much has he left ?   Willie has six turkeys and sells two of them for three dollars, and the rest at a dollar a pair, how much money does he receive altogether ?   Several columns of numbers may be given, the sum of no column exceeding 6 : *e.g.*,

1	2	3		2	1	3	0				
2	2	1		1	2	1	2		2 tens	=	20
3	1	2		3	3	1	4		3 tens	=	30
									1 tens	=	10
									6 tens	=	60

4. Similarly, pupils may be asked to tell all they can about *e.g.*, the number six : five and one are six, $(5+1=6)$; two and four are six $(2+4=6)$, etc.   There are three twos in six ; there are two threes in six, etc.   And so on with the pictures for larger numbers ; as, *e.g.*, *twenty* represented by four   How many fives? How many fours ? How many twos, etc.

5. In a similar way, such practice may lead to the mastery of the multiplication table: *e.g.*:

    Once 3 is 3.

    Twice 3 is 6, etc., etc.

The foregoing are simply thrown out as suggestions.   The thoughtful teacher, who prepares his lessons, will be able to present an endless variety of interesting self-instruction work.   The rule is : **All at work, and always at work.**

NOTE.—The Kinder-Garten Guide (which has been referred to) ought to be in every teacher's hands; Published by E. Steiger & Co., from whom all sorts of Kinder-garten material can be had at reasonable rates.

CHAPTER XIII.

OUTLINE METHODS IN SPECIAL SUBJECTS.

I. Geography.

1. Objects of the Study.—Apart from its practical utility Geography when properly taught, affords an excellent means of mental discipline and general culture. It appeals to the imagination, strengthens the memory, and stimulates the reasoning powers by inducing the habit of discriminating facts and forming real relations. It supplies invaluable information about innumerable familiar objects and aspects of nature, and excites an interest in these that gives a new charm to every country walk.

2. Preparatory Object Lessons.—Object Lessons on plants, animals and minerals, should be begun as soon as the pupil enters school, and may be continued throughout the whole course. An object lesson for geographical purposes may have more of the character of an *information lesson* (imparting fact-lore). Such lessons shoul l include the geographical classification of animals and plants, as for example those of the Hot Region, those of the Temperate Region and those of the Cold Region. Those animals and plants which **do not** come under the observation of the children, should receive most attention.

3. Cardinal Points of Compass.—(1) *Sun at Noon.*—Draw attention to the position of the sun at noon and inform the pupils that when we face the sun at that hour, we look toward the *South*, and that our backs, are to the *North*, the left hand to the *East* and the right hand to the *West*.

(2) *Sun at Rising and Setting.*—Inform the pupils that the sun rises in the East and sets in the West.

(3) *Shadow of Stick.*—Set up a stick about four feet long in a vertical position in the yard. At noon the shadow points North and South.

(4) *Diagram upon Floor.*—Draw upon the floor a long line pointing North and South. Bisect this by another of the same length, pointing East and West. Causing a pupil to take the centre, give directions "Go North," "Go South," "Go East," in quick succession. Now, put in lines for the intermediate directions and proceed as before. Again—Place a map directly over the diagram with the top to the North. Now, after resting an instant the end of the pointer upon the central part of the map, move it towards the sides, the pupils describing the movement as N, S, E, &c., &c. Inform the pupils that it is for *convenience* we hang the map against the wall.

T

4. Developing Idea of Map.—(1) *Boundaries.*—Let the teacher secure the assistance of the class in drawing a plan of the school-room floor, marking the place of the doors, windows, etc. This plan may be drawn first upon the floor, then the pupils should draw it upon their slates. Deal with the school yard in the same manner.

(2) *Scale in Maps.*—The teacher draws a horizontal line about two feet long upon the board, and says "Let us call this the North side of the room." "Who will come to the board and draw lines for the other sides?" The sides being drawn, the teacher calls upon others to mark the places for the doors, windows, desks, etc. The teacher then draws a horizontal line *one* foot long and says, "Let us call this the North side of the room ;" "Who will come to the board and put in the other sides?" Proceeds as before. Next a line *four inches* long is drawn and the teacher calls this the North side and proceeds as in the other case. The pupils thus see that the school room can be represented by pictures of *different* sizes.

(3) The teacher hands a boy a foot rule and asks him to measure the North side and the East side of the room. Supposing it is found that the measurements are 20 feet and 24 feet, the teacher says "If I call every foot *one* inch, how many *inches* long will be the lines to represent those sides?" Let these be drawn upon the board, etc. Now let another pupil take the foot rule and find the length of the teacher's desk. Supposing it proves to be 5 feet, get the pupils to decide that it will take a line 5 *inches* long to represent it in the plan. The school yard may now be represented, taking one inch to represent a **yard**. (These processes employ child's own activity, pp. 129, seq. ; they define fundamental ideas, pp. 80-81 ; they base representation on presentation, pp. 93-94 : they connect the new with the old, p. 171.)

5. Definitions of Natural Divisions of Land and Water.—(1) *Pupils to form Definitions.*—Be careful that the things defined are thoroughly understood, and that the pupils as far as possible form the definitions for themselves. (Page 49.)

(2) *Presentative to Representative.*—From adjacent hill lead the pupil to the conception of a mountain. From well known creek, to the idea expressed by "river." (Page 74.)

(3) *Moulding-Board Representations.*—Letting the blue surface of the moulding-board represent the sea, form islands, capes, peninsulas, etc., with river sand.

(4) *Pictorial Representations.*—Lead the pupils to examine pictorial representation of islands, bays, capes, etc.

6. Map Notation.—The pupils should be taught to read the map as one does the newspaper. Many of the facts given in most so-called descriptive parts of geographical text-books, are clearly stated upon the map and do not need further expression. In order that the pupils may feel at home with a map, they must be familiar with the manner of representing not only capes, bays, peninsulas, towns, etc., but plateaus, lowlands, etc.

The pupils should be led to discover for themselves the important physical features of each country. This will compel him to think while studying the map, and lead to self-activity and independence of research. (Pages 92 and 105.)

7. Developing Ideas of the Earth's Shape and Size.—(1) *Shape of the Earth.*—Let the teacher provide peas, marbles, oranges, or other spherical bodies. Holding the marble and the pea up to view, "In what respect do they resemble each other?" (Shape). "In what respect do the orange and the ball resemble each other?" The marble and the orange? So, too, this globe (school-globe) resembles the world in **shape.** (Page 58.)

(2) *Size of the Earth.*—How long would it take a man to walk around it? How long would it take a train running forty-five miles an hour to run around it, etc.?

8. Basic Ideas in Mathematical Geography.—(1) *Poles, Axis, Equator, Latitude, etc.*—Causing an ordinary black globe to spin, call on pupils to draw a line through those points upon the surface which move most quickly. The line drawn through those points represents the equator. "What points move most slowly?" These two points are the poles. The straight line joining these is called the axis. All points between the equator and the North Pole are said to be in North Latitude. All points between the equator and the South Pole are said to be in South Latitude. Lead the pupils to see the necessity of lines of latitude and lines of longitude, by asking them to describe the position of points made with the crayon upon the surface of the black globe.

(2) *Hot Region, Cold Region, Temperate Region.*—Show the pupils the location of those regions. "Why does the belt around the middle of the earth become so hot, and why does the temperature become lower as we move towards the poles?"

9. A Map as an Enlarged Picture of a Portion of the Globe.—*Map and Globe taught together.*—The teacher says "On this map of the world, I see two large portions of land, joined by a narrow neck. (Here point to map of North and South America). "Who will come to the globe and find the same?" Again—"On this map of the world you perceive this large island (Australia)." Will you find the same island on the globe? etc. etc.

10. Interest in Map Work.—*Connection between Places and Characteristic Animals and Plants.*—In dealing with a map of the world, the grand divisions should be connected with such people and with such productions as may be characteristic. The teacher should make the dead matter of maps fairly glow with interest.

Pointing to a map the teacher says " Here is the home of the Negro." A few words upon the customs of the negroes in Africa will secure the closest attention. When the attention is rivetted, the teacher says " This country is called : " here write the word Africa upon the board ; do not pronounce it till all have looked at it. If pronounced at first, the pupils will not care to examine the spelling. Pupils then called upon to pronounce and spell the word. The teacher may now throw in—" It is also the home of the hippopotamus and the giraffe." " Who will find the home of the Negro on the *globe*." Other regions dealt with in a similar manner.

11. Causes Affecting Climate.—*Distance from the Equator. Height above the Sea-level.*—Before entering upon the continents the pupils should be made familiar with the principal causes determining the climate of a place.

(*a*) The distance from the equator.

(*b*) The height above the sea-level.

(*c*) The nature of the winds sweeping over it.

(*d*) Slopes towards or away from the equator.

(*e*) The nature of the currents (warm or cold) washing its shores.

12. The Continents.—(1) *Topical Method.*—(*a*) The Topical Method should be followed. (Analytic Method, p. 167.) Teacher and pupils enter upon the study of the different topics. This method properly carried out, requires wide reading on the part of teacher and pupils. The pupils must have access to the best books of reference and also to the best books of *recent* travel. The books of reference will be especially useful as giving information for the ordinary recitation in geography ; and an hour should be set apart each week for the reading by the pupils of interesting items found in the books of travel.

(*b*) The desire of the class to enter upon the study of any prarticular division or country, may be aroused to a state of enthusiasm by exhibiting pictures of its striking characteristics, as regards scenery, great works of art, people, animals, plants, etc. The solar camera, of course, surpasses all other apparatus for this purpose. Specimens of productions will also prove very useful. Specimens and pictures will be gladly collected by the pupils. (Page 76.)

(*c*) Since Political Geography rests upon and is largely determined by physical conditions, it follows that physical Geography should be first learned. The natural order of topics would be (1) Outline and coast features, (2) Surface, including the great highland regions, slopes, mountains, rivers, lakes. (3) Climate and productions. (4) People.

(2) *Map-work in General.*—The most effective means of making the pupils familiar with part of a map, is to practise them in drawing the part from memory. (Page 91.) Map-drawing should, however, be regarded as a **means** not as an **end**. It is not necessary, then, that the maps of the pupils should be *very* accurate. The energies of the pupils should not be wasted in learning any of the so-called systems of map-drawing by *construction* lines.

Although it is not necessary that the maps drawn by the pupils be absolutely correct, the maps from which the pupils **learn** geography should be accurate. An outline rapidly drawn upon the board by the teacher is almost certain to give erroneous ideas of relative position and of proportion. A true outline *painted* in some bright color upon the ordinary blackboard, or better still, upon a movable blackboard of slate-cloth, is almost indispensable in teaching maps. For a similar reason the pupils should use pasteboard outlines of the continents. The *true* form of the boundary being thus retained, the pupils are not likely to go far astray in putting in the other map-work.

Whenever possible life should be thrown into the dead matter of maps, by connecting the places with something of permanent interest, as for example : Trafalgar, with the naval engagement—The Bay of Fundy, with its wonderful tides, etc. Maps should be so taught as to enkindle the imagination and stir the feelings. (Transference of Interest, page 113.)

(3) *Map-Drawing as Desk Work.*—Map-drawing furnishes one of the most useful forms of Desk work. This arises from the following considerations :

(*a*) It keeps the hands employed.

(*b*) The work done by the pupils in a given time may, by changing slates, be brought to a speedy test.

(*c*) By this means the teacher, while employed with other classes, can cause the pupils constantly to *review* maps, thus keeping map-work already taught, fresh in the memory.

(4) *Map-Drawing as a means of Education in Geography.*—Map-drawing is one of the most speedy and effective means of examining the pupils either

for the purpose of promotion, or for the purpose of testing home work. When used as an instrument of examination, map-drawing should not be confined to mere physical features and political matters : the animals, plants, minerals, &c. of a region, may be as readily indicated on the map, as can be gulfs, capes, islands, countries, towns, &c.

(5) *Coast Features.*—As in the work of drawing the outline, the pupils have already drawn the coast-features, it follows, that these should be learned in this connection.   Capes, islands, peninsulas, bays, gulfs, etc., are a part of the coast-line and should be learned when this element is dealt with.

(6) *Surface.*—It is impossible to give a clear conception of the structure of the surface of a country by mere description, or even by pictures.   For this part of the work we require *raised* maps.   The raised maps offered for sale are rather expensive ; but by means of the ordinary moulding board* such maps may be easily made by teacher and pupils.   In the work of form-ing the sand-maps on the moulding board, the teacher would be greatly assisted by having on his desk the "Royal Relief Atlas," published by Messrs. Sonnenschein and Allen, London.

While looking at the sand-map, the pupils should be required to des-cribe the position of the great highland regions, give the boundaries of the great slopes, etc.   In other words, the pupils should be led as far as possible to discover the facts for themselves, by examining the map.   This is true of all map-work, and leads to independent habits of investigation. The best way of fixing these divisions of the surface in the memory, is to have the pupils construct them.   (Pages 95 and 129.   Doing defines Ideas.)   For this purpose, each should be supplied with a pan and a small quantity of putty.   A few minutes should be given for examining the large map, and then the work should be done entirely from memory.

The description of a Highland Region should include an enumeration of its mountain chains, rivers, and lakes ; and the description of a Lowland Region should include an enumeration of its rivers and lakes.   Now this is the connection in which the names of the mountains, rivers, and lakes should be taught, that is, their position should be described with reference to *natural* divisions of the surface, not (at first at least) to the *artificial* divisions of political geography.

(7) *Climate and Productions.*—The Climate and Productions naturally follow the surface.   General views should first be given.   (See Guyot's Common School Geography).

---

* A board 4 x 3 ft. painted blue and swung between two upright pieces will answer every purpose.   The front edge should be provided with a hinged leg so that the board may be presented at any angle to the pupils.

(8) *Political Divisions.*—As in the case of other map-work, the political divisions should be fixed in the memory by drawing them.

(9) *Great Towns.*—When the greatness of a city is the outcome of some obvious natural cause, the attention of the pupils should be directed to the fact by *questions,* For example, the city of Para is likely to flourish, as it is the sea-port for the produce of the Amazon Basin. Towns should be grouped upon their respective rivers and coasts. Coupling what a town is noted for with its name, makes the work more interesting and useful.

13. Political Geography.— (1) *Interest ; how aroused.*—The desire of the class to enter upon the study of any particular country, should be aroused by exhibiting pictures of its striking characteristics, as regards scenery, people, animals, plants, great works of art, etc., also by exhibiting speci- mens of its productions. The Solar Camera is of great value to excite in- terest in the study of a country. (Secures unity of interest and prepar- atory adjustment, pp. 60-61.)

A few words as to the history of the people, citing especially any great historical events will prove interesting.

(2) *Surface.*—The nature of the surface of the country should, as far as possible, be elicited from the pupils. This eliciting is now perfectly reasonable, because the pupils have only to remember what general division of the surface the country is a part of. The teacher supplements at his discretion what can be drawn from the pupils.

(3) *Climate and Productions.*—In a similar manner, the climate and productions of the country should be elicited. A little information by way of supplement, is all that is required.

(4) *Occupation of the People.*—The occupation of the people should be derived, as far as possible, from a consideration of the natural productions, etc.

(5) *Commerce ; Great Cities.*—Foreign or Domestic Exports, Imports, Commercial Towns—Routes of Commerce. In learning about the great cities, good pictures will be helpful in many ways.

(6) *Journeys.*—These should be made very interesting by pictures.— Solar Camera of great value.

(7) *Comparison.*—Comparison should be carried out in every subject. The continents drawn on the same scale should be always before the pupils. The pupils should be constantly exercised upon these, and also upon the chart, showing the comparative volume of trade of different countries, the comparative wealth, the comparative population, military strength, etc. The teacher can easily form such charts by enlarging the diagrams given in

some family atlas of recent date. (Composes the most perfect form of attention, pages 58 and 59.)

NOTE.—The following books are recommended for teachers :—Geikie's Teaching of Geography, MacMillan & Co.; Dr. King's, Aids and Methods in Geography, Lee and Sheppard, Boston.

II. Arithmetic.

Remarks on General Principles of the Method.—It is strictly in line with psychology :

1. It begins with the *presentative* and advances to the *representative*. Number is, of course, pure abstraction ; in the method here outlined, the pupil begins not only with concretes, but with intuitions that *make* them concrete. That is, the arrangement of each number-form is an analyzed one which makes relations distinct. Present seven things in a row, say, and the resulting idea is vague ; it will have to be made definite by analysis and synthesis. Symmetrical arrangement, with different intuitions of the same form, leads to clear *perception*, and so aids the higher mental processes.

2. It follows, that this actual partition and re-combination of things call out gradually the analytic and synthetic functions of mind.

3. Since number is not so much a *relation* as a *relating*, the method gives the pupil a clear idea of number—an idea which in the highest mathematics is not to be corrected, but only to be made *explicit*.

4. The *varying* forms give both novelty and distinctness. The child sees that the *relation* is the same although the form is different. He is *abstracting*, and abstracting in the natural psychological way, simply and unconsciously. He is learning to *think* relations from *seeing* them.

5. Giving the symbol as soon as the idea is mastered, is justified by common sense as well as by psychology. There is variety and therefore interest ; dealing with the objects too long, becomes monotonous ; symbols open up a new field. There comes also a feeling of *power*, of advance, etc. There is *economy* of time and power for both teacher and pupil. It affords means of *self-instruction*. In short, the justification is on the same ground for the child as for the race. The human mind *always* economizes by means of some condensed symbol as soon as the idea is familiar. It is worse than useless to be always going back to beginnings ; this would render progress extremely slow.

GENERAL SUGGESTIONS.

1. Arithmetic is taught for the sake of (*a*) its value in discipline, (*b*) its value as knowledge, *i.e.*, its utility in the affairs of life.

2. To secure these VALUES as thoroughly as possible, all arithmetical study is to be a training in thinking ; all *merely* mechanical work is to be banished. There must indeed be mechanical drill, but this must be founded on *intuitions*.

3. For this training in thinking, as well as for acquiring skill, *systematic* training in Mental Arithmetic, from first to last, is absolutely indispensable. Indeed, so far as Arithmetic is concerned, the principal work of the teacher in the Public School is to practise the children in Mental Arithmetic.

4. At each and every stage Mental Arithmetic must precede, and lead up to Written Arithmetic. As compared with the effectiveness of written Aritmetic alone, it may be fairly said that with the *systematic teaching of Mental Arithmetic*, **twice the Knowledge and twice the Power** will be acquired in a given time.

5. In mental work, rapidity, correct language, and logical order of thought and statement must be constantly aimed at.

6. In mental Arithmetic it is desirable that the teacher should follow the sequence of some book. Otherwise the " course " is likely to be without logical method ; disconnected problems are of but little use in mental training. At the outset, children need no book ; when they have advanced to division, and its applications, they may prepare assigned lessons in some text-book. But a book supplies only *type-questions ;* many similar questions should be framed by teacher and pupils.

7. In Mental Arithmetic there should be frequent *written-examinations*.

8. Good counters are cubes (black and white) with faces a centimetre (about $\frac{2}{5}$ inch) square ; *ten* of them are represented by a rectangular prism (units, black and white alternately,) which makes a convenient *ten-unit*. For making the number-forms, a blackboard may be used having holes bored two inches apart in horizontal and vertical lines. With this are 100 white (wood or bone) buttons with short stems for inserting in the holes. The number forms can be built up, for teaching, or copying by the pupils.

A.—*First Stage.*—*The Numbers One to Five.*

1. The numbers 1 to 5, inclusive, taught *intuitively* by NUMBER-FORMS and by counting—these " forms " being presented through (*a*) dots or

points on blackboard, slate, etc., (*b*) arrangement of balls of abacus, (*c*) arrangement of *cubes*, etc., used as counters. Number-forms are to be used because the *intuition* of a number of objects in a group is *clear* and comparatively easy if there is a *symmetrical* arrangement ; *e.g.*, the perception and ultimate conception of *five* are easier from *this* arrangement

than from this • • • • •

2. It will be found useful to run over the number forms from one to eight, or even ten, to give a *general* idea of the numbers represented ; then begin to make these ideas *definite* making 1—5 the first stage. It is not necessary to spend time, first of all, in learning to count. That 5, *e.g.*, follows 4, and precedes 6, is *seen* from the intuitions, and but little, if any, formal drill in counting is necessary.

3. From principles which have already been set forth, it will be well, after reasonable drill on *one* form, to make other presentations of a

Number Form, *e.g.*, of *five :—*

4. Practice is to be had in *all the combinations* of the several numbers (*see table below*), *first*, the additions, then the subtractions, etc. ; and every number is to be mastered before the next number is taken up. This means (*a*) the *addition* of pairs of numbers, by Number Forms in various ways (see above), *e.g.*, (*b*) *subtraction* or the resolution of numbers into pairs by similar means, (*c*) the multiplication and division (exact) of pairs, as *e.g.*, three times two are six ; the twos in six are three.

Note.—(*c*) *May* be left till the combinations from 1 to 10 are learned. PRACTICE IN COUNTING BACKWARD AND FORWARD.

5. Of course, this includes practice in number-forms, on board, slate, etc.

For example :— etc.

6. Give the *figure* (symbol) as soon as an idea of a number is clearly grasped.

7. When sufficient practice has been had with blocks, dots, etc., give practical problems, for example : Charlie paid one cent for a pencil, and four cents for an orange, how much did he spend ? etc., etc. When drilling on *addition*, let the practical problems be in addition ; when in *subtraction*, let the practical problems illustrate subtraction. Then, problems

illustrating both operations. So with multiplication and division. By using the number-forms the operation can be *seen*, and this leads to *understanding*.

8. There should be exercises in rapid mental work, *e.g.*, $5 - 1 + 2 - 1 + 3 - 2$, etc.

9. Have practice in the corresponding written (word and symbol) exercises as soon as the children have mastered the mental process.

For example :— ⦂ | ∴ | ∴ : in words, *two* and *three* are five ; in symbols, $2 + 3 = 5$.

B.—*Second Stage.—Numbers Six to Ten.*

The numbers 6 to 10, inclusive, to be taught intuitively, all the steps given in the first stage being followed. This includes especially

(1) Practice in the addition of two numbers whose sum is not greater than ten ; see table given below. Practical problems as before.

(2) Subtraction. Practical problems.

(3) The multiplication and division of numbers within the above-named limits. This practice means

(*a*) The *multiplication table* of numbers from 1 to 10 ; this supposes (as before) much " drill," but drill grounded on intuitions.

(*b*) *Division* of the products obtained in (*a*) by an abstract divisor ; (*b*) division in the sense of distribution, the converse of the operation in (*a*) : in (*a*) the factors are given and the product is to be found ; in (*b*) the product is given and the factors are to be found. It cannot be too often repeated that these processes are to be rendered VISIBLE—there must be intuitions through number-pictures.

(*c*) Measurement of the products of the *multiplication table*, *i.e.*, division in the sense of being contained in ; *e.g.*, 2 is contained in 4, 6, 8, etc.

(4) Practice in the corresponding written exercises as soon as the children have mastered the processes mentally. Practice, also, in solving and in constructing practical problems.

(5) After ten has been learned, the *tens* may be run over : twen-ty, thir-ty, for-ty, etc. Then, 5 tens $= 4$ tens $+ 1$ ten, $= 3$ tens $+ 2$ tens, etc., etc.

The following table, which exhibits all combinations of number from 1 to 20, shews substantially the work to be done in these two stages, and is the basis of all combinations.

C.—Third Stage.—Numbers from One to Twenty.

1. TABLE OF COMBINATIONS ON NUMBERS FROM 1 TO 20.

1	2	3	4	5	6	7	8	9	10
1	1+1	2+1	3+1	4+1	5+1	6+1	7+1	8+1	9+1
			2+2	3+2	4+2	5+2	6+2	7+2	8+2
11		1+2			3+3	4+3	5+3	6+3	7+3
	12		1+3	2+3			4+4	5+4	6+4
10+1		**13**		1+4	2+4	3+4			5+5
9+2	10+2		**14**		1+5	2+5	3+5	4+5	
8+3	9+3	10+3		**15**		1+6	2+6	3+6	4+6
7+4	8+4	9+4	10+4		**16**		1+7	2+7	3+7
6+5	7+5	8+5	9+5	10+5		**17**		1+8	2+8
	6+6	7+6	8+6	9+6	10+6		**18**		1+9
5+6			7+7	8+7	9+7	10+7		**19**	
4+7	5+7	6+7			8+8	9+8	10+8		**20**
3+8	4+8	5+8	6+8	7+8			9+9	10+9	
2+9	3+9	4+9	5+9	6+9	7+9	8+9			
1+10	2+10	3+10	4+10	5+10	6+10	7+10	8+10	9+10	10+10

2. The upper part of the table gives the combinations of the numbers to ten inclusive ; the lower part, the combinations of the numbers from 11 to 20 inclusive. The ways of forming five are.—4 and 1, 3 and 2, besides the related forms, 2 and 3, and 1 and 4. In all, there are 55 different combinations, and no more. The other combinations, forty-five in all, are simply different ways of *expressing* some of these as *e.g.*, 3 and 2 are 5, may be also expressed by 2 and 3 are 5. In the table, the *equivalent* forms are separated from the fundamental forms by wider spacing, *e.g.*, 1 + 2, so separated from 2 + 1.

The plan to be followed is the same as that of the preceding stages. Number forms of all the numbers from 11 to 20 are to be given by means of balls on Frame, dots, etc.; and by means of these the partitions and recombinations are to be shown. Take, *e.g.*, the number eleven. From the table, the *different* combinations for eleven are 10 and 1, 9 and 2, 8 and 3. 7 and 4, 6 and 5. Then with the following number-form for eleven, all the *unit-forms* of which are now familiar to the child, we have :

$$10 + 1 = 11 \quad = \quad 9 + 2 \quad = \quad 8 + 3 \quad = \quad 7 + 4$$

$$= \quad 6 + 5$$

All these forms may be made upon the ball form, by simply moving some of the balls of the original figure, so that, as in all the preceding forms, pupils see that these five forms are identical. And similarly with the other forms up to 20. Making these partitions and combinations, and expressing the process in words and figures, afford good self-instruction work.

3. (*a*) This table includes the usual forms :—1 plus 2, 3, 4, etc. ; 2 plus 1, 2, 3, etc. ; 3 plus 1, 2, 3, etc. If thoroughly learned from intuitive-teaching, it will prove a solid foundation for all primary work.

(*b*) It is applicable to the higher combinations of numbers, *e.g.*, take those of 5 ; 4 + 1 leads to 14 + 1, 24 + 1, 34 + 1, etc. ; 2 + 3 leads to 21 + 3, 2 + 23, 23 + 3, 24 + 3, etc.

D.—*Fourth Stage.*

1. The genesis of numbers from 1 to 100, inclusive—the method of intuition being followed as in the preceding stages.

2. Make the pupil familiar with combinations of *tens* as *units ; e.g.*, as in the combination of five, 4 + 1 = 5, so, 4 tens + 1 ten = 5 tens ; this by visible and tangible objects. Call attention to the fact that thirty = three-ty, is 3 tens ; forty is four-ty, *i.e.*, 4 tens, etc. In fact, practice on the *tens* (using intuitions) may be had as soon as ten is learned.

3. Teach the *intermediate* numbers, *e.g.*, 21 = 2 tens + 1 ; 22 = 2 tens + 2, etc.; 31 = 3 tens + 1, 32 = 3 tens + 2. Give practice in counting backwards and forwards by 2's, by 3's, etc. : 2, 4, 6, etc. ; 3, 6, 9, etc. Give notation and numeration to 100, inclusive. Throughout, keep prominent the composite character of the numbers, viz. **tens** and *units ; e.g.*, 35 = 3 **tens** and 5 *units.*

4. Give practice in the addition of a number of one digit to one of two digits ; the higher number to be exhibited as so many *tens* and *units.* Form *series* of numbers, *e.g.*, give two or three terms, and have the children continue the series, 12, 14, 16, etc. ; 9, 12, 15, etc. ; 21, 25, 29, etc.

5. Practice in the subtraction of a number of *one* digit from one of *two* digits. As in the preceding exercises, *intuition* is necessary, especially in such cases as 43 + 7, 62 + 9, etc.

6. Practice the multiplication table till the pupils have obtained a ready knowledge of it, but, in *every instance* give by *intuition a clear insight into the meaning of each combination ; e.g.*, the meaning of 4 times 7 is 28, must

---

NOTE.—Call attention to the fact that *thirteen* is three-teen, *i.e.*, 3 and *ten* ; fourteen, 4 and *ten* etc. The pupil may run over the numbers from 11 to 20, to get a general idea of them, before proceeding to a definite knowledge of them by analysis and synthesis.

be made perfectly clear by means of the "ball-frame," etc.   But this *clear insight* being had, drill till the children can give the *combination with scarcely an effort of thought.* The pupil may be taught to construct and practice the table for himself, by means of the balls, the counters, dots, etc. : *e.g.,*

●	●	⦁	one	3
●	●	●	two	3's
●	●	●	three	3's

etc., etc.

In written work the order should be (*a*) multiplication by a number of one digit ; (*b*) do., by·10 ; (*c*) do., by a multiple of 10 (*d*) do., by a number formed of units and tens.

7. Give practice in the division of the products of the multiplication (as in Stage B, 1 b), (*a*), by an abstract divisor, *i.e.,* division in the sense of distribution ; and (*b*), measurement of the *products, i.e., division* in the sense of *being contained in.*   In written work the order will be (*a*), division by a number of one digit ; (*b*) by 10 ; (*c*), by a multiple of 10 ; (*d*), by a number consisting of *tens* and *units.*

8. The children are now prepared to deal formally with (*a*), the factors of a number ; (*b*), the factors common to two or more numbers ; (*c*), the G. C. F., of do. ; and (*a*) with the multiples of a number ; (*b*), a multiple of two or more numbers, and (*c*), the L. C. M. of two or more numbers.

The course of work above exhibited shews, in the main, the whole course of instruction in elementary arithmetic, and constitutes the basis of all subsequent work.   Unless, therefore, the work outlined has been thoroughly mastered, subsequent progress will be uncertain and unsatisfactory.

E.—*Fifth Stage.*

This stage is mainly a continuation of the preceding stages, which cover the ground of the first seven sections of Mental Arithmetic, Pt. I.   Details, therefore, are not necessary.   A few hints may be noted.

1. Children must understand the value of numbers before they use them. This is the fundamental principle in the preceding stages, in which intuition has the first place.   In Stage D, when intuition is no longer expedient, the number should be clearly analyzed into *hundreds, tens* and *units,* etc.

2. In written work with large numbers—*i.e.,* numbers too large for mental operations, note the following points :—

(*a*) Avoid working with *very large* numbers. Do not waste nervous force in drudgery. Long mechanical operations, especially of multiplication with large *factors*, have little practical value. Who needs to multiply millions by millions, or hundreds of thousands by hundreds of thousands? Instead of questions involving hosts of figures, give many questions of moderate length, and aim at *accuracy* and *rapidity*.

(*b*) To prevent mere mechanical drudgery, and to awaken the interest which grows out of *intelligence*, every process must be thoroughly explained.

(*c*) As already implied, in mental work, insist on good language and logical and concise order of statement ; in written work aim at *neatness, accuracy, rapidity*.

(*d*) Some of the tables of weights, measures and money, will of course be mastered, and use made of them in " Practical Problems."

F.—*Sixth Stage.*—*Fractional Arithmetic.*

I. Vulgar ; II. Decimal.

1. Begin with the now familiar idea of the *division* of a NUMBER *into equal parts*, the underlying principal in all teaching of fractions. Show, *e.g.*, that to divide 6 by 3 is to obtain one of the 3 equal parts (2) that compose 6. Show that " to take *one-third* of 6 " is the same as " to divide 6 by three ; " there is a change of *name*, but no change of idea or of operation. Give practice in finding $\frac{1}{2}$, $\frac{1}{3}$, $\frac{1}{4}$, $\frac{1}{5}$, etc., of a number. (See page 211).

2. Lead to the facts that a number has *two halves, three thirds, four fourths*, etc.

3. The children have already learned that *twice* one unit of *any kind*, is *two* units of the *same kind ;* three times one unit of *any kind* is three units of the same kind, etc. They are, therefore, now prepared to find $\frac{2}{3}$, $\frac{3}{4}$, $\frac{4}{5}$, etc., of a number ; *e.g.*, they find *one*-third or 6 to be 2, and therefore *two*-thirds of 6 to be 4.

4. Lead to the fact that thus to take (*e.g.*) $\frac{3}{4}$ of a nnmber is the same as to take one-quarter of three times the number, *i.e.*, to *divide* 3 times the number by 4. Lead to the facts 3 lbs. divided by 4 is 12 ounces, $\$3 \div 4 = 75$ cents, etc.

5. Show that $\frac{1}{2}$ of a number $= \frac{2}{4}$ of it $= \frac{3}{6}$ of it ; that $\frac{1}{3}$ of a number $= \frac{2}{6}$ of it, etc. ; and that $\frac{2}{8}$ of a number $= \frac{1}{4}$ of it, etc., *e.g.*, $\frac{1}{2}$ of 24 $= 12 = \frac{2}{4}$ of 24 $= \frac{3}{6}$ of 24.

NOTE.—Vulgar fractions form a principal subject in Mental Arithmetic. Both from common experience and from operations in the preceding stages, the children have become familiar with some of the ideas and nomenclature of Fractional Arithmetic. The formal and systematic instruction is now to begin. Give the *notation* as soon as the conceptions are clearly gained.

6. Now proceed to show that not only a *number* of things, but also a *single thing* may be divided *into equal parts*. Base the instruction on intuitions, by a divided line, rectangle, or other concrete object. Apply the ideas developed in 2, 3, 4, 5, above.

7. Show (*a*) how to change a whole number into the form of a fraction; (*b*) how *inexact* division gives rise to a mixed number; and (*c*) *conversely* how a mixed number may be changed into an indicated division, *i.e.*, an "improper fraction;" (*d*) how the quotient of one number divided by another equals the sum of the quotients of the parts of the dividend by the divisor, as *e.g.*, $\frac{24}{4} = \frac{16 + 8}{4} = \frac{16}{4} + \frac{8}{4}$, etc., and conversely.

8. Use ideas of 5, above, to show how to change fractions with different denominators into fractions having a "common denominator."

9. Addition and subtraction.

10. Multiplication and division.

For methods and type-questions, see chapter on fractions in McLellan's Public School Mental Arithmetic.

II.—Decimal Fractions.

The Teaching in Decimal Fractions follows the order observed in vulgar fractions, so that every "rule" in decimals finds its explanation and demonstration in the corresponding rule in vulgar fractions. Guard against rule-of-thumb work; explain every process.

G.—*Seventh Stage.*

Application of the foregoing to analysis and to "Commercial Arithmetic."

The unitary method, which has been followed in the simple analysis of the previous stages, is to be followed here. It is to be applied to

1. Solution of " Rule of Three," problems.
2. " Simple Interest.
3. " Profit and loss in all its "cases."
4. Other Percentage Problems.
6. Proportional parts and Partnership.

NOTE.—While special stress has been laid on the necessity of beginning with intuitions for the acquisition and development of the first conceptions in the several stages, it is very desirable that the pupils should pass as soon as possible to the abstract and the general.

For method and type-questions under these heads see McLellan's Higher Mental Arithmetic.

NOTE.—In this stage the fundamental principles of ratio and proportion, with applications, may be given.

III. PRIMARY READING.

Methods.—The problem of teaching to read is doubtless a difficult one ; but some writers greatly exaggerate the difficulty. It requires no great learning or skill to frame a strong "indictment" against the English alphabet. It is safe to say that the actual difficulty is inversely as the strength of the indictment. It is usual to name four methods of teaching primary reading, viz.: the *alphabetic*, the *phonetic*, the *word*, and the *phonic*. As the alphabetic method is now but little used and the phonetic requires a special alphabet, we may confine our notes to the *word* and the *phonic* methods.

Word method.—The method, as practised, begins with teaching words as wholes : it connects familiar spoken words with their written or printed forms, and passes sooner or later—generally not soon enough—to phonic analysis ; that is, the spoken word is resolved into its separate sounds, and these are associated with the letters which represent them in the written or printed word. The so-called word-method is, therefore, a combination of the word method and the phonic method.

1. It claims to be analytic, proceeding from "whole to part." It is undoubtedly analytic when it introduces phonic analysis of words, and connects the sound-elements with the letters which represent them. As pure word-method it is analytic—proceeding from whole to part,—only in the fact that the child's vague idea of sound is made definite by calling his *attention to the sound of the word*. The whole that the child starts from is the vague idea of sound ; the "part" is the *articulate*, *i.e.*, the definite sound.

2. It claims to proceed from the "known to the unknown," *i.e.*, from the known sound-word (word as spoken) to the unknown form-word—word as written or printed. But the *word*, as a *word*, is an arbitrary symbol having no significance of its own. How can an idea of *sound* be used to assimilate an unassociated idea of *form ?* The best that can be said is that the method awakens some interest by showing the child that *written* words, like spoken, are means of expressing his ideas of things. It is pure assumption that because the form-word is before the child he *knows* the word. He no more knows the word till he has made his vague idea definite by analysis, than he knows the number ten before he has made his vague idea definite by partitions and recombinations of the objects before him. He *knows* the word only through analysis into its element.

3. The method—as word-method—is mechanical ; there must be a vast amount of telling, and a vast amount of guessing. For vague perceptions lead to feeble memory. The mind is, therefore, driven to form merely sensuous associations. And thus, when the word-method, as such, is too faith-

U

fully followed, the child memorizes whole pages of the "readers" and simply recites when he seems to be reading.

4. This perpetual telling tends to produce a mere passive as opposed to an active and energetic habit of mind. He is not taught to *use* the knowledge acquired yesterday to gain new knowledge to-day; he does not learn *with* what he *has* learned ; *e.g.*, yesterday he was told about the word *cat*, to-day he is told about the word *mat* : yesterday's lesson does not help him with to-day's. Is not this a waste of power, a direct violation of "learn *with* what you *have* learned."

5. Before the child can gain power to recognize or form new words he *must* unconsciously follow the phonic method. When he comes to a new word, it is not a question of using the phonic method, or not using it. He cannot form or recognize the new word unless he has learned the sounds of its letters from unconscious phonic analysis.

6. It is only a question, then, whether the child is to be *taught* the phonic method, and so get all the benefits, practical and disciplinary, that flow from it ; or whether he shall be left to discover the method for himself. If he is left to himself, there must be a great waste of experiences, endless corrections of hasty inductions, etc., in order to acquire even moderate power of word-recognition, *i.e.*, in order to learn even the mechanical part of the art of reading.

7. In reading, as in all primary work, the child should not be left to his own weak powers of analysis and synthesis. There must be exercise of both these mental functions before the power of word-recognition is gained, and here, as everywhere, it is the business of the teacher to direct the mental activity so that the desired results may be reached with the least waste of power.

The Phonic Method.—The *phonic* method begins with *elements*, that is, the *sounds*, or powers of the letters, and then combines them into words. It is, therefore, commonly called a "synthetic" method.

1. It is, in fact, both analytic and synthetic, and may, therefore, be rightly called the analytic-synthetic method. The recognition of the sound *ă*, or *ā*, is an analytic act. In making the exact sound *ă*, the pupil's *attention* is called to what he has for a long time been doing, and like all attention, *analyzes* ; the result is the *definite* idea of the sound *ă*. It is here, as elsewhere, a mistake to suppose that because the sounds are definite in themselves, they are definite to the child. The vague "whole" in this case is the undifferentiated *mass of sound* and corresponding undifferentiated ideas of sound—those which he has made led by impulse or imitation, and

the process of making one out of this mass *definite*, is one of analysis. There is also synthesis in combining the several *definite* elements into a significant word.

2. The *phonic* (analytic-synthetic) method best obeys the law of unity of attention, "one thing at a time." The child's attention is fixed first upon one kind of sensations, the *auditory*, and *then* upon the corresponding *visual* sensations. In the word method, attention is divided between the look, the sound and the meaning of the word, and in some cases the distraction is increased from the attempt to associate the form of the word *immediately* with the "object," (See page 168.)

3. It has been said that this method is without interest because the isolated sounds have no meaning. This is pure theory. The *forms* of letters are interesting to children, then why not sounds? Besides, there is *(a)* interest in the teacher's uttering of the sounds, *(b)* interest in the pupil's own activity in *making* the sounds ; in elementary education it is scarcely possible to over-estimate the interest of the child in what *he himself does*. *(c)* Intellectual interest arising from the exercise of the analytic function. *(d)* Interest from the sense of new power, or capacity, and this is of the highest value. Left to his own hap-hazard inductions from the word-method, the pupil must spend a long time before gaining the power and sense of power, to recognize new words. *(e)* It ought to be remarked that the child is not kept dwelling on the isolated sounds till all are learned ; as soon as he has mastered a few sounds, and the letters which represent them, he is set to work to use his knowledge. In the very first lesson he learns *a*, and *t*, and *c*, and experiences the thrill of *discovery* when, combining these, he *recognizes* the sound *cat*, with which he has long been familiar.

4. The objection has been made to this method that it is impossible to isolate the sounds of the consonants ; that in the attempt to do so they are partially vocalized, and so mislead the children ; *e.g.*, in isolating the sound of *c* in *cat*, it becomes *kĕ*. To this objection the answer is : *(a)* In the case of a final consonant there is a slight vocalization, *e.g.*, the *t* in cat. In the case of an initial consonant the thing is to get the pupil to place his vocal organs in proper *position* for *articulating* the consonant-sound. This is secured even if there is a slight vowel-element. Besides *(b)* It is not necessary to isolate the initial consonants ; with right teaching, the child is led to get for himself the idea of the sound, and the power to form it.

5. The difficulty arising from the same letter standing for several sounds is much magnified. Besides, this is not peculiar to the phonic method. The word method *proceeds* to analysis, and, therefore, has to face the difficulty.

The word method assumes that the child will get the sounds of the letters by unconscious inductions; well, learning the different circumstances under which the same letter stands for different sounds, is not nearly so difficult; *e.g.*, the child has learned, say, the "hard" sound of *c* (as in *cat*), has he to make a very *wide induction* in order to *know* where it has the "soft" sound? Again, his *experience* is available for many cases. Suppose he has learned the siblant *s*, and comes to the sentence, "the cat is on the mat," he is not likely to pronounce *is* "iss;" if he does so at first, he speedily corrects himself: nor does he trouble himself about the "inconsistency" over which the philosopher grows so eloquent.

6. The analytic-synthetic (phonic) method is, therefore, psychologically justifiable. Indeed, it stands to reason that any method which quickly puts into the hands of the child the *power* of recognizing and constructing new words, is better than one that leaves him wholly dependent on memory and vague inductions from past experiences.

7. Finally, the method has stood the test of experience. It has been used with excellent results in the Ontario Normal Schools. It is used in the Toronto schools where the results may challenge comparison with those of any other schools or any other methods.

Suggestions.

1. The teacher should remember that much *drill* is necessary, no matter which method of teaching reading may be used. The aim is to gain ability to recognize and pronounce words without conscious mental effort. When a child has mastered the multiplication table the symbols 6×8 suggest the result without mental effort; so, in primary reading, the association of sounds and symbols must be *perfect*. There must be no stopping to *think*, *e.g.*, what sound any letter in *band* stands for, or what sound they all together represent. So long as any such thinking has to be done, there cannot be *good* reading; the mechanical association between sign and sound is not complete, and the reader has to take time and expend energy in re-making such association. So long as this is the case there cannot be expressive reading.

2. From the beginning, writing is to go with reading. Imitating the teacher, the pupils utter the short sound of *a* (as in cat); the teacher makes the letter and drills to associate sound with sign; the pupils then write the letter on blackboard, etc.

3. The *names* and sounds of the letters are not to be given together. One thing at a time is again the order. Indeed, it will not, in general, be necessary to give formal lessons on the *names*. These are learned incidentally;

and it will be found that by the time the Second Part of First Book (Ontario Readers) is reached, the pupils *know the names of the letters.*

4. Transition from *script* to *print* will be made with little effort. If the blackboard and tablets (or primers) are used together from the start the print-form will come with the script-form. When a word is written on the blackboard, have children point it out on the tablet. Show the word on tablet and have children write it, etc.

5. Pupils must be taught, from the first, to read every sentence with expression. As already intimated, *perfect familiarity with the words of the sentence is necessary.* There should be many exercises involving questions and answers. With simple devices the thoughtful teacher will lead the children to read every sentence with the right expression.

6. Instead of using only ready-made pictures (in tablets, etc.), the teacher should, as far as possible, make blackboard drawings of objects. This increases interest of class.

7. Diacritical works are not necessary ; the different sounds of a letter are learned from comparison of different forms, *e.g.,* cap, cape ; mat, mate ; fat, fate, etc. Of course, there are some words that must be taught as wholes.

8. It is unnecessary—rather it is unwise—to associate objects with written words. The order is : the idea, the spoken word, the written word. That is, perfect association is formed between the idea and its spoken word, then perfect association between the spoken word and its written form. To attempt to form a new and *direct* association between the idea (object) and the *form* is to violate the law of unity of attention.

Practical Suggestions—The following suggestions may be useful to the young teacher :

1. Choose some element, say *at*, as starting point. Give sound of *a* in *at*, and have children repeat the sound individually and collectively. Make the letter on blackboard and have children make it on slates, etc., helping them to easiest way of doing this. Drill to associate sound and sign : Make letter and call for sound, make sound and call for letter. Proceed similarly with the letter *t*. Then sound elements *a*, *t*, at first slowly, then more rapidly, till the word *at* is produced. Illustrate meaning of *at* (*at* the door, etc.) Have pupils write word.

2. Show picture of a cat. Children pronounce the word *cat* ; then slowly so as to separate into two sound-elements (a *known* and an *unknown*) represented by *c-at*. Write word *cat* on blackboard. Call attention to the parts : Sound *at* ? (or what does *at* say, etc.) Sound the whole word ? Then

sound the part *c*? (or sound the letter that makes *at* into *cat*?) Have children make the letter. Drill to associate form and sound. For desk-work have the children write the several letters and the *word*, on properly ruled slates or paper, giving directions as to how the letters can be best formed. In a similar way, proceed with the words bat, cat, fat, hat, mat, nat, pat, rat, sat, vat.

3. Constant exercise in using acquired knowledge to gain new words, which are significant, or which can easily be made significant, to the child. For example: (1) the teacher writes the word *pan*, and asks the pupil to pronounce it. (2) He pronounces the word *fan* (or gives picture of the thing) and has them *write* the word. (3) He leaves them to *discover* new words, *e.g.*, *cap*. In such way may be treated such words as tan, tap, cab, can, cap, fan, has, ham, man, map, nap, ran, ram, rap, sam, sap, van, trap, strap, bran, ant, pant, grant, span.

4. Similarly, the short sounds of the other vowels can be taught : bit, fit, hit, mit, pit, sit, *or* in, bin, fin, pin, sin, tin, spin ; cot, hot, not, pot, *or* fop, hop, lop, mop, sop, top ; bet, met, net, pet, set, *or* hen, men, ten, pen ; but, cut, hut, nut, rut, *or* bun, fun, sun, run, etc., etc.

5. The other consonants may be taught as in (2) and (3)—ba-d, ha-d, pa-d, po-d, ho-d, so-d, bi-d, hi-d, di-d, d-in, din-ner, etc., ba-g, na-g, ra-g, bo-g, fo-g, do-g, g-ad, g-ap, g-un, big, pig, gig, etc.; l-ad, b-ag, l-ap, let, let-ter, etc.; and, sand, band, land, stand, etc. Of course the teacher will not confine himself to monosyllables. He will introduce into his simple sentences and "stories" longer significant words, *e.g.*, dinner, dipper, dig-ger, dimmer, dagger, sadder, sinner, summer, softer, butter, bitter, better, pepper, supper, rub-ber, rob-ber, red-der, lad-der, man-ner, ban-ner, pic-nic, sis-ter, riv-er, nev-er, cutter butter, etc.

6. As already intimated the long vowels can be taught inductively ; the pupils will soon see that the final *e* is silent and makes the medial vowel long : bat, bate ; mat, mate, etc.; bate, fate, mate, pate, rate, date, gate, hate, late, grate, skate, slate, grated, plated ; cane, lane, mane, sane, vane ; fade, jade, made, glade, blade ; came, same, tame, lame, name, blame, fame, dame, game, flame, etc. Fin, fine ; din, dine, etc.; fine, line, mine, nine, pine, vine, wine ; time, grime, lime, crime, clime ; hide, ride, tide, side, glide, pride, etc. Mole, stole, dole, bole, sole, poke, woke, broke, yoke, spoke ; bone, tone, lone, alone, crone, drone, cone. Met, mete ; pet, pete ; cede, re-cede, im-pede. Tun, tune, cub, cube, etc.; mute, lute, fume, tune, clue, blue ; latest, plated, skating, etc.; biting, glided, etc.; con-sume, vol-ume ; mop-ing, grop-ing, sloped, com-plete, severe ; strong, long, etc., etc.

7. It will be convenient to have for use a large number of words, classified according to similarity of vowel sounds. For example, other ways of representing long vowel sounds :

Long a—*ai*, as : ail, bail, fail, jail, mail, nail, pail, rail, sail, wail, fail, frail, snail, trail, etc.; aim, air, hair, chair, pair, lair, re-pair, rain, pain, gain, plain, grain, ex-plain, etc.

Ay—As : bay, day, gay, hay, jay, lay, may, nay, pay, play, ray, say, way, pray, dray, gray, a-way, de-lay, pray-er, Sun-day. *Also* a few in *ey* : prey, they, obey, con-vey, etc.

Long e—*e*, *doubled* (e e), as : bee, fee, lee, see, thee, flee, free, tree, three, feed, deed, need, seed, deem, seem, queen, seen, be-tween, six-teen, etc., etc.

In the combination *ea*, as : lea, pea, sea, tea, flea, plea, leaf, sheaf, mead, read, beak, leak, heap, leap, each, peach, teach, reach, etc., etc.

Long o—*ow*, as : bow, low, mow, sow, tow, blow, flow, glow, grow, etc.

Oa, as : oats, oak, oar, roar, soar, foal, goal, shoal, foam, roam, loam, loan, moan, groan, hoarse, ap-proach, etc.

The oi sounds as : oil, boil, coil, foil, soil, toil, broil, spoil, noise, voice, con-join, appoint, etc. *Some in oy*, as : boy, coy, joy, toy, annoy, destroy, oyster.

And so proceed with other analogous sounds.*

The teacher should keep in mind that in teaching primary reading he is to put his pupils as quickly as possible in possession of the power of word-recognition, ability to pronounce words without a conscious effort of thought so that the pupils may quickly pass to **interesting** reading matter. But of course he is not to drill simply on isolated words till the forty sounds and their representatives are learned. He should have the words as fast as learned used in sentences and easy stories. It requires skill to form these properly. *No lesson requires more careful preparation by the teacher than the primary reading lesson.*

Let no teacher follow any plan which takes from four to eight months to learn by the "word-method," "some two hundred words." The school life of the child is too short and too precious to be thus frittered away. By *following the analytic-synthetic (phonic) method his pupils in "from four to eight months," will have acquired the ability to pronounce at once any ordinary English word,* that is, **The main difficulty in primary reading will have been mastered.**

---

* In making classifications of words, and framing sentences, &c., the teacher will get much help from *Meiklejohn's* "English Method of Teaching to Read," *Macmillan & Co.* To help in sentence and story-reading, the teacher should have different primary readers.

IV.—TRAINING OF LANGUAGE POWER.

I. General Principles.—Importance of language has been dwelt on pp. 107, 184, 215.

1. The instrument for expression of thought.

2. The instrument of thinking process.

(*a*) It records thoughts. (*b*) It shortens the thinking process. (*c*) It analyzes thought. (*d*) It reacts on thinking.

3. Language, is, therefore, the complement of reason—that without which reason would not and could not be what it is. Progress in thought, therefore universal progress, depends upon language.

4. It follows that language is the *test* and the condition of the cultivation of reason :

(*a*) In perception, there must be for the percepts, *words*; (*b*) In judgment (the thinking of relations), there must be *propositions*. (*c*) In relating judgments (reasoning, etc.) there must be connected propositions, or *discourse.*

5. Hence **every lesson should be a lesson in language.** (*a*) Power of expression is test of thinking ; clear expression means clear thought. (*b*) Disconnected (occasional) "language lessons" are useful but not sufficient. (*c*) Reproduction in oral and written language indispensable. (*d*) Hence mistake of having large classes especially in primary work.

II. Method in Outline.—There may be considered : 1. Indirect Influences ; 2. Reproduction ; 3. Original Work.

1. Indirect Influences.—The teacher should :

(1) *Use Correct Forms of Speech.* Child, a creature of imitation. Outside influences form habits of incorrect speech : school-room influences should correct bad habits of speech, and form good habits. In all questioning, exposition, stories, narratives by the teacher, there should be (*a*) good grammar, (*b*) correct pronunciation, (*c*) educated accent, or cadences of voice, which are "the commentary of the emotions on the propositions of the intellect."

(2) *Insist on Correct Forms.* No imperfect answer to be accepted. Blunders in grammar, slovenly enunciation, fragmentary speech, not to be tolerated in either teacher or pupil.

(3) *Study Correct Forms.* Teachers should study *con amore* the best writers. Pupils should have abundant reading of such authors ; the scrappy lessons of the ordinary reading book are totally insufficient. To become good readers, and good users of English speech and lovers of English lit-

erature, they must read and study good literature. There ought to be much supplementary reading in every school. There is not half enough practice in reading in any school class, and the power to read well and love for good literature will not be developed without libraries of choice literature.*

(4) *Exercise in Correcting Faulty Forms.* There should be practice in correcting prevailing errors of speech. Pay no attention to the nonsense poured out against the practice of correcting "false syntax." There is no need, however, to imagine incorrect forms. There is plenty of false syntax in every-day speech and writing, and habits of right speaking must come from correcting opposite habits.

(5) In this connection, *grammatical analysis* may be mentioned as a valuable means of language training. It is necessary also to intelligent reading, because it is necessary to the clear apprehension of thought.

2. Reproduction.—The importance of this has been emphasized.

(1) *All lessons* supply material for such exercises. The primary pupil is to (*a*) write new words and sentences he has been taught. (*b*) Make new sentences in which given words are to occur, such as *new* words, irregular verbs (go, went, etc.) on which lessons have been given. (*c*) Copy maxims and proverbs which are worth remembering. (*d*) Give substance of what has been said in lessons on such proverbs and maxims. (*e*) Give Sentences expressing observed facts.

(2) *Silent Reading.* This should be practiced from the beginning. Give a reasonable time for class to read over silently a few sentences, a short narrative, etc., and then have them close books and reproduce the thought. Capital exercise for all classes. Power of concentration cultivated, etc.

(3) *Stories.* From pictures, and reproduction of stories told by teacher. Train children to "translate" pictures (orally) as well as they can, to tell the story as well as they can, and finally to write out the thought as well as they can. Advanced classes should give abstracts, narratives, paraphrases, etc.

(4) Object lessons. (*a*) *Perceptive* ; (*b*) *Reflective.*

(*a*) *Perceptive.*—Have object lessons on size, weight, form, etc., and common objects, etc.; and make every such lesson a language lesson. Learning the facts about a cube—faces, corner, edges, etc., these must be properly ex-

---

* An excellent and remarkably cheap series of "Classics for Children," is published by Ginn & Co., Boston. The whole set ought to be in every school and in every teacher's library.

pressed.   Lesson on *table*, *e.g.*, the facts taught about *top*, *frame*, *legs*, *uses*, *material*, etc., must be properly expressed orally and in writing.   If a lesson, *e.g.*, (by means of pieces of wood, stone, wool, etc.) has been given to develop ideas of *hardness* and *softness*, the results should be expressed in such language as : "Because the stone does not yield easily to the touch, it is said to be *hard*, to have (or possess) the quality of *hardness* ;" similar sentences about the wood, &c.; then expression of the generalization.   (*b*) *Reflective*.—Lessons on truthfulness, justice, charity, industry, patriotism, etc.   Such lessons may farily be called (subjective) "object" lessons because they appeal directly to the child's *experience*.   Wisdom and goodness embodied in maxims, proverbs, literary, gems, etc., to be the subject-matter of lessons.   Such lessons can be made more interesting than *external* object lessons, and are of the highest value in education.   For example, lessons on such selections as the following :

> " A soft answer turneth away wrath, etc."

> "Kind hearts are the gardens,
> Kind thoughts are the roots,
> Kind words are the blossoms,
> **Kind deeds** are the fruits."

> " All things that you do, do with your might,
> Things done by halves are never done right."

> **"Dare to be true, nothing can need a lie."**

> " Be good dear child, and let who will be clever,
> *Do* noble deeds, not dream them all day long,
> And so make life, death, and the vast forever,
> One grand sweet song."

> " *Politeness, like great thoughts, comes from the heart.*"—

" What is it to be a gentleman ?   It is to be honest, to be gentle, to be generous, to be brave, to be wise, and, possessing all these qualities, to exercise them in the most graceful manner."

> " Define a gentleman you say?
> Well, yes, I think I can !"

> " He is as gentle as a woman,
> And as **manly as a man**." etc., etc.

(5) *Memorizing*.—Selections in Poetry and Prose.   The Intelligent learning by heart of masterpieces of our literature is a most effective means of education ; now greatly neglected owing to re-action against mere *rote*-learning.   Should be *in every school ; part of the work of every class.*

(*a*) It trains the language faculty and the memory.

(*b*) It stores the mind with good and beautiful thoughts which will tell powerfully on character.   (*c*) It helps towards expressive reading.   (*d*) It tends to develop a taste for good literature, one of the highest results the teacher can aim at.

Something in this line should be done every day; and every week part of a day should be specially devoted to readings, recitations, etc.

3. Original Work.—The work being graded according to the stage of advancement of class, there should be : (1) Letters and Business Forms. (2) Narratives of personal experiences, descriptions of journeys, etc. (3) Biographical sketches and historical narratives.   (4) Accounts of current events.   (5) Criticisms of well studied selections.   (6) Formal Essays.

V. GRAMMAR.

General Remarks.—Grammar is one of the *thought-subjects* of the school course.   It has, perhaps, stronger claims than Arithmetic to be called "the logic of the common schools."   But beside its disciplinary value, it has great practical value.   The science of the sentence (the unit of thought), its study *helps* to make the student a good reader, and a good speaker and writer.   The teacher should be on his guard against the prevailing attempts to belittle the study of Grammar and Analysis.

General Method.—Begin with the *bare* sentence, the two-word sentence, subject and predicate.   Then, as Prof. Whitney says, "Having the nucleus of the sentence well understood, it is easy to go on and teach the other parts of speech and their offices ; the substitute for the noun (pronoun) the two kinds of qualifying words (adverb and adjective) and the two connecting words (preposition and conjunction), and with such clearness as to be thoroughly comprehended.   Dealing as we do with a known and familiar language, we can accomplish all this before we proceed to take up the several parts of speech themselves for a *more detailed* treatment."   This is the true method, and the preliminary work indicated can be done in almost the lowest classes.   The child begins to form *judgments* before he is two years old, and to express them (in *propositions*) before he is *three*.   Before a sentence can be properly read, it must be understood, *i.e.*, there must be analysis of it, conscious or unconscious.   Begin then with the sentence, and let the process be one of analysis and synthesis.

For public school work the following points should be kept in view :

I. Classification of Words (Parts of Speech) —Word-functions :

    1. Something thought (and talked) about........Subject or noun.

    2. Somewhat thought (and said) about this......Predicate or verb.

3. Noun-substitute .... Pronoun.

4. The Subject-qualifier...................... Adjective.

5. The Predicate-modifier .... Adverb.

6. The Noun-connector .... Preposition.

7. The Sentence-connector. .... Conjunction.

8. The Emotion-word .... Interjection.

In this is indicated the *essential* function of each part of speech, that which is necessary to its *definition*. The noun, *e.g.*, may be *object* of a verb, or with a preposition may make a "modifier;" but its distinguishing character is *to name the thing thought of*. After abundant examples of the *uses*, the *definitions* should be given. The examples, in fact, lead up to accurate definition; this is essential to accurate thought.

Examples.—Plants grow.   Flowers fade.   Flowers bloom.

(*a*) Leaves fall—flutter—rustle.   Birds sing, fly, chirp.   Boys play, run, jump, learn.   Grass grows.   Time flies, etc., etc.

(*b*) *Little* birds sing, *pretty* flowers fade, *all* men die, *good* boys obey, *dead* leaves fall, etc.

(*c*) Birds sing *sweetly*, boys run *fast*, roses fade *quickly*, etc.

(*d*) The little child weeps bitterly, the sun shines brightly, etc.

(*e*) The yellow bird sings *in* the tree, the boy writes *with* a poor pen, etc.

(*f*) The girl sings *because* she is happy, the sun rose *and* the clouds dispersed, etc.

By inductive teaching there will be no difficulty in getting even pupils in " Second Reader " to learn the " parts of speech."

II. Keep prominently in view the fact that the use of a word in a sentence determines what part of speech it is.   *Walking* is a healthful exercise, hand me my *walking* stick.   There is *rest* for the weary, they *rest* from their labours, etc.

III. *Grammatical Equivalency*—make this also prominent.   For example :

(*a*) An adjective, or an adverb, or an infinitive, or a prepositional phrase, or sentence (as quotation) or dependent proposition may fill the office of a noun ; *e.g.*, *That* you have wronged me doth appear in this : From fame to infamy is a beaten track, etc., etc.

(*b*) The office of adverb may be filled by a single word, or a prepositional phrase, or a noun, or an infinitive phrase, etc.

(*c*) The "adjective" may be a single word, or a noun in the possessive case, or a prepositional phrase, or a "participle phrase," or a dependent preposition, etc.

Inflexions, *Number, Gender, etc.*—A good many inflexions will be learned incidentally, but there should be many lessons and copious exercises on the subject.

Classification of the different kinds of *nouns, verbs, adjectives,* etc.

There should be much analysis, but eschew "diagramatic" analysis as an invention of the deviceful empiric. This "diagramming" is supposed to help the pupil to apprehend at a glance the relations of words, clauses, etc., as if these relations had not to be apprehended *before* the *disjecta membra* could be placed in the right "compartments," etc. There ought to be occasional exercises in written, but much practice in oral, analysis. Analysis trains to power of rapid apprehension, of expressive reading, and of clear and concise expression of thought.

Note.—In addition to books prescribed by the Department, and those already named, the teacher should possess the following books. But he should accept nothing on "Method" which he cannot justify on psychological principles: "DEWEY'S PSYCHO-LOGY" (Harper Brothers) ; Sully's "Psychology for Teachers ;" Preyer's "Mind of the Child" (D. Appleton & Co.); Compayré's "Lectures on Pedagogy" (D. C. Heath); Payne's "Contributions to the Science of Education" (Harper & Brothers)

Brook's "Normal Methods of Teaching," Laurie's "Primary Education" (Jas. Thin, Edin.) ; Sinclair's "First Year at School ;" Hughes' "Securing and Retaining Attention and Mistakes in Teaching ;" "Kindergarten Guide" (Steiger & Co.)

Compayré's "History of Pedagogy" (D. C. Heath) ; Mahaffy's "Old Greek Education" (Kegan, Paul & Co.) ; Laurie's "Comenius" (Macmillan & Co.)